Interactive Multimedia

Practice and Promise

Edited by
Colin Latchem, John Williamson and
Lexie Henderson-Lancett

KOGAN
PAGE

London • Philadelphia

First published in 1993

Kogan Page Limited
120 Pentonville Road
London N1 9JN

British Library Cataloguing in Publication Data

A CIP record for this book is available from the British Library.

ISBN 0 7494 0815 4

Typeset by Witwell Limited, Southport.
Printed and bound in Great Britain by Biddles Ltd, Guildford and King's Lynn.

Contents

CONTENTS

Contributors

Ian Conboy
Ian Conboy is Senior Projects Officer with the Department of School Education, Victoria, and has specific responsibility for telematics and distance education. He is Victorian schools representative on the Australian Education Council working party for the establishment of a National Open Learning Technology Corporation. His research interests include distance education, educational technology and media studies.

John Frylinck
John Frylinck is Head of Public Services in the Library of Curtin University, Perth, Western Australia. He is accountable for the management, planning and development of the Curtin Library's information, lending and instructional services. He has worked at senior management level in specialist, national and university libraries in various countries and has a special interest in CD-ROM applications in libraries. He has recently introduced an integrated CD-ROM network at Curtin.

Lyn Henderson
Lyn Henderson, PhD, is a Lecturer in Education and the Academic Coordinator of the Remote Area Teacher Education Program (RATEP) at the James Cook University of North Queensland, Townsville. She has developed a number of Diploma of Teaching subjects for delivery to students in remote communities through interactive multimedia courseware. Her research interests involve the interrelationships among interactive multimedia, cultural difference, cognition and learning theories.

Lexie Henderson-Lancett
Lexie Henderson-Lancett was formerly a Lecturer in Education at Macquarie University in Sydney, New South Wales. Seconded as a consultant to the Federal Government in 1985, she prepared national

7

policy guidelines for computers in Australian primary schools. She then entered private enterprise and became National Sales Manager: Education for Apple Computer Australia Pty Ltd. Returning to lecturing at Curtin University in Western Australia, she took a leading role in facilitating the development of a number of interactive multimedia projects. She currently consults to two universities and a major Australian bank on trends in learning and interactive multimedia courseware development.

Stephen Heppell

Professor Stephen Heppell is Director of the Xploratorium, a multimedia learning laboratory in the Faculty of Education at Anglia Polytechnic University, Brentford, Essex. He has for many years been closely involved in the area of educational computing and its impact on the classroom and is highly sought after as a speaker at international conferences. His current research is in integrated media.

Colin Latchem

Associate Professor Colin Latchem is Acting Head of the Teaching Learning Group (TLG) at Curtin University in Perth, Western Australia. He is involved in academic staff development, instructional design and media, distance education and research and development in interactive multimedia and compressed digital videoconferencing. He has worked in the UK, Nigeria, India and Australia and has conducted educational technology consultancies for the Council for Educational Technology for the UK and State and Federal governments in Australia. His research interests relate to technology applications in classroom and rural/remote settings.

Peter Olaf Looms

Peter Olaf Looms is a member of the Danish Broadcasting Interactive Media Unit working on the use of CD-ROM, CD-I, laser disc and recordable optical discs in information and education systems and the design of large-scale image databases. He also has extensive experience in instructional design and evaluation in educational broadcasting. He is the Scandinavian correspondent for three journals and newsletters on interactive multimedia.

Eric Lugtigheid

Eric Lugtigheid is a staff member of the Department of the Secretary of State of Canada in Ottawa and has worked as a Senior Policy Analyst in the fields of multiculturalism, corporate policy and planning, and education. In 1991, he was appointed to the position of Executive Co-ordinator, Jean Talon Project in the Education Support

Branch of the Department. The Jean Talon Project proposes to create and distribute a series of electronic products on Canada in the twentieth century and, by so doing, to stimulate the creation of an environment conducive to the electronic publishing of information in Canada.

Philip McAra

Phil McAra is Computer Systems Manager within the Learning Systems Division of the Scottish Council for Educational Technology. He is responsible for programming and technical computing activities within the division and providing consultancies and workshops for industrial and educational customers with special reference to the use of hypertext and multimedia systems in support of education and training. Current projects include an interactive videodisc on appraisal management and an information disc, *The Multimedia Solution*, a guide to multimedia and its jargon.

Ann Nguyen

Ann Nguyen is a Lecturer in Computing in the Division of Business and Hotel Management at Griffith University–Gold Coast in Queensland. One of her main research interests is sensory perception in multimedia-based education.

Nigel Paine

Nigel Paine is the Chief Executive of the Scottish Council for Educational Technology, a national body charged with developing educational technology solutions for education and industry in Scotland and beyond. He is involved in the development of innovative learning and training systems. He recently edited the UK National Extension College's 25th Anniversary Book *Open Learning in Transition*, and has written two other books on open learning. He chairs or serves on bodies involved with educational broadcasting, training standards and educational technology and innovative teaching in UK higher education.

Jenny Preece

Jenny Preece, PhD, is Senior Lecturer in Human–Computer Interaction in the Computing Department within the Faculty of Mathematics at The Open University in the UK. She has published over 30 papers in this field and is the author of two books on human–computer interaction and closely related subjects.

David Raitt

David Raitt, PhD, is a systems engineer in the Systems Design Section of the European Space Agency in The Netherlands which provides support in advanced information systems and technology. He is a recognized authority on leading-edge information technologies and is the Chairman of the International Online Information Meetings held in London each December and the founder and editor of *The Electronic Library*, which covers the applications and implications of new information technology.

Thomas C. Reeves

Thomas C. Reeves, PhD, is Associate Professor of Instructional Technology at The University of Georgia. He teaches programme evaluation, instructional design and research methods courses and directs a wide range of funded research and development projects for business, industrial, military, medical and government clients. He has also planned and evaluated numerous interactive programmes including the Acute Combat Training Life Support programme for the US Navy and sales/support training for Apple Computer, Inc. He has been an invited speaker at conferences in Australia, Bulgaria, Finland, Peru, Burma, Switzerland, Taiwan and throughout the United States.

Alexander Romiszowski

Alexander Romiszowski, PhD, is Professor of Instructional Design, Development and Evaluation and Director of the Training Systems Institute at Syracuse University, New York. He is the author of several books on instructional systems design, media selection and instructional materials development. His current research involves instructional design, new technologies and AI in education and distance education media. He has worked extensively as a consultant and project manager on a variety of educational and training technology projects in many parts of the world.

William Tan

William Tan, PhD, is Multimedia/Network Specialist in the Distance Education Centre, University of Southern Queensland, Toowoomba. He has extensive experience in the design and implementation of computer-based instructional courseware and local area networks.

John Williamson

John Williamson, PhD, is Associate Professor of Education and Head of the School of Teaching Studies at Curtin University, Perth, Western Australia. He has published in the areas of curriculum implementation and evaluation, classroom processes and practices and the professional development of teachers. He is a Fellow of the Australian Teacher Education Association and coedits *The South Pacific Journal of Teacher Education*.

Preface

This book is about developments in interactive multimedia (IMM) in the early 1990s. It seeks to explore issues, raise concerns, question actions, point out pathways and direct our thinking and practice in the uses of IMM in education, training and library and information services. Its genesis lay in the International Interactive Multimedia Symposium held in Perth, Western Australia, in January 1992. This brought together a wide range of technologists, educators, trainers, information providers and researchers to consider the opportunities and challenges presented by this new technology and to stimulate changes in traditional attitudes, particularly in education, that would lead to the wider adoption of IMM. It was widely recognized by the delegates that there was need for more clarity, in both concept and purpose, if the potential of IMM was to be fully realized.

Several of the chapters in this book are based on papers presented at the IMM Symposium. Others have been specially commissioned from experts in the field. The aim is to provide educators, students, trainers, librarians, managers and practitioners with an overview, not only of the directions and uses of the technology, but also of the research foundations and educational and contextual issues that need to be addressed if it is to be widely and appropriately adopted.

'Interactive multimedia' is an umbrella term for a range of videodisc-, compact disc- and computer-based systems that allow the creation, integration and manipulation of text, graphics, still and moving video images, sound and feedback clues for many diverse applications in education and training, public information and archiving, and point-of-sale and marketing. End-users can control the links, determine the paths of navigation, set their own speed of information handling and construct the content in accordance with their needs. Chapter 1 provides an overview of IMM. It discusses the components of IMM courseware and their design; the introduction of the technology into various learning environments; and the critical issues of research, development and adoption. These topics are expanded by the other contributors.

In Chapter 2, Nigel Paine and Philip McAra provide a guide to current developments in IMM technology. This is a field in which there are so many new developments, technicalities, acronyms and buzzwords that it is important to clarify terms and technologies, and the authors' recent involvement in the creation of an information disc, *The Multimedia Solution*, has allowed them to provide this up-to-date guide to IMM and its jargon. Technical developments have out-stripped many non-specialists' understanding of the terminology used in the field of IMM and the editors are grateful to Alex Kasten of the US *Multimedia and Videodisc Monitor* for permission to draw on the Monitor Information Services' publication *Multimedia and related technologies: A glossary of terms* to provide a glossary at the end of the book.

In Chapter 3, Alexander Romiszowski explores a range of key issues in regard to IMM in education. He begins by analysing what is meant by 'interactivity' and 'multimedia'. He then distinguishes between instructional IMM systems and informational IMM systems and discusses the issue of design, development and dissemination. He concludes by examining the convergence of information technology and telecommunications technology and the potential of IMM in conjunction with computer-mediated communication to provide the 'virtual learning community'. This latter issue is taken up by Ian Conboy in Chapter 10.

In the rush to bring new IMM products to market or develop prototype courseware, the need for a solid research base has been largely ignored. In Chapter 4, Thomas C. Reeves describes some research foundations upon which IMM should be based and recommends new directions for research to guide the development and use of IMM programmes. He challenges us to examine very carefully the idea that IMM 'automatically' supports learning and provides guidelines for the conduct of case studies and research utilizing computer modelling. He argues that the uniquely powerful data collection capabilities of IMM lend themselves particularly well to the conduct of this kind of research.

The rapid development of educational computing presents a direct challenge to educators. In Chapter 5, Stephen Heppell traces the history of computers in the classroom from the early days when the computer itself was the focus of attention, through the outclassing of 'useful little programs' by sophisticated generic software tools, to modular software and 'integrated media'. He offers a developmental taxonomy which encompasses the narrative function, the interactive function and the participative function. He argues that it is inevitable that pedagogy will change radically, given the rate of change in computer technologies, and discusses possible scenarios for future educational computing.

In Chapter 6, Peter Olaf Looms maintains this focus on the school and surveys the uses of interactive multimedia in North American and European classrooms. Having analysed the reasons for the disappointing reception IMM has had to date in these environments, he defines the obstacles that need to be overcome and refers to the ways in which IMM products are being developed and introduced into Danish schools. He concludes by sketching a scenario for the development of IMM in education over the next few years, making particular reference to Europe and the United States.

Human–computer interaction is a major design issue for developers of computer-based courseware. To date, little of the research in this area has focused on IMM. In Chapter 7, Jenny Preece discusses the general theory, knowledge and techniques that can support and guide multimedia and hypermedia development in pursuit of information-seeking and knowledge acquisition. Her discussion covers the important issues of navigation, metaphors, guides, maps and other aids.

In Chapter 8, William Tan and Ann Nguyen examine the costing of IMM practice. They propose a classification for computer-based instructional systems which takes into account interactivity levels, complexity of implementation and developmental costs and then show how to calculate the lifecycle costs of these different levels of application. These examples provide some basic rules of thumb for educators, trainers or managers contemplating the development and implementation of IMM.

The high costs of IMM courseware development seem likely to result in an emphasis on generic courseware and a search for worldwide markets. New information technology such as IMM may also be seen as providing answers to educational and training needs in developing as well as developed countries and in meeting the needs of ethnic minorities or disadvantaged groups. In Chapter 9, Lyn Henderson explains that IMM courseware can never be culturally neutral and that cultural appropriateness has to be achieved through something far more than mere tokenism or cosmetic changes. She describes how IMM has been developed and applied for higher education study by Aborigines and Torres Strait Islanders in remote offshore communities and how the processes and products have had to incorporate culturally appropriate ways of learning to empower these minority culture students.

In a second Australian case study, Ian Conboy describes the use of audiographics technology to create what Alexander Romiszowski describes in Chapter 3 as a 'virtual learning community' by clustering Victorian schools and colleges into decentralized self-help groups to improve rural and remote educational provision. The story of this 'electronically extended classroom', using Macintosh computers, voice and fax, provides some important lessons about the links between government policy and technology-based change in education and the factors that will encourage teachers to implement such innovation in schools.

Many libraries already have substantial investments in non-print material and associated hardware and, while IMM may be currently regarded with ambivalence by some librarians and information providers, the technology has the potential to transform resource collections and information networks. In Chapter 11, John Frylinck and David Raitt look at the barriers and constraints to the adoption of IMM in libraries, the possible applications and advantages of the medium and the innovative technologies that are becoming available.

One of the issues considered by the delegates to the IMM Symposium in Perth was the need for a 'national agenda' which would act as a catalyst for, and encourage inter-sectoral cooperation in, electronic publishing and the development of multi-purpose products. One country that has taken such an initiative is Canada, and in Chapter 12, Eric Lugtigheid describes the Jean Talon Project, which will involve government agencies at the national and provincial levels, educational institutions and the private sector in the development of products that will enable Canadians to learn more about their country, feature resources that are otherwise difficult to access in museums and other public information collections and help to encourage a market, and therefore an industry, for multimedia. The chapter describes the studies that led to the decision to proceed with the Jean Talon Project and conduct a pilot project in Alberta.

These are early days for IMM. The technology is in transition; national economies are in recession; and educational and training bodies, libraries and other agencies are going through a period of massive change. This international group of authors recognize how these and other constraints may affect the adoption of IMM, but they establish firm foundations for the case that IMM is a significant new technology. It places end-users in control of their learning; it is highly motivational and supportive of 'deep learning'; it parallels the ways in which we learn best – by interacting and by participating; and it can provide more equitable and more cost-effective educational, training and information services.

The editors wish to thank the authors for their contributions and for so speedily developing and revising their chapters by means of disk, fax and E-Mail; the organizers of the International Interactive Multimedia Symposium for permission to draw on some of the papers from this event; and Judy Gaebler, Philomena Porter, Terri Crowe, Sharon Bailey, Kathy Matthews and Jim Mitchell, for their unfailing patience and word processing and graphics skills.

Colin Latchem
John Williamson
Lexie Henderson-Lancett

Perth, August 1992

Acknowledgements

The editors acknowledge that:

Adobe Premiere and the Adobe Premiere logo are registered trademarks of Adobe Systems Inc.

Audio Visual Connections (AVC) is a registered trademark of International Business Machines Corporation.

Apple, Macintosh and QuickTime are registered trademarks of Apple Computer Inc.

Authorware Professional and Plus are registered trademarks of Spinnaker Corporation.

CD-I is a registered trademark of NV Philips.

CDTV is a registered trademark of Commodore Electronics Ltd.

Convertit! is a registered trademark of Heizer Software.

CourseBuilder and MacroMind Director are registered trademarks of MacroMedia Inc.

Designs Work Bench (DWB) is a registered trademark of LaserMedia UK.

DVI is a registered trademark of Intel Corporation.

Guide is a registered trademark of Owl International.

HyperCard is a registered trademark of Apple Computer Inc, licensed to Claris Corporation.

IBM PC, PC-AT, PC-XT, PC-DOS, PS/2 and LinkWay are registered trademarks of International Business Machines Corporation.

Interactive NOVA is a trademark, and NOVA is a service mark, of WGBH Educational Foundation.

MS-DOS and Windows are registered trademarks of Microsoft Corporation.

OS/2 is a registered trademark of International Business Machines Corporation and Microsoft Corporation.

Photo CD and Kodak are registered trademarks of Eastman Kodak Co.

PictureBook is a registered trademark of Digithurst Ltd.

SuperCard is a registered trademark of Aldus Corporation.

TenCore is a registered trademark of Computer Teaching Corporation.

ToolBook is a registered trademark of Asymetrix Corporation.

1 IMM: An overview

*Colin Latchem, John Williamson and
Lexie Henderson-Lancett*

Introduction

Interactive multimedia (IMM) comes in various forms: as an interactive videodisc (IV) or compact disc programme run in tandem with
a computer program; as a desktop computer program offering colour,
sound and video as well as text and graphics; or as virtual reality (VR).
IMM technology combines all the processing power and control
capabilities of the modern microcomputer with the motivational and
presentational capacities of traditional audiovisual media. It offers
more storage capacity, greater speed and flexibility of access, more
intermingling of various forms of mediated information, greater
durability, less maintenance and greater ease of use than any of the
more traditional media. However, the real strength of IMM lies not so
much in the technology but in the courseware which provides
browsable 'chunks' of information connected by predetermined 'links'
and enables the end-user to access and navigate this information and
build, test and apply knowledge in logical and personally meaningful
ways. IMM can provide a wide range of surrogate experiences with
situations, equipment and materials and can require extensive
decision-making and thinking skills on the part of the user.

IMM may be a technology whose time has come. There are growing
concerns throughout the world about the performance and costs of
existing educational systems. Changing student populations and
course structures and the expansion of distance and open learning call
for new modes of delivery. In industry and the professions there are
pressing needs for more flexible training pathways and the integration
of workplace and off-the-job training. Libraries, archives, museums
and other information providers are seeking new ways of handling the
information explosion in all forms of media. While IMM may still be
seen as being at the exploratory phase, current investigations provide

some basic premises and principles about the development and delivery of interactive multimedia products in all these applications. These are summarized in this chapter and expanded on by the other contributors to this book.

The components of IMM

IMM products typically have three interrelated and interdependent components: computer-based, video-based and text-based. An IMM package can take any of the following forms:

* A videodisc providing still and moving images, audio, graphics and text controlled by a keypad or a light-pen wiped over bar-coded commands within training notes, workbooks, charts, exhibition panels, etc;
* a videodisc or compact disc providing still and/or moving images and audio interfaced to a personal computer providing text, graphics and audio; or
* a personal computer providing text, colour graphics, animation, photographic still images and compressed digitized motion video.

Conventional peripheral devices and/or other media may also be part of such systems.

In such IMM packages, all the computer-based alphanumeric, graphic, audio, video and instructional design elements are capable of being updated and altered. The videodisc or CD material is fixed but discs can be re-purposed by developing different interface information for specific needs. There are also WORM (write-once/read many times) optical storage systems that allow users to record a blank disc but do not allow for any subsequent erasure or modification. The computer, video and textual elements of IMM have their own technological characteristics, symbol systems and cognitive processing capabilities. Together, they provide a powerful motivational tool and enable learners to construct knowledge by connecting their mental representations to the real world and integrating mediated information with information already stored in the memory.

The computer elements of IMM

The computer elements of an IMM system have the capacity to:

* store, manipulate and present a range of information forms (eg,

databases, alphanumeric material, graphics, animation, stills and video, voice, sound effects, music and synthesized sound);

- juxtapose information or transform information from one symbol system into another (for example, convert numerical values into graphs or convert typed material into speech through a voice synthesizer);
- allow various forms of computer-based information to be accessed in linear and non-linear ways;
- control a videodisc or CD-based disc for the purposes of, for example, access, play, pause, rewind, fast-forward, replay, slow-motion;
- provide graphics overlay;
- enable learners to work independently through tutorials/ dialogues, drill and practice sequences, simulations/ models and exploration/problem-solving;
- assist and guide learning and inquiry by means of maps, pathways, navigation tools and browsing tools;
- facilitate learning by presenting dynamic, symbolic representations of non-concrete, formal constructs and relationships;
- monitor and track learner usage and performance;
- provide feedback to the learner;
- act as an electronic notebook (cut-and-paste storage); and
- print out screen material.

These computer elements may be commercially produced or generated by teachers, trainers or other end-users. The main strengths of the computer lie in its information processing and human interface capabilities and in its ability to empower the learner. However, computer-based instruction (CBI) is more closely associated with training than with education and the computer is still an unfamiliar learning mechanism for many people. Greenberger (1990, p2), suggests that the computer is a prodigious and versatile tool but that until recently, it was 'intellectually precocious, mighty in feats, yet weak in senses'.

The video elements of IMM

The term video properly refers only to the picture, but as a generic term, it usually embraces audio and other signals which are part of a complete programme. The video elements of an IMM system may be commercially produced or developed in-house by educators or trainers (for example, by using a write-once system or the QuickTime option on a Macintosh). The video elements have the capacity to:

- provide the motivation for cognitive engagement;
- present authentic, simulated or dramatized behaviour, processes, situations and events;
- demonstrate motion and the effects of time and change;
- provide access to the inaccessible by means of location work at remote or dangerous sites; aerial, space or underwater photography; microscopy and endoscopy; time-lapse and slow-motion photography; freeze-frame, split-frame and computer-enhanced imagery;
- incorporate or overlay captions, graphics and animation;
- communicate and engineer affective states;
- develop pattern recognition skills in regard to visual and auditory cues in problem-solving and problem representation;
- assist learners with deficiencies in language skills;
- present linear constructs or information structured into small chunks; and
- allow learner-controlled access, replay and freeze-framing to analyse information that would otherwise be transient and unsuited to the individual's cognitive constraints.

The main strengths of video lie in its connotations of enjoyment, its wide acceptability as a source of information and its ability to convey complex situations and feelings. Video can provide the auditory and visual dimensions which the computer has so far been unable to supply. The main problems with video are that learners may have been conditioned to watch this medium passively and that relatively few educators will accept the enormous gains in understanding that can be achieved through film, TV and video (see, for example, *Daedalus*, 1982).

The textual elements of IMM

The textual elements in an IMM package can appear on the screen or in print. These can:

- provide the user with the primary symbol system used in scholarship and learning;
- provide a stable arrangement that aids comprehension and learning;
- assist and guide learning and inquiry through the provision of abstracts, contents tables, chapter headings, subheadings, footnotes, indexes, further references, etc;
- allow the user to vary the rate and move back and forth when studying unfamiliar or difficult material;

- be combined with pictures or diagrams to aid comprehension and retention; and
- take the form of supplementary reading/'take home' copy, assignment and evaluation materials, etc.

Textual material can be commercially produced or developed by teachers or trainers. Learners can also generate response material in this medium; for example, by writing assignments in an on-screen 'notebook' or creating hypotheses from the video segments, an activity that Mazur and Gay (1990) describe as 'inferactive writing'. The main strengths of the medium of text are its familiarity and association with learning. Its main weaknesses lie in the difficulties that poor readers may have in decoding text and the problems of understanding that may be experienced by users in general when reading in unfamiliar domains.

The aim of IMM courseware development is to draw on the various strengths of the elements described above and to compensate for any of their disadvantages by integrating these elements into a single environment which enables users to view, hear and utilize information in ways which complement or reinforce each other.

Applications

Interactive multimedia products have the capacity to shift the locus of 'ownership' and 'control' in learning. Whereas learning has traditionally been 'controlled' by the teacher, the instructor or the computer-based instructional system, the end-users of IMM courseware can be empowered to own and control their own learning. They can work in their own time and at their own pace, choose their preferred navigational pathways and delivery systems and develop their own mental models and schemata.

IMM courseware can be designed for use by individuals or small groups. It can provide opportunities for experiential learning, brainstorming and problem-solving and for the learners to evaluate and modify their schemata. It can provide representations and semantically rich problems for the exploration of concepts, principles and procedures. Environments that are dangerous, expensive or otherwise unsuitable for the users' current competency levels can be simulated to provide hands-on learning, as for example with Apple's *Animated Dissection of Anatomy for Medicine* or *ADAM*, which allows medical students to perform surrogate, desktop surgery (Boyle and Doyle, 1992).

In corporate applications, IMM can reduce training times, travel costs and disruption to work schedules. IMM simulations can allow trainees to work in potentially dangerous environments without risk to themselves. For example, at Bethlehem Steel in the United States, trainees use IBM Multimedia to simulate working with molten steel and hydraulics. Walk-up IMM kiosks with touch screens, video and stereo audio are increasingly being used for applications such as customized destination maps in department stores or tourism offices, product brochures and corporate profiles.

IMM can provide anonymity and confidentiality as well as achieve personalized instruction and cost savings. For example, in Tulane County, California, the Department of Social Services now uses IMM to guide applicants for welfare assistance. In the health context, a unique IBM Multimedia product called THINKable has been designed to foster cognitive rehabilitation for clients suffering from injuries, developmental disabilities, substance abuse, degenerative disease or neurological disorders. The programme also generates progress reports for case managers, doctors, families and insurers.

IMM has many applications in libraries, archives and museums. All these systems are undergoing fundamental changes and are progressing from an exclusively curatorial role to a role which embraces interpretative and attention-seeking functions. IMM can bring knowledge in all of its media formats into condensed, accessible forms capable of being used for reference and educational applications.

Instructional design issues

The developers of IMM courseware need to be highly skilled in applying ideas from behavioural psychology, cognitive psychology, adult learning, systems theory and media technology. Earlier CBI models were essentially behaviourist, concerned with modifying users' behaviour to achieve predictable outcomes. In contrast, the trend in the theory base of IMM is towards a greater integration of cognitive theory which is essentially concerned with the development of metacognitive skills, knowledge transfers within and across various domains and solving novel problems within a domain. Merrill (1991) suggests with his second generation instructional design theory (ID^2) that the aim is to build a technology that enables the learners to construct appropriate mental models, not via an extreme constructivist approach, but through a combination of effective experimental learning environments enhanced by more directed instructional strategies and prespecified interactions that are known to be necessary for the acquisition of particular knowledge, attitudes and skills. IMM has the potential to facilitate 'deep learning', defined by Biggs (1987, p15) as that learning in which the learner is self-motivated and self-directed, searches for meanings within the task, personalizes the task, integrates it into a whole, and tries to theorize about the task and form a hypothesis. To give an idea of how IMM may embody such learning strategies, an interactive videodisc-based case study, *A Right to Die? The Case of Dax Cowart*, places students in a situation where they have to decide whether a blind and seriously burned young accident victim should be subjected to lengthy and extremely painful treatment or allowed to die. The learners consider the various issues involved by 'talking' to the patient, his mother, the doctors, a nurse and a lawyer (Covey, 1990). Thus, the designers of this package aimed to encourage deep and meaningful learning by a process of questions and challenges to misconceptions through which the students constantly have to construct and re-examine their conceptual frameworks. IMM is a particularly effective medium for providing such search-through-problem environments. Another example of such an environment, this time designed for younger learners, is to be seen in *Palenque*, a product designed for 8- to 14-year-olds, which enables the students to use the simulated tools of the archaeologist to research Mayan ruins, engage in such tasks as reconstructing fragmented glyphs, search for the tomb of Pacal, a 12-year-old boy-king, and thereby learn to analyse and synthesize data and solve realistic problems (Wilson and Tally, 1990).

So effective is IMM for significant learning that it can actually become a research tool in its own right. For example, an IMM system known as *The Global Jukebox* has been developed at Hunter College of the City University of New York to aid the work of Alan Lomax, doyen of American folklore study, and his fellow researchers. Comprising a Macintosh computer and CD-ROM and laser disc players, *The Global Jukebox* enables a vast collection of filmed and taped music and dance from over 400 cultures to be accessed for the purposes of tracing migrations from one culture to another and establishing correlations among performance styles and cultural traits (Watkins, 1992).

The other central issue in IMM instructional design is the design philosophy of increasing learner control over the 'what' and the 'how' of learning. Hooper-Woolsey (1989, p137) suggests that it is important for designers of IMM products to provide the end-user with 'a handful of simple ways to travel from one object to another (by keyword, object search, text type or random choice) which lets people create many paths through a rich territory without getting lost or hitting a dead-end'. The three key issues in optimizing IMM design are *linking, human interface and content.*

Linking

IMM links need to be set up in ways that are both non-linear and non-hierarchical. The aim should be to provide the end-user with optional and implicit navigation routes which facilitate freedom of movement within the environment for the purposes of search and cognitive processing. The links should also allow for the use of extensions or support information wherever unfamiliar or difficult concepts are encountered. 'Chunking' the content into meaningful pieces and creating meaningful and logical links presents a real challenge to courseware developers with a background in other media. 'Concept mapping' has been found to be an effective tool for conceiving information in chunks, seeing possible relationships between these chunks and understanding the cognitive processes the users are expected to apply.

Human interface

When the concept of interface first emerged, it was simply thought of as the hardware and the software through which a user and a computer could communicate. Today, the concept has broadened to include the cognitive and affective aspects of the user's experience with the total environment presented by the product. The graphical user interface (GUI), developed and popularized by Xerox, Apple and Microsoft, facilitates intuitive navigation by the user. The basic tenets of human interface design are now well established. The user, not the computer, should initiate all actions. 'Cards' or 'screens' provide the 'front door' to the various forms of information. The user accesses and manipulates the various elements of the product by clicking on buttons, icons or metaphors with a mouse or other pointing device. Interface design should be consistent where appropriate and differentiated where needed so the user can rely on recognition rather than recall. The user should always be given immediate auditory or visual feedback. User activities should be broken into small steps where tasks are complex and, wherever possible, these activities should be reversible to minimize errors or any fears that the user may have about using the system. The interface design should be aesthetically pleasing, appropriate to the content and suited to the learner's culture and prior knowledge.

Designing 'event-driven' and 'content-driven' IMM interfaces should involve much more than providing users with endless opportunities to traverse hierarchies of menus. Hooper (1988, p9) suggests that the 'experience of following links' needs to be considered by designers, together with the 'experience of examining linked knowledge' and should be facilitated by a variety of forms – pictorial, diagrammatic and acoustic, as well as textual. For example, maps, diagrams and illustrations can be used both as concept explanations and as points of departure for further access.

Content

Sculley (Greenberger, 1990, p45) observes that while the main issues in computing today are how to store more information, increase memory size and obtain greater capacity, these are not the key issues in IMM. Here the main challenge lies in locating and creating the mass of information that can be stored in the products and utilizing this information in ways that promote understanding. It is all too easy to be over-ambitious and to underestimate the complexity of the production to be undertaken, the sourcing problems, the up-front or rights fees and the sheer labour intensity of the task. For example, Gaffney, Favrolo and Sicker (1991) reported that when they required 500 slides for the development of the *Interactive NOVA: Animal Pathways* videodisc, they discovered that the average photographic library was simply not accustomed to handling requests for such large numbers of slides. They also found that the typical cost of a 35mm slide was US$100–150. Fortunately they found cheaper alternatives in universities and wildlife agencies, but such options may not always be available to the developers. The time factor is another prime consideration. Brand (Greenberger, 1990, p105) cites a HyperCard project of 10,000 cards, monochrome and without video or animation, that took an estimated one person per hour per card and cost US$150,000. It clearly pays to be selective. The focus needs to be on those chunks of information that will maximize the motivation and the learning of the end-users. Gaffney, Favrolo and Sicker (*op cit*, p9) described their methodology for selecting material for *Interactive NOVA: Animal Pathways* thus:

> The way we chose content was analogous to stocking a new kitchen. We didn't fill the kitchen with a random assortment of foods (i.e. animals). Instead, we selected foods that could be used in recipes (i.e. environments). Eggplant, apricots and peanut butter wouldn't get us one good meal. But milk, flour and eggs could be the ingredients for many. In other words, we selected animals, habitats and behaviours that would lend themselves to multiple cross-references.

With the content identified, decisions need to be made about the cost, time and resource implications of representing this content in various mediated forms.

Introducing IMM into learning environments

Kuhn (1962) portrayed scientific progress as a series of changes in 'world view' that compete with older frames of reference and crystallize into a 'paradigm shift' rather than a linear accumulation of verified hypotheses. Fjeldstat (Greenberger, 1990, p38) believes that we are now experiencing a paradigm shift in multimedia and that what the PC did for the 1980s will be dwarfed by IMM in the 1990s. She suggests that IMM will totally change the ways in which we think, work and learn. However, a word of caution is necessary here. Caterall (Greenberger, 1990, p65) reminds us that instructional technologies, including computer-based instruction, have histories of lofty promises, low levels of adoption and even lower levels of use. Little it seems has changed since the 1970s, when Coldevin (1977) suggested that, with the exception of the case of open learning, instructional technology had failed to reorientate values or create new structures in education. Despite all the major advances and investment in the technology, computers have not radically changed classroom pedagogies and are typically used to add to existing practice rather than replace it.

The more complex the innovation, the greater the changes required of the system, and the widespread adoption of IMM in educational systems will require change at many levels. Governments and administrators will need to change the often rigid ground rules that exist for resource allocation. Educational institutions will need to revise their organizational structures, pedagogies and modes of delivery. Teachers will need to move from providing face-to-face teaching and text-based learning to facilitating individualized, interactive, media-based learning, and learners will need to be empowered to accept far greater responsibility for their own learning.

In the light of these observations, it is interesting to note that, as a first step towards adopting IMM, the state of Texas, the second largest American textbook market behind California, revised its purchasing policy in 1991–92 to allow interactive multimedia to compete with the science textbooks traditionally used in its elementary schools. One of the preconditions was that the costs of the multimedia packages for each grade had to be comparable with those of class sets of textbooks. This was the first instance of instructional technology being permitted to compete against textbooks in a US state adoption procedure. It resulted in Optical Data Corporation's 11-videodisc *Windows on Science* curriculum, supported by more than 6,000 print pages of teaching and learning materials, being taken up by 65 per cent (2,200) of the elementary schools in 44 per cent of the Texas school districts. This gave ODC a market share of 35 per cent. The *Windows on Science* courseware was designed for front-of-the-class presentation by teachers controlling videodisc players. This minimized the hardware costs and the operational problems and, in the words of ODC president William Clark, 'presented the lowest possible learning curve to a largely technophobic teacher population' (*MMD*, 1992a). However, having broken the mould, Clark was confident of a second stage of adoption, with learning stations around the perimeters of the classrooms featuring laser disc players interfaced to computers featuring student-centred activities and management capabilities for teachers. Utah soon followed the Texas lead in purchasing multimedia products with textbook funds (*MMD*, 1992b).

Hardware costs have undoubtedly been an inhibiting factor in the adoption of the microcomputer in the classroom. However, Hebenstreit (1992, pp7–9) suggests that rapidly reducing costs are going to break the 'computer-room syndrome' which prevents students from using computers as personal tools for individual purposes. He suggests that this will open up a completely new set of possible uses about which we presently know almost nothing, because, as the Stanford/ UNESCO Symposium Report (1986) stated, no conceptual framework exists to evaluate the relevance of results obtained in a computer-saturated environment against those obtained in a computer-scarce one. Hebenstreit believes that courses will become 'meta-courses', focusing on the foundations of fields of study rather than mere facts, figures, methods and techniques, and that in the delivery of these courses, teachers will provide the 'know-why' and computers will provide the 'know-how'. He also foresees (p8) the 'present-day catastrophic patchwork situation' of educational software coming to an end and an amalgamation of electronic and print publishing taking its place:

> I think that in ten years from now, no publisher will (agree) to publish a school manual without a set of diskettes for a multimedia computer including software for assisting the teacher, software for assisting the teaching/learning process and software for assisting the learner as well as a clear definition of the pedagogical strategy and objectives implemented in the book *and* the software. A teacher may not like an author's strategy and in that case, he may choose another manual exactly as he does today or even use more than one manual. What is important is that software should come in complete sets, like the chapters of a book, implementing a coherent pedagogical strategy which avoids the teacher (having)

to rush around gathering small pieces from here and there and avoids also (having) to test each separate piece of software in great detail to make sure that the pedagogy is sound.

There are many potential applications for IMM in non-school settings. Universities, colleges and libraries are well placed to utilize this technology to improve opportunities for study and information access. In business environments, IMM can be used for point-of-sale promotion of products and delivering training and productivity improvement programmes into the workplace. The potential of IMM for public information, displays and museums seems boundless. For example, in the visitor centre in the remote Cape Range National Park in the far north of Western Australia, a solar-powered touch-screen interactive videodisc display provides a guide to the ecology of the Ningaloo Coral Reef maritime reserve (Temple, 1990). At the Gondwana Rainforest attraction in Queensland, multimedia displays within a simulated volcanic crater inform visitors about Australia's environmental, Aboriginal and European history.

As governments and organizations search for more efficient and cost-effective modes of delivery, there is the potential for a paradigm shift. IMM developers and educators need to map out the pathways for educational change, rather than be led by the technology.

Research

Researchers such as Clark (1983) and Reeves (1986) have clearly demonstrated that comparative research methods using experimental or quasi-experimental paradigms cannot accurately assess the effectiveness of instructional media or technology and that new directions are needed. Kozma (1991) states that little research, particularly process research, has to date been conducted on learning with multimedia environments, partly because most of the effort in this field has been focused on development and partly because the field is itself still evolving. He does, however, point the way forward by suggesting that learning with media is a complementary process within which representations are constructed and procedures are performed, sometimes by the learner and sometimes by the media, and that these media should therefore be researched in terms of the cognitively relevant characteristics of their technology, symbol systems and processing capabilities and the ways in which these relate to cognition and learning. Reeves (1986, p105) suggests that the 'no significant differences' problem which has plagued research on the effectiveness of innovations in education is at least partially the result of failing to describe and measure the unique dimensions or characteristics of the innovations under study. He suggests that it is important to construct causal models of the influence of the critical dimensions of interactive multimedia on learning outcomes and suggests that researchers should use new research models such as 'explanatory observational studies', 'the method of controlled correlation', 'instructional treatment modelling' and 'systems-oriented evaluation'.

Nix (Nix and Spiro, 1990, ppix–xi) sees problems in conducting such investigations, problems that parallel those of creating 'solutions teams' of specialists from essentially different backgrounds to develop IMM courseware. He suggests that the innovative exploration of computer-based learning systems presents enormous difficulties even for people with computer expertise; for people without such expertise, computers are often intractable or at least a major sidetrack to consideration of the issues that brought them to the computers in the first place. Nix questions how many philosophers, psychologists, academics, teachers, educators, researchers and developers know what a fundamentally different and effective instructional medium should be like and how to program this new medium in unique ways without having to interact with computer specialists who are not equipped to comprehend computer applications from a human, educative point of view. However, Nix suggests that it is important for people who are researching cognition, learning and education to explore the value of computers in education and to determine whether new guidelines might be developed to augment, amplify, clarify, nullify and/or replace guidelines both from traditional approaches and from newer approaches to computer-based instruction and classroom education.

Research into IMM will also need to take into account social background, race/ethnicity and gender issues and the ability of the medium to assist disadvantaged students and users who are not predisposed to learning. Sutton (1991) suggests that, because of the hardware costs, the use of computers in schools has maintained or even exaggerated social differences. On the other hand, she postulates that shortages of hardware have meant that earlier fears of anti-social computer-based environments have been allayed. Hawkins et al (1982) established that more social interaction might actually occur when students worked in groups with computers than when they worked without them and Pease-Alvarez and Vásquez (1990) found that group work with computers could give rise to new forms of student–student and student–teacher interaction. An American multimedia programme designed to alleviate illiteracy, *Principles of the Alphabet Literacy*

Systems (*PALS*) was shown to have high motivational appeal and to have enabled students to progress three grade levels in 20 weeks (Karlstein, 1988). Anecdotal reports of teachers working with minority groups as diverse as Mexican-American students and Australian Aborigines suggest that these students like computers because 'they never get angry' and 'are always fair'. Such evidence implies that there may be scope for IMM intervention programmes for minority, disadvantaged and underperforming students. However, further research will be needed in regard to eurocentric and gender considerations in the technology, procedures and practices of IMM.

Research will also need to be conducted into the ways in which various users of IMM can visualize, access and manage what Barker and Tucker (1990, p9) refer to as 'the multi-dimensional knowledge structures' of this medium, as opposed to the more familiar 'two-dimensional book metaphor'. Researchers such as Spiro and Jehng (1990) contend that hypertext facilitates cognitive flexibility because it allows topics to be explored rather than intact schemata to be retrieved. On the other hand, Charney (1987) suggests that the non-linear features that make hypertext so appealing may also make it more difficult for less able students or users who are new to a domain. Working with books, the learner silently interrogates text in ways analogous to dialogue (Palincsar and Brown, 1984). The learner creates chunks of variable word size to achieve a reading pace commensurate with the familiarity or meaningfulness of the information (Simon, 1974) and is supported in this task by such devices as tables of contents, indexes, chapter headings and subheadings, page numbers and footnotes. Research will be needed to ensure that learners of different ages and different abilities can function within IMM environments, because these environments will typically contain a great deal more information than many learners may actually need or have ever encountered with other media, combine the stability of text with the transience of sound and video, feature multiple symbol systems and have no boundaries to the information flow. Most users are not familiar with IMM or even comfortable with computers and so the technology has to be inviting to users at all levels.

Developmental issues

As multimedia production becomes less dependent on arcane computer languages and achievable through event-driven authoring environments, including systems for the desktop capturing and manipulation of audio and video, opportunities arise for computer-oriented teachers or trainers to create or customize courseware for specific contexts. However, the time entailed and the range of knowledge and skills required suggest that 'solutions teams' are a more sustainable model for development if IMM is to achieve successful applications and competitive advantage in wider markets.

IMM courseware development is a hybrid born of education and technology. It depends on the value-added services of content experts, cognition and cognitive mapping specialists, computer software and media professionals, artists and producers, researchers and the users themselves. Hooper (1988, p2) suggests that the principal challenges in IMM are those of pedagogy and design. Minsker (Greenberger, 1990, p87) reminds us that authoring systems cannot shoot film or video, write scripts or design interactive programmes. Only people can do this. Developing and designing IMM is not a simple linear process, moving on from content specialist to instructional designer to script-writer to video producer and so on until completion of the product. Content and design are interdependent and successful product development not only encompasses scientific principles but also artistic perspectives which can accept and exploit the unpredictable. For example, in developing *Interactive NOVA: Animal Pathfinders*, Gaffney *et al* (1991) admit that the process required a balance among availability, beauty and utility. There was constant give and take. Sometimes the text set the agenda and sometimes the video footage – because it was spectacular, because it was needed or simply because it was readily available. Working in such a setting, new styles of project management and product conceptualization are required. A highly skilled project manager is needed to ensure that deadlines and budgets are adhered to and that the work is coordinated. There also needs to be a conceptualization chief designer to take the project from concept to realization and make sure the project works as a whole. At the same time, specialist boundaries have to be blurred and leadership has to pass from individual to individual, depending on the task in hand. New methodologies are needed where developers are not working to a template or courseware has to be capable of being updated or customized by a range of end-users. Such methodologies transcend the duality of the traditionally distinct research and practice roles and call for the use of the action–research paradigm in courseware development.

James Finkelstein of George Mason University in the United States suggests that universities have a great potential to provide leadership in developing IMM. However, he stresses that the culture of such institutions will need to change because collaborative works are typically discounted by tenure and promotion committees and creative work in new media may be regarded as outside the accepted definitions of research and scholarship (Bitomsky, 1992).

Winter (Greenberger, 1990, p23) suggests that the IMM production enterprise can be far-flung and chaotic because, unlike the more traditional book trade, people are uncertain of their roles and publishers have not only to worry about production, but also about which hardware which will best serve the products and which channels will provide the best sales outlets. Therefore IMM 'solutions teams' not only need to encompass skills in instructional development but capabilities in all stages of product development, from market research to training end-users and providing after-sales service.

IMM courseware creation entails considerable investment in time, money and other resources. Further, there is often a need to involve specialists from very different traditions, such as education, training, research, libraries, archives, museums, audiovisual production, publishing, computing, marketing and project management. Sculley (Greenberger, 1990, p201) and Barker and Anthonisz (1992) suggest that 'strategic alliances' and inter-sector/inter-institutional cooperation are necessary to achieve viable production units and to take IMM from its current 'emergent' state to a mature stage of development. These writers see advantages in collaboration between the public and the private sectors. Governments have an overall view of the educational and training needs of their economies and these overlap with industries' perceptions of their human resource development needs. IMM producers, on the other hand, need a mass market capable of adopting or adapting their courseware and may need 'seed funding' or the expertise of educators for innovative but educationally sound product design. Systems are also needed to assist key people in institutions and organizations to incorporate multimedia applications appropriately and to review forward planning in the light of this new technology. Given these circumstances, it is important that all those people interested in making IMM work should develop a climate of mutual trust and form creative partnerships to open up new horizons in education and training.

Technological issues

The pioneering technology for IMM was the analogue videodisc developed by NV Philips. Valuable lessons were learned from this technology and it still has its place in the market, but hardware and software platforms are changing rapidly and radically as consumer electronics migrates from analogue to digital and as information technology and communications technology converge at the desktop, laptop and palmtop levels. Compact disc systems, such as the Philips/ Sony CD-I, Commodore's CDTV and Intel's DVI, offer integrated text, graphics, sound and motion video capabilities. Multimedia software environments, such as Apple's HyperCard and QuickTime and IBM's Audio Visual Connections (AVC), are stimulating growth in computer-based courseware development and video integration and Apple and IBM have formed partnerships (Taligent and Kaleida) to compete against Microsoft in endeavouring to gain the market edge in IMM for the next generation of home computers. Apple has also recently demonstrated software that enables Macintosh machines to read handwriting and 'hear' whole sentences and 'converse' with almost anyone (Boyle and Doyle, 1992). Satellite, fibre optic and integrated services digital network (ISDN) provisions make it possible to access information-providers on a national and global scale. Little wonder that Microsoft chairman Bill Gates sees all these developments as forming 'the new digital world order'.

Given the dramatic progress in computing technology over the past few years it can be confidently predicted that there will continue to be significant increases in memory densities, mass storage densities and processing speeds and that these will be employed to achieve more sophisticated IMM systems. What is less easy to predict is whether IMM will become a ubiquitous, standardized and democratizing technology like TV or video, or remain a technology characterized by proprietary standards and limited by its costs and functions to an élite minority.

Currently the manufacturers are placing a lot of emphasis on high performance, relatively inexpensive player-only systems in an attempt to open up multimedia to a wider range of consumers and people who do not currently use personal computers. To date, for all the many millions of microcomputers sold, the computer revolution has only reached into about 15 per cent of American homes and the penetration rate has been lower in many other countries. In the home context, excluding those many users who actually work at or from home, the computer's functions and capacities far outweigh what most consumers actually need. In educational environments, on the other hand, the costs of providing enough learning stations and the limited range of suitable courseware have inhibited the growth of self-study applications and most computers in these environments are used for word processing, desktop publishing, spreadsheet, database and graphics applications rather than for computer-based instruction. The relatively low levels of domestic sales and profitability in desktop computers combined with the effects of the current recession are forcing the computing companies to look for a new, high-growth consumer electronics product. The industry needs another big hit like the VCR, which knows no socioeconomic bounds and has generated whole new hardware and software production, retail and rental industries. Thus Commodore's CDTV and Philips/Sony's CD-I are initially being aimed at the domestic market and will then be targeted on the training and educational markets. High-demand 'edutainment' titles at affordable prices are critical to the success of these consumer electronics products. So too is the price point set for the hardware. Bushnell (Greenberger, 1990, p81) argues that prices still need to be lower to achieve mass sales and that thousand-dollar machines are only likely to be taken up by needs-driven people with relatively high levels of education, annual incomes of over US$40,000 and discretionary money to spend. Stein (Greenberger, 1990, p85) also raises the interesting question of how potential purchasers will become aware of, and then be able to browse, multimedia programmes. Books can be browsed in a bookstore; videos piggyback on reviews and cinema and TV marketing; and music is pre-sold via radio and MTV. It is interesting to speculate on the channels and outlets through which IMM products will be marketed.

The educational and training markets will require authoring systems that enable good production values to be achieved inexpensively. Baseline technology standards and multimedia platform compatibility will also be important factors. Where funds are limited, potential purchasers are easily deterred by any possibility of early obsolescence and fears of 'backing the wrong horse'. David Nagel (1991), who heads Apple's Advanced Technology Group, asserts that proprietary standards are not acceptable in IMM. He suggests that the criteria for selecting a platform for IMM should be: support for cross-industry products (computing, consumer electronics and telecommunications); persistence and 'graceful ageing' (a life of 10 to 15 years); a rich applications programming interface that will support separate but related authoring and playback environments; ease of use; and a powerful development environment for all levels of end-user. Toshi Doi (*MMD*, 1992c) of the Sony Corporation, speaking at the Seventh International Conference and Exposition on Multimedia and CD-ROM, stated that 'we need a universal multimedia standard by 1995, or the industry will experience disaster'.

Educators have largely ignored the potential of computers to revolutionize learning and most of the development of the technology has lacked input from academe. This time, educators, trainers and information providers should endeavour to be in on the ground floor. If the aims of the industry can be realized and there can be a confluence of the entertainment, educational and information technologies there will be a far wider acceptance and understanding of IMM as a powerful tool for learning and there will be a widespread demand for courseware and developers with the requisite knowledge and skills. If IMM is to confer real benefits, it is not only the integration of the media that will be called for, but the integration of the technological and the creative, the logical and the sensorial and the theoretical and the opportunistic.

References

Barker, J. and Tucker, R. (eds) (1990). *The interactive learning revolution: Multimedia in education and training.* Kogan Page, London/Nichols Publishing, New York.

Barker, J.E.D. and Anthonisz, K. (1992). Developing an interactive multimedia industry. Paper presented at the International Interactive Multimedia Symposium, Perth, 27–31 January.

Biggs, J. (1987). *Student approaches to learning and studying.* Australian Council for Educational Research, Melbourne.

Bitomsky, M. (1992). Universities urged to maximise IT strengths. *Campus Review Weekly,* 2(39), 7.

Boyle, C. and Doyle, D. (1992). Casual multimedia and IMM technology. Presentation at the International Interactive Multimedia Symposium, Perth, 27–31 January.

Charney, D. (1987). Comprehending non-linear text: The role of discourse cues and reading strategies. In J. Smith and F. Halasz (eds), *Hypertext '87 Proceedings.* Association for Computing Machinery, New York, 109–20.

Clark, R. (1983). Reconsidering research on learning from media. *Review of Educational Research,* 53, 445–59.

Coldevin, G.O. (1977). Educational media implementation: Strategies for initiating change in formal learning environments. In P. Hills and J. Gilbert (eds), *Aspects of educational technology XI: The spread of educational technology.* Kogan Page, London, 371–9.

Covey, P. (1990). *A Right to Die? The Case of Dax Cowart.* Paper presented at the Annual Meeting of the American Research Association, Boston, April.

Daedalus (1982). Print culture and video culture. *Journal of the American Academy of Arts and Sciences,* III (4).

Gaffney, D., Favrolo, A. and Sicker, E. (1991). *Producing Interactive NOVA: Animal Pathfinders.* Apple Computer Multimedia Lab, Cupertino, Calif.

Greenberger, M. (ed) (1990). *On multimedia: Technologies for the 21st century.* The Voyager Company, Santa Monica, Calif.

Hawkins, J., Sheingold, K., Gearhart, M. and Berger, C. (1982). Microcomputers in schools: Impact on the social life of elementary classrooms. *Journal of Applied Developmental Psychology,* 3, 361–73.

Hebenstreit, J. (1992). *Trends in the development of technology for flexible learning.* Paper presented at the Seminar on Distance Education, Lyngby, 22 May. Ministry of Education, Denmark.

Hooper, K. (1988). *Interactive multimedia design.* Technical Report 13. Apple Computer Multimedia Lab, Cupertino, Calif.

Hooper-Woolsey, K. (1989). *Visual almanac: Technical report.* Apple Computer Multimedia Lab, Cupertino, Calif.

Karlstein, P.J. (1988). Fighting high school illiteracy: The PALS project in Brooklyn.

Technology Horizons in Education, IBM PCs and Compatibles Special Issue, 49–54.

Kozma, R.B. (1991). Learning with media. *Review of Educational Research*, 61 (2), 179–211.

Kuhn, T. (1962). *The structure of scientific revolutions*. University of Chicago Press, Chicago.

Mazur, F.E. and Gay, G. (1990). Distinct video crafting of multimedia programs for inferactive writing. *Journal of Interactive Instruction Development*, 2 (4), 18–20.

Merrill, M.D. (1991). Constructivism and instructional design. *Educational Technology*, 31 (5), 45–54.

MMD (1992a). Videodisc-based curriculum for Texas. *Multi Media Digest*, 1 (3), 9.

MMD (1992b). Utah adopts Windows on Science and English Express. *Multi Media Digest*, 1 (5), 11.

MMD (1992c). Special report: Microsoft Conference San Francisco 1992. *Multi Media Digest*, 1 (5), 15.

Nagel, D. (1991). Presentation at Platforms for the Multimedia Industry: The Sixth International Conference and Exposition on Multimedia and CD-ROM, San Jose, Calif, 18–20 March. Videotape, Reed Publishing (USA).

Nix, D and Spiro, R. (eds) (1990). *Cognition, education and media*. Lawrence Erlbaum, Hillsdale, NJ.

Palincsar, A.S. and Brown, A.L. (1984). Reciprocal teaching of comprehension-fostering and comprehension-monitoring activities. *Cognition and Instruction*, 1, 117–75.

Pease-Alvarez, L. and Vásquez, O.A. (1990). Sharing language and technical expertise around the computer. In C.J. Faltis and R.A. DeVillar (eds), *Language minority students and computers*. Haworth, Binghamton, NY, 91–107.

Reeves, T.C. (1986). Research and evaluation models for the study of interactive video. *Journal of Computer-Based Instruction*, 13, 102–6.

Simon, H.A. (1974). How big is a chunk? *Science*, 183, 482–8.

Spiro, R. and Jehng, J. (1990). Cognitive flexibility and hypertext: Theory and technology for the nonlinear and multidimensional transversal of complex subject matter. In Nix and Spiro (1990), 163–206.

Stanford/UNESCO Symposium (1986). *Computers and education: Which role for international research?* Report of the Stanford/UNESCO Symposium, Stanford University.

Sutton, R.E. (1991). Equity and computers in the schools: A decade of research. *Review of Educational Research*, 61 (4), 475–503.

Temple, A. (1990). Amiga in the Outback. *Amiga User International*, March, 48–9.

Watkins, B.T. (1992). A folklorist's material on more than 400 cultures to be available on a multimedia 'Global Jukebox'. *The Chronicle of Higher Education*, XXXVIII (36), Washington, DC, A21–A22.

Wilson, K. and Tally, W. (1990). The Palenque Project: Formative evaluation in the design and development of an optical disc prototype. In B. Flagg (ed), *Formative evaluation for educational technologies*. Lawrence Erlbaum, Hillsdale, NJ, 83–98.

2 Interactive multimedia technology: A summary of current developments

Nigel Paine and Philip McAra

Introduction

The IBM PC was announced on 12 August, 1981. This computer boasted 16Kb of RAM, expandable to 64Kb on the system board. With two memory-expansion cards you could get up to 256Kb, an impressive amount of RAM when compared with contemporary machines such as the BBC Model B or Apple II computer. This was serious personal computing! We were living in a text-based monochrome world where learning on the computer was a novel but low-level experience. The IBM XT machine was soon to arrive. Equipped with a colour graphics adaptor, 512Kb RAM and an Intel 8086 processor this machine marked a considerable advance.

What has changed this useful, but nevertheless limited, tool into an engine which can drive moving digital video, multi-track sound and text in a thousand different typefaces and control a host of external delivery platforms is processing power – access to massive storage and third and fourth generation processing ability which can import and export vast amounts of data at speeds of many megabytes of information per second with the ability to store and replay real-time video in digital format at 25 frames per second. Today, users can select from and interact with an enormous reservoir of materials stored in multiple magnetic and optical formats.

A number of elements have encouraged the development of electronic multimedia up to, and including, its logical endpoint – virtual reality. We see the following as the key elements:

- The arrival of laser disc technology which enabled the user to access high-quality analogue images on the computer screen. The ability of interactive video systems to deliver computer-mediated training which included full-frame motion video altered our perception of what the technology might deliver.

- The concept of the graphical user interface (GUI), popularized by Apple Computer, Inc, which was essentially about visual metaphors, intuitive 'feel' and pooling information on the virtual desktop. Only additional power was needed to move into multimedia. The concept was already in place.

- The steep fall in hardware costs and the unprecedented rise in computer speed and memory which transformed the personal computer into an affordable machine capable of combining audio and colour video in exciting ways.

- The release of Windows 3.0 by Microsoft into the mainstream IBM clone world, which accelerated global acceptance of the GUI as the standard mechanism for communicating with small computer systems.

- The development by NV Philips of optical digital technologies built around the compact disc (CD). This raised the interesting questions – 'If sound, why not data? And if data, why not images?' – questions which brought us to the very brink of interactive multimedia. A CD-ROM's 640Mb of storage opened up real possibilities for courseware development and packaging of myriad information if you could process that information and decode and display digital video material in real time.

Each of these elements added pressure on the others to speed up integration and development, and the technical solutions were solved at the interface between the GUI, the storage medium and the processor itself. When Windows 3.0 was launched, the GUI moved into the mainstream of personal computing. The economies of scale thus offered by the huge installed hardware base triggered the development of IBM-compatible multimedia applications. Microsoft Windows 3.0/3.1 has sold over 9 million copies worldwide. No piece of software has ever exceeded this level of market penetration, and third-party software houses must now produce Windows-based products in order to remain competitive. Rival graphical operating systems (for example IBM's OS/2.2) may be technically superior to Windows 3.1, but technical superiority alone no longer guarantees a product's success in the marketplace. Market share is a prime consideration and Windows is currently the *de facto* world standard graphical user interface for IBM clones. The huge market dominance of Windows is illustrated by the widespread installation of this product on hard disk drives at the point of manufacture.

The virtual disappearance of the 80286 processor from the motherboards of desktop and notebook PCs is attributable to the fact that Windows and Windows-based applications require an 80386 processor to operate in a satisfactory manner. The future demands of multimedia databases and courseware may soon require that the 386DX and 486DX chips, featuring 32-bit processing, are adopted as a minimum standard.

In the remainder of our chapter, we shall look at the main hardware and software systems used in interactive multimedia and discuss some of the strengths and weaknesses of interactive multimedia as it exists today.

Hypertext and hypermedia

The term 'hypertext' v as coined by Theodore Nelson in the 1960s to encapsulate the idea of packaging knowledge and information in non-linear ways that can be explored by self-determined linkages (Nelson, 1967). In developing hypertext courseware, use is made of specialized computer software, commonly referred to as 'authoring systems', to manipulate and link text and graphics within the computer environment. Hypertext-based authoring systems allow documents to be built by defining and manipulating objects on-screen. The author defines 'buttons' (which enable predefined links to be built into the hypertext document), 'fields' (which are set up to contain text) and 'graphical objects' (which can be created within the document or imported from other sources).

Typical hypertext documents allow the user to browse materials via a computer's GUI. The user navigates through the document by 'clicking' on the buttons or 'hotspots' defined by the author. The simplest way of understanding hypertext is to imagine a series of file 'stacks' made up of 'cards'. As the user browses one card, ideas or links suggest themselves and other cards or stacks can be immediately accessed for this information. The user can jump from one card to another in any order, guided by intellectual curiosity or prior knowledge rather than any linear arrangement preordained by the product's developer. The hypertext model supports the concept of learners enhancing or deepening their knowledge base by establishing new links and new dimensions to understanding by interacting with the material under consideration. Hypertext documents can also provide users with the tools to alter or add to existing material, thus blurring the distinction between the developer, the teacher and the learner.

The term 'hypermedia' describes hypertext applications extended to include such elements as animation, audio, still pictures and motion video. The terms 'hypermedia' and 'multimedia' are sometimes used interchangeably, but Romiszowski (1992) argues that these are, in fact, different concepts (see also Chapter 3).

Authoring systems

Authoring systems are software packages which enable hypertext-based multimedia applications to be created by non-computer specialists. Authoring systems simplify the developmental process by utilizing graphical user interface (GUI) systems. A GUI is a visual metaphor which uses icons to represent actual desktop objects that the user can access and manipulate with a pointing device. Using such systems, courseware developers do not need to be expert in writing computer codes or conversant with the technical functionality of computers' operating systems. The functionality of the scripting interface is dependent on the authoring system being used. Today's authoring packages offer multi-level access, ranging from the simplest level of page creation to advanced scripting with interfaces to program codes and data external to the package.

Numerous multimedia authoring packages now subscribe to the hypertext model. These systems are built using an object-oriented approach to application development. With the most recent products, developers can link segments of text, graphics, video and sound into sequences by building up storyboards on the screen using icons to depict each element and time codes to determine duration. The hypertext model provides a valuable conceptual framework which aids the management of the various elements of a multimedia system for dynamic applications in learning, reference, simulation, marketing and entertainment.

Today's authoring packages provide an integrated collection of software tools for the control of CD-ROM, laser disc or videotape players, video cameras and other multimedia devices. However, while the construction of courseware using such tools is more or less intuitive, any claims of 'instant courseware development' seriously underestimate the complexity of the task of designing quality materials for use in education and training. The educator or trainer embarking on the creation of interactive multimedia courseware needs to recognize the multi-disciplinary skills entailed in such work.

Global interest in the potential of hypertext authoring within the personal computer environment was triggered by the arrival of the Apple Macintosh in the mid-1980s. The Apple's object-oriented interface provided the conceptual launch pad for a number of hypertext-based authoring tools. HyperCard, with its intuitive user interface, has become a widely used and familiar hypertext application for in-house development of courseware. Such is the consistency in user interface design set by Apple Computer that the teacher or the developer can use HyperCard to develop effective interactive materials by utilizing skills honed on other Macintosh applications. Under licence, Apple Computer provides HyperCard free with every Macintosh. This is attractive to single or small-scale developers who may distribute completed 'stacks' in the knowledge that no run-time payments are required. However, serious developers will require the full version of HyperCard which must be purchased from Claris Corporation. The latest version of HyperCard has full colour implementation as in SuperCard and MacroMind Director, as well as scripting behind objects. This will clearly give HyperCard an advantage over other authoring tools on the Macintosh platform.

Other authoring tools for the Macintosh platform which are claimed to exceed the functionality of HyperCard include Plus, SuperCard and Authorware Professional. Plus, from the Spinnaker Corporation, is a HyperCard clone which supports colour and is also available for running under Windows 3.0 on the DOS platform. Original implementations of Plus running under Windows were unsatisfactory in terms of speed and later releases of the package require authors to pay run-time fees on the distribution of completed materials. SuperCard is a low-cost HyperCard alternative for the Macintosh, offering full colour (from 256 to millions). No run-time fees are required for this product, an attractive feature for authors.

In 1989, IBM launched LinkWay, a hypertext tool for personal computers running under MS-DOS. At the time of writing (1992), LinkWay is still being marketed in the UK as an inexpensive entry point system for educational users. However, the cumbersome nature of LinkWay's authoring interface made this a time-consuming way of developing serious applications. A true graphic user interface for the IBM platform was the necessary launch pad for serious developments. The 1990 launch of Windows 3.0, Microsoft's GUI for DOS-based PCs, provided this opportunity.

A large number of products are already on the market which offer similar functionality to HyperCard for the PC, running under Windows in VGA or Super VGA mode, and providing a palette of 256 colours. Examples of products running under Windows 3.0 include:

PictureBook (Digithurst Ltd), ToolBook (Asymetrix Corporation), Guide (Owl International), Authorware Professional and Plus (Spinnaker Corporation). These tools cover a wide price range, some requiring royalties on the distribution of finished applications.

Some of the more expensive packages allow multimedia authoring to be conducted via an iconic interface. The overall structure of the materials being developed is represented by an on-screen flow chart built using design icons. Each icon represents a hypermedia element and can be opened by the author to reveal settings and tools for working with that element. Such icons represent, for example, animation sequences, sound sequences or full and still video displays. Authorware Professional hosts an iconic interface, as does CourseBuilder for the Apple Macintosh.

IBM now provide a professional level multimedia authoring tool for use on personal computers running under DOS or OS/2. The Audio Visual Connection (AVC) authoring system lets the author design hypermedia materials by manipulating objects via an 'object-oriented' language. The current release of AVC supports the playback of Digital Video Interactive (DVI) files.

A current trend is the ability of authoring systems to produce dynamic applications which can be delivered on both the Macintosh and Windows platforms. Authorware Professional is an example of a package which is available for both platforms. ToolBook has the ability to read HyperCard files (stacks) and convert them under Windows into ToolBook files (books). The migration of applications from HyperCard to ToolBook is implemented using a third-party utility called Convertit! (Heizer Software, California, 1990).

A good example of a large hypertext information system now available for both Macintosh and Windows is the *Europe in the Round* stack, a project funded by the Learning Technology Unit of the UK Department of Employment as a database for all countries in the European Community. The 18Mb of data on geography, politics, tourism and training (normally distributed on CD-ROM) were converted from HyperCard to ToolBook format using Convertit!

Professional developers of multimedia materials tend to develop on the Macintosh platform, with applications being 'ported' to Windows for delivery to a wider audience on completion. The 'seamless' operation and general ease of use of the Macintosh-based tools for multimedia authoring should continue to make this platform a natural choice for developers.

MacroMind Director, a tool initially designed to create animation sequences, is now commonly used to manage multimedia resources on the Macintosh. MacroMind Director facilitates the development of complete multimedia presentations by creating graphics, text and animation, synchronizing them with sound and video, and adding interactive control for the user.

The advent of QuickTime, described later in this chapter, adds a new dimension to multimedia authoring, enabling movies to be integrated into presentations and courseware.

The Multimedia PC

A minimum specification, defined by Microsoft, has established a unifying multimedia standard. Microsoft Windows 3.1 software is at the heart of the Multimedia PC (MPC). The multimedia upgrade for Windows 3.0 was initially available, at additional cost, on CD and offered extensions to the Windows desk accessories which enabled the direct control of sound resources. The upgrade also features an interactive hypermedia guide to Windows. Release 3.1 of Windows now features the multimedia extensions as standard. This is a significant development, registering acceptance of multimedia in the mainstream. The important issue here is that the MPC definition lets developers know the minimum specification for delivery platforms. The MPC minimum specification is as follows:

80386 SX microprocessor (or better)
2Mb of RAM
30Mb hard disk
Video Graphics Array (VGA)
CD-ROM drive with audio output

8-bit sound input and output
Audio synthesizer
Musical instrument digital interface (MIDI)
Joystick controller
Stereo speakers

We stress that this is a minimum specification and that a platform equipped with 4–8Mb RAM, 100Mb+ hard disk and a 486 DX processor is more suited to development work.

Apple Computer claims that any machine in their range of products will deliver multimedia functionality when interfaced to the appropriate additional devices – for example, a CD-ROM drive. Indeed, every Apple computer from the Classic II model upwards comes complete with a microphone and the on-board ability to record and play back wave form audio. In reality, the Apple LCII, with 4Mb of RAM and colour monitor, represents a sensible minimum platform for multimedia activities.

AVI (Audio Visual Interleave)

This is an extension of the Microsoft Windows graphical user interface which allows the display of software-based full-motion video running in a window. This innovation enables short sequences of real-time video to be delivered on the MPC without the need for extensive additional video processing hardware. AVI can be seen as the PC's competitor to Apple's QuickTime, which was launched worldwide early in 1992.

QuickTime

QuickTime is a software extension to the Apple Macintosh operating system which allows on-screen motion video and audio to be cut-and-pasted into any existing Macintosh document through the use of software-based compression and decompression techniques. QuickTime's ease of use has led to extensive experimentation by developers in the fields of education and training. Using QuickTime, short motion sequences can be incorporated into text-based programs, and E-Mail can be enhanced by the inclusion of movie 'snippets' displayed in a window, as in an Open University trial system which uses a movie snippet to illustrate the functioning of a mechanical device to aid wheelchair users in mounting low steps. The quality of QuickTime images still falls short of video from traditional analogue sources and there are problems with lip synch. However, these shortcomings will doubtless be overcome as the technology advances.

Adobe Premiere version 2.0 has extended dramatically the concept of QuickTime. It is a digital movie-making tool which allows the user to create his or her own QuickTime movies and much more besides, including support for international video standards. There are also plans for a Windows version of QuickTime which at the time of writing was in beta release.

CD-ROM (Compact disc read-only memory)

CD-ROM is a laser-encoded optical memory storage medium with the same constant linear velocity (CLV) spiral format as compact audio disc. It was developed by NV Philips and the Sony Corporation. Up to 640Mb of data can be stored on one 12cm compact disc. CD-ROM is typically used as a mass storage device and is a key element of the

MPC. Large quantities of information are stored in digital format for access by the computer and the information held on the disc may represent data, sound and images. Because the information is held in digital format, the content is independent of the storage medium. The limitations of CD-ROM include slow data retrieval time when compared to a hard disk and an inability to deliver full-motion, full-screen video. The standards for this format are known as the 'Yellow Book'.

CD-ROM XA (Compact disc read-only memory, extended architecture)

CD-ROM XA is an extension of the CD-ROM standard, promoted by Sony and Microsoft as a hybrid of CD-ROM and CD-I. The CD-ROM XA standard allows audio and video sequences to be stored and retrieved from the same disc. The standard supports the use of compression and decompression techniques to increase the storage capacity of a CD-ROM disc. An example of an application delivered via CD-ROM XA is the *Reading Disc* produced by Cambridge Training and Development in associated with NeXT Technology. This disc combines all the elements of multimedia (photographic stills, graphics, sound and motion video) within about 200 hours of learning material. The disc runs on MS-DOS-based PCs equipped with CD-ROM XA hardware.

DVI (Digital Video Interactive)

DVI technology allows real-time compression and decompression and displays of digital graphics and full-motion video (FMV) with audio on an 80286, 80386 or 80486 PC. Developed by RCA's David Sarnoff Research Centre and now marketed by the computer chip manufacturer Intel, the current DVI solution has two components. The Action Media DVI board will enable the playback of full-motion video on a PC. The development platform requires the addition of a video capture module, allowing audio, still images and motion video to be captured from live or recorded sources.

DVI systems permit the storage and replay of video material held on the PC's hard disk drive in digital format as a DOS data file. However, file sizes are extremely large. A file containing a few minutes of digitized full-screen video can occupy 60Mb of hard disk storage space. Intel and Microsoft have agreed to a specification which expands the current media control interface (MCI) to work with digital video, thus giving rise to yet more initials – DV MCI. The new standard has been endorsed by sixteen companies, including Asymetrix, Fast Electronics, Fluent Inc, IBM and Iterated Systems. Intel is joining forces with Asymetrix (producers of ToolBook) to produce the necessary software development kit to allow the capture and editing of DV MCI applications in a Windows environment.

Professional developers are now using DVI technology alongside CD-ROM technology. Applications which include large data files for decoding and delivery via a DVI system can be stored on CD-ROM. An example of such an application is the *Multimedia Encyclopedia of Mammalian Biology* from McGraw-Hill. Users with an MPC equipped with a DVI delivery board can view video clips of mammalian behaviour as well as static visual information. In another application, DVI was selected by London-based HoDos Ltd to deliver a low-cost desktop simulator for training British Rail drivers in a project funded by the UK Department of Employment's Learning Technology Unit. Previous simulators for British Rail used videodisc technology. DVI technology was chosen for this project for a number of reasons. Firstly, it could integrate full-screen motion video, multiple sound channels and CD-ROM storage in the PC-based system, thus avoiding the need for overlay cards, videodisc players and additional sound generators. Secondly, the developers predicted a fall in price of DVI technology, a prediction which proved to be true (Intel now offers a DVI chip-set to equipment manufacturers for US$100). This further satisfied the low-cost criterion.

Thirdly, DVI offered greater flexibility, because of its ability to vary the frame-rate dynamically in real time. The prototype delivery system uses a large hard disk (DVI video takes up about 10Mb per minute) with the DVI Action Media delivery board installed in a 386-based VGA PC. The developers now intend to commit both data and programs to CD-ROM storage.

The cost of a Multimedia PC equipped with DVI delivery board is approximately US$5,000. The cost of upgrading an existing 386-based PC to MPC status with DVI capability is approximately US$3,200 (1992 prices). Even though prices are falling, it is unlikely that the MPC with ability to process real-time video will cost less than twice the price of the standard non-multimedia box.

Toshiba Europe and Fast Electronic GmbH have developed the first DVI solution for the colour laptop market. Video can be played from CD-ROM or hard disk and displayed on a built-in LCD screen. This system comes with 9cm CD-ROM drive, 200Mb hard disk, colour screen and DVI delivering card at the 1992 price of DM20,000 (Barker, 1992).

CD-I (Compact Disc Interactive)

CD-I, developed by NV Philips and Sony, is a 'one-box' entertainment and information system based on a CD-ROM drive with an on-board computer which utilizes the 68000 processor from Motorola. Rivalling Commodore's CDTV, CD-I subscribes to the interactive TV set philosophy, whereby materials are viewed on a television monitor and interactivity is gained via an infra-red joystick device. The TV set determines the standards of video display, which are poor by today's computer standards. CD-I is specified by the 'Green Book', a document agreed among Philips, Sony and Matsushita.

CD-I was launched on to the US domestic market in October 1991 and in the UK in April 1992 at list prices of US$1,000 and £599 respectively. The US launch was supported by more than 50 titles from such publishers as American Broadcasting Corporation Sports, Britannica, Caesar's Palace, Children's Television Workshop, Hanna-Barbera, Polygram, Rand McNally, the Smithsonian Institution, the Audubon Society and Time-Life. UK VAT-inclusive prices for CD-I titles range from £14.95 for storytelling, games and music discs to £34.95 for titles such as *Time-Life Photography*, *Treasures of the Smithsonian* and Rand McNally's *Atlas of America* (*MMD*, 1992a). Full-motion video (FMV) and other enhancements will increase the functionality of CD-I. There is now an intense focus on palmtop CD-I players by Sony, Sanyo, Matsushita and Kyocera. Sony's system, due to sell for about £840, plays unmodified, full-size CD-I and 12cm and 9cm CD audiodiscs, has a 10cm colour LCD display and weighs about 1.2kg without its batteries (*MMD*, 1992b).

Non-professional authoring of materials for delivery on a CD-I platform is not yet a realistic proposition for small-scale developers. While object-oriented authoring tools are starting to appear (for example, Mediamogul) such systems require an expensive array of hardware for effective material production. In the US, a CD-I starter system for developers currently costs about US$16,000 (1992). The Designs Work Bench (DWB) from LaserMedia UK is a CD-I authoring system which features a package from Script Systems Inc and offers a point and click interface to all functions required during CD-I title development. This system automatically generates the C-code required to drive the CD-I applications. LaserMedia claim that DWB reduces development times by up to 80 per cent, dramatically reducing the costs of title production. CD-I machines will also read and display ROMs Photo CD.

CDTV (Commodore Dynamic Total Vision)

CDTV is a consumer multimedia system from Commodore based on the interactive TV set philosophy and a rival to CD-I. Aimed at the home entertainment market as well as the educational and commercial sectors, CDTV is a 'one box' solution. CDTV is basically a non-keyboard Amiga computer with a CD-ROM drive. The graphics and level of interactivity in early CDTV titles were disappointing and CDTV tends to be primarily perceived as a delivery mechanism for games and entertainment titles.

A CDTV unit can be purchased in the UK for £599 and for less in the US. It outputs directly to a standard TV set. Users interact with the system with a hand-held infra-red remote control. In addition to the delivery of CDTV titles it can also be used as a stand-alone CD audio player. The product is based on a Sony/Philips type CD-ROM with a data capacity of 540Mb and, like CD-I, utilizes the Motorola 68000. The system hosts three coprocessors dedicated to handling video, sound and graphics.

A limited range of interactive entertainment and educational CDTV titles is currently available. In the US, titles sell in the US$30–50 price range and include: *The Holy Bible, The Complete Works of William Shakespeare, The Guinness CDTV Disc of Records, The World Vista Atlas* and the 21-volume *Grolier Electronic Encyclopedia* with its 9,000,000 words, 33,000 articles and 2,000 images on a single CD.

Commodore have set up the Commercial Developer Support Program in an attempt to encourage the creation of CDTV titles. Authoring can be conducted using a Commodore Amiga computer with Amiga Vision, a hypermedia authoring tool. The final product can be emulated on the host computer but in-house mastering of CDTV discs is not currently possible. CD manufacturing facilities in the US, Europe and elsewhere are available for mass production and one-off runs.

Write-once systems

Write-once/read many times (WORM) systems allow the user to record information on a blank 'writeable' optical disc but do not allow any subsequent erasure or modification to that disc. Sony and Philips produce units capable of recording CD-ROM XA, CD-I and CD-Audio.

Photo CD

This technology has been developed by Eastman Kodak. It allows the storage of up to 100 positive or negative 35mm images on one CD ROM. It is multi-session compatible which means that after an initial storage of images further images can be added until the disc is full. The Kodak Photo CD player allows the images to be viewed on a standard television. The images can also be read by a CD-I player or even an adapted CD audio player. It is possible to export the images from the ROM into bitmaps and from there into other software applications. There is evidence that some software applications will incorporate Photo CD import facilities in new versions of their software. CorelDraw 3.0 have done this already. This is an extremely cheap (about £35 per 70 images and pro rata) method of digitizing images for multimedia use at very high resolution.

IV (Interactive videodisc)

Interactive videodisc is now an ageing rather than an advancing technology but it remains supremely effective in delivering full-frame, full-colour moving video. The new digital technologies, such as DVI and CD-I, have as yet failed to deliver motion video as a cost-effective option. Barker (1990, p50) stated that

> IV is now old technology but it will be given a new lease of life by the coming of interactive multimedia . . . the old IV (interrupted video) will be given the kiss of life by HyperCard. IV did not put you in the driver's seat. HyperCard allows multiple paths through the material – a much more accurate simulation of the real learning situation.

Interactive videodisc technology can be used to hold up to 55,500 still images and deliver up to 36 minutes of full-frame full-motion video and two sound channels from a single side of a 30cm diameter laser disc. The laser disc player, being a random access device, can be instructed to seek and play video sequences without the time delays associated with tape-based systems. The basic components of an IV workstation are a PC, a laser disc player and a monitor. The PC is equipped with additional hardware which enables the laser disc player to be controlled by the computer. A typical IV workstation costs about US$5,000.

Products from VideoLogic are commonly used to upgrade 80286 and 80386 PCs to IV workstations. The MIC (Multimedia Interactive Control) 3000 card from VideoLogic allows computer-generated graphics to be integrated with full-frame motion video, the combined graphics and video picture being displayed on a TV-style monitor.

VideoLogic now produce the DVA (Digital Video Architecture) 4000 card, which digitizes the analogue video signal from the laser disc and integrates the video picture with the computer graphics in real time for display on the PC's standard VGA monitor.

The commercial authoring of IV materials is often conducted using TenCore, a long-established programming environment for developing computer-based training materials. PC OpenSoft from the Scottish Interactive Technology Centre is an inexpensive and easy-to-use hypertext-based tool for building interactive sequences using a laser disc video source. Hypertext-based authoring systems, including HyperCard and ToolBook, now provide users and developers with the ability to build exciting new front-ends for access to existing laser disc resources.

Successive waves of investment by the British government have failed to stimulate an anticipated UK demand for IV solutions. The Interactive Video in Schools (IVIS) project and the Interactive Video in Industry and Further Education (IVIFE) project are but two examples of centrally funded IV schemes which have had little impact in the British scene. The disadvantages of IV include the high cost of equipment and the expense of mastering laser discs. A predicted fall in the cost of hardware has never materialized, primarily because of the absence of a consumer boom. However, IV is far from dead. For example, Pioneer Video Manufacturing Inc. in Los Angeles have the capacity, after a recent enlargement, to stamp out 1.3 million discs per month and have plans to increase this capacity still further, and there are several other manufacturers with the same investment and capacity elsewhere in the US (Large, 1992).

IV applications continue to be successfully developed, marketed and utilized, particularly in the world of training, where new knowledge and skills need to be delivered flexibly and cost-effectively. For example, British Telecom has used IV technology to deliver a half-day training programme on staff appraisal and counselling which effectively replaced a three-day face-to-face training programme, thus achieving enormous savings in time and money. A large number of generic training titles are available from commercial providers such as Longman Training. Titles can be expensive but organizations may hire titles and IV equipment for the periods of time they are needed.

VR (Virtual reality)

Virtual reality (or Cyberspace) is an interactive, three-dimensional audiovisual computer-generated 'reality' which users may 'enter' or experience in the desktop mode. The origins of VR systems lie in the flight simulators used in pilot training and space research. The arrival of VR systems in amusement arcades has given rise to a great deal of media hype and speculation about VR. So what exactly is VR, and what can it offer the educator, trainer or information provider?

VR provides a totally new interface between the computer user and the application. Two classes of VR systems have now evolved, *immersive* and *desktop*. Immersive systems require the user to wear a headset. The current generation of headsets employ low-cost LCD TVs to good effect, but the limited resolution (360 x 230 pixels) is restrictive. However, the images displayed are generated and controlled by powerful computers and the user experiences the illusion of being within an alternative environment. Magnetic sensors located in the headset track the motion of the user in the real world, the data collected being used to control the movement of a virtual embodiment of the user in the 'virtual world' or 'artificial reality'. Glove sensors enable users to grasp and manipulate virtual objects in their vicinity. User immersion is further enhanced by stereo head-phones which create an atmosphere of ambient sound and facilitate communication between individuals sharing the 'virtual world'. While today's off-the-shelf VR systems enable the users to see, hear and manipulate objects, VR demonstration systems have featured gloves fitted with small pneumatic actuators which provide force feedback so that in future systems the user will also be able to 'feel' virtual objects.

Immersion VR systems are popular in the entertainment industry, but from a practical standpoint, they have a number of problems. The equipment is bulky, the headsets are cumbersome and the display is of low resolution. Sensor lag can cause a delay between head movements and view updating, causing user disorientation and frustration. Initial costs are high and maintenance is expensive.

Desktop VR, which allows interaction with virtual environments on a microcomputer, avoids many of the inherent problems of immersion systems while retaining the power of real-time visualization and interaction. The user views a three-dimensional environment on a high-resolution monitor and navigates through this using a 'space ball'. Desktop VR systems are now used in architecture, art, education and research and applications ranging from molecular modelling to numerical analysis can use VR to convey the correct visualization of objects and relationships within three-dimensional environments.

Desktop VR is a very real option for the developers of educational and training materials. Software tools for controlling and creating the virtual environment are now available and developers are beginning to explore the possibilities. For example, West Denton High School on

Tyneside has embarked on Europe's first student-based VR project and, in another project, Dimension International's SuperScape toolkit has been used to create a 'virtual factory' which students and trainees can explore to gain experience of a dangerous workplace and better appreciate the need for health and safety programmes.

VR is an exciting technology which is redefining the human–computer interface. Barlow (1992, p20) describes the challenge before us thus: 'Cyberspace remains a frontier region across which roam the few aboriginal technologists and cyberpunks who can tolerate its savage computer interfaces, incompatible communications protocols, proprietary barricades, cultural and legal ambiguities, and general lack of useful maps or metaphors.' As educators and trainers, can we afford to dismiss VR because it gets in the way of 'real' computing? We think not.

Strengths and weaknesses of interactive multimedia

So what of multimedia? What are the strengths and what are the weaknesses? Interactive multimedia is hugely attractive for a number of well-rehearsed reasons: authoring software; powerful delivery engines; good development tools; cheap storage media and high resolution graphics. Interactive multimedia provides a powerful means of enhancing learning and information provision. There are, however, a number of cautions which need to be heeded if the full potential of IMM is to be realized. These can be listed in priority order:

- *Lack of world standards:* there are a number of competing standards for the technology and this will inevitably mean winners and losers, particularly in the CD area. CD-ROM, CD-ROM XA, CDTV and CD-I are, to all intents and purposes, non-compatible. This means that if all one's development eggs are put into one basket, there is an element of risk in the longevity of the technological base. In a fast-moving world this may or may not be a factor in determining whether to get involved. IV may be seen as technically obsolete but its delivery platforms are still serviceable and successful applications continue to be developed. For example, British Telecom still uses IV while actively investigating alternatives.
- *Technical problems:* all the IMM technologies have 'technical teething problems'. Things do not always work exactly as specified and development teams must often take risks. For example, the

British Rail desktop simulator project team experienced problems with early implementations of the DVI solution. After building and testing the simulator with data stored on a large hard disk drive, the video files were committed to CD-ROM. Limitations were then encountered when the video files exceeded a certain size and were being read from CD-ROM. The latest implementation of DVI has overcome this problem.

- *Platforms:* it is now possible to develop IMM courseware on one platform and deliver on multiple platforms. However, there are exceptions. DVI was developed by Intel, which means that it is an IBM-clone machine product. Using that technology limits the developer to one platform. The integrated Apple/IBM model is attractive but limiting in terms of range and installed base.

- *Technolunacy:* this can be defined as the pursuit of technological solutions irrespective of the problems. There are still too many unrealistic claims about the potential of IMM technology and its ability to 'replace' other delivery methods. It has to be recognized that there are limits to the appropriateness of the applications and that a poor application does nobody any favours. Unfortunately, the market is currently overrun with technologists rather than educators and salespeople rather than IMM designers. Much 'high tech spec' is, in fact, 'low-level learning', a sophisticated version of computer-based learning. There will be no future for multimedia, other than in games software, unless the epistemological and pedagogical issues are thought through and it can be demonstrated that deep learning can be achieved through this medium.

- *Building successful teams:* a multi-skilled team is critical to the successful development of IMM applications. With divergent media, the audiovisual production teams and the text developers can work more or less independently of each other, only coming together to review progress. Interactive multimedia is, by definition, a totally integrated technology and must be developed by a team which possesses instructional design, programming, authoring and design skills as an absolute minimum. These teams, by and large, do not exist and have to be created. Any weakness within a team will impair the product or prevent it from reaching the marketplace. This has serious implications for product management and control and often imposes new disciplines on the organization.

- *Developmental costs:* these are high and, given the extent of non-automated processes, will not reduce appreciably. Video has to be produced to high standards. Graphics and programming are expensive and text, the cheapest element to produce, may be minimized by the very nature of IMM. The costs of developing educational and training materials can easily escalate to a point beyond cost-effectiveness unless the number of users is high. The high developmental costs also increase the risks for organizations producing or selling material speculatively.

The confluence of powerful microcomputers, GUIs and the optical storage and retrieval of digital information creates a situation in which spectacular growth seems possible in courseware development by commercial companies and by educational and training institutions. The technology also places a valuable tool in the hands of the learner, who can structure information and thereby create a unique artifact, a multimedia essay which captures, transforms and integrates snippets of text, sound and video. What we need now is firm evidence that the multimedia revolution is actually under way and that the manufacturers and the technologists can provide new means of facilitating learning as opposed to generating yet more products in search of a market.

References

Barker, J. (1990). Interactive video is dead, long live interactive video. In J. Barker and R.N. Tucker, *The interactive learning revolution: Multimedia in education and training.* Kogan Page, London/Nichols Publishing, New York.

Barker, J. (1992). Desktop video in the fast lane. *Inside IT*, 63, 3–4.

Barlow, J. P. (1992). Enhanced sensory perception. *The Journal of the Virtual Reality User Group* 1(1), 20.

Finney, A. (1991). Going Green. *Multimedia*, 31–2.

Large, I. (1992) Oracle . . . which Oracle? *Multi Media Digest*, 1 (2), 12–13.

MMD (1992a). CD-I bandwagon starts to roll in UK. *Multi Media Digest*, 1 (5), 13.

MMD (1992b). Japan Inc. shows its CD-I colours. *Multi Media Digest*, 1 (5), 13.

Nelson, T. H. (1967). Getting it out of our system. In G. Schechter (ed), *Information retrieval: A critical review.* Thompson, Washington, DC.

Romiszowski, A.J. (1992). Developing interactive multimedia courseware and networks. In *Proceedings of the International Interactive Multimedia Symposium*, Perth, 27–31 January, pp17–46.

3 Developing interactive multimedia courseware and networks: Some current issues

Alexander J. Romiszowski

Establishing concepts and contexts

This chapter is organized around ten issues identified by Kristina Hooper (1988) in her summary chapter to the proceedings of a 1986 Apple Computer conference on interactive multimedia (IMM) in education. These issues were:

- What is the nature of interactivity?
- The integration of the media
- Information databases or storytelling or what?
- Instructional design issues
- The question of emotion in education
- A language to describe the IMM experience
- Interfaces and metaphors
- Production and dissemination issues
- Implementation and management issues
- The synergy of converging technologies

Before addressing these issues, however, I should clarify my interpretation of the terms used in this chapter's title.

Interactivity can occur between teacher and learner, learner and learner and learner and a computer-based system. To understand interactivity qualitatively, we need to consider the various dimensions of such interactivity, from surface-level recall to 'deep processing' of knowledge.

In using the term *multimedia*, it is important to realize that the concept of using several media in concert to provide learning packages

Philosophy	vs	Pragmatism
The non-sequential multi-dimensional storage of information is characteristic of the human mind. Associative linking is a characteristic of creative thinking. So it should be 'natural' and more 'useful' to structure external knowledge bases in a similar way.		It is impossible to predict the information needs of any individual reader, so it is more effective and more economical to structure a knowledge base so that it can serve the information needs of any reader, under 'user-control'.
Constructivism	vs	Objectivism
Knowledge structures are personal unique representations of reality which are formed through interaction with one's environment, colleagues, etc. A hypertext is an external record of the unique structure imposed on a domain of knowledge by an individual or a collaborative group.		A given domain of knowledge may be analysed, structured, and therefore presented in a manner which will be optimal for both initial learning and later reference. The network of information nodes and the links between them represent the inherent structure of the knowledge domain.
Collaborative Creativity	vs	Systematic Design
The network of information nodes and the links between them are therefore the result of an act of creativity or insight on the part of the author(s). Any user should be free to annotate or otherwise add to the hypertext.		The preparation of hypertext is a specialist task to be performed by a few skilled designers for the benefit of many readers. Additions or changes to this structure will be the result of the systematic creation of new knowledge.

Figure 3.1: *Some variable dimensions of the hypertext concept* (from Romiszowski and Abrahamson, 1992).

is by no means as short lived as the 'multimedia revolution' implied in some writings (see for example, Barker and Tucker, 1990). As computer technology has made inroads into image processing, just as it earlier progressed into text processing, it has been natural to incorporate the ability to store information in a variety of media within a network of information, giving rise to the concept of *hypermedia*.

Hypermedia is the more recent connotation of Nelson's concept of 'hypertext', which may be summarized by two terms, 'nodes' and 'links'. Nelson (1967) and, before him, Bush (1945), promoted the concept of storing textual information as a network of documents linked together by meaningful 'pointers'. It is important to distinguish between the concept of hypermedia and the concept of multimedia. The use of a variety of media to improve communication of a particular topic is one issue. The storage of information (in whatever medium) in a network so that it can be more easily cross-referenced to other relevant information is another. Such a distinction is not always clear to many practitioners in our field.

The term *courseware* has been born in the context of computer-based software. However, it may be useful to remember that computer-delivery is only one of many ways of presenting information and exercises to students. I argue for the expansion of use of the term 'courseware' in order to fight the misconception that if one is using computers as part of an instructional delivery system, then the use of other media, such as group interactions or paper materials, is a sign of failure on the part of the designers.

Networks can be construed in at least three quite different senses. The meaning that probably first comes to mind is 'local area networks' or even 'wide area networks' to enable the sharing of materials, or the sharing of comments on materials, between distant participants. However, another interpretation of the term 'networks' relates to the structure in which a set of topics has been stored and interlinked to create a particular example of hypermedia courseware. Yet a third connotation is the network of concepts and ideas that exist in a person's mind on a particular topic. All of these meanings are valid and will be addressed in this chapter.

What is the nature of interactivity?

One may usefully approach this question by comparing interactivity as it may be experienced within a multimedia programme with interactivity as it is experienced on a day-to-day basis in human interactions or conversations. Let us examine a series of typical scenarios. In the first scenario, a technical instructor restricts information presentation to practical demonstrations and explanations of key points to be remembered in the execution of a given task. The learner is expected to follow the demonstration and explain the key points back to the instructor. The instructor's feedback is limited to corrective actions where the learner's performance is, in any respect, below expectation. One may notice the similarity between this account of human interaction and the methodology commonly used in linear programmed instruction.

In the second scenario, dealing with more complex tasks and content, the instructor may not simply correct and demonstrate anew the poorly performed elements in the original demonstration but may use alternative examples or analogies and other tactics to overcome specific learning difficulties experienced by the learner. We are now observing an example of human interaction analogous to the branching model upon which most computer-assisted instruction (CAI) is based.

Proceeding to a third scenario, we may witness a conversation which is more student-led than instructor-led. The student approaches the expert with a specific question. When this is answered, a further question is raised by the student. Again the instructor responds to this need. In this scenario, the instructor is a resource, supplying information requested by the student in the light of that student's current understanding of the topic and current needs for deeper understanding. Such a conversation is analogous to a student-led search of a hypertext or hypermedia package.

In the last scenario, the student may ask for help over a particular issue and, in replying, the instructor takes the conversation beyond the student's initial request. By posing challenges and asking questions, the instructor is probing the cognitive structure that the student has formed. By supplying extra, uncalled-for information, the instructor is extending this knowledge structure in ways which (from superior expertise and knowledge of the domain) the instructor realizes will be beneficial to the student. This form of dialogue has often been referred to as 'Socratic'. The equivalent machine-based models would be those arising from attempts to create intelligent tutoring systems. An intelligent tutoring system should be able to handle both system- and student-initiated questions and should be able to learn from a given student and adapt in a manner that has not been predicted and planned for in some preconstructed courseware. Taking this description as the ultimate goal in IMM, it is fair to say that, as yet, no practical project has modelled all aspects of intelligent tutoring.

To summarize, the value and nature of interactivity in the instructional process can best be described by the 'depth of processing' or the quality of thinking that is demanded of the student. In the four scenarios I have outlined above, we can see a continuum from surface-level interactivity (where simple responses are observed and commented on) through to deep-level conversational dialogues, where both learner and teacher are gaining insights into each other's thinking. This dimension (surface-processing to deep-processing) may be one of the most useful ways of evaluating the nature of the interactivity that has been built into a given instructional product.

From the research literature, it is possible to see increasing attention being given to exploring aspects of cognitive science that may throw light on how to proceed in order to achieve deep cognitive processing on the part of students. However, if we look at the practical field of development, we may be somewhat disheartened in that even the most recent products in the area of interactive multimedia are mostly employing surface-level interactivity. There is much basic research yet to be done. We are still a long way from translating into practice the principles of learning that the cognitive sciences have to offer us.

The integration of the media

The concept of utilizing media in combination is not new. The use of multimedia presentations and packages in education derives from the belief that differences in learning modalities of students can be matched in some way to the provision of audio, audiovisual and textual versions of a particular topic. A further factor that would indicate the use of a variety of media is the content to be transmitted. A third viewpoint is that certain media can teach more effectively than others. This has led to a large body of research, built up over more than half a century, that has compared the effectiveness of teaching a particular topic to a particular type of student by different media. Of late, much of this work has been attacked, notably by Richard Clark (1985), who re-analysed much of the research and the meta-analyses and demonstrated that when other factors are controlled, very little, if any, variability in learning is demonstrably due to alternative media choices. This led Clark to formulate his now-notorious comment that the contribution of media to the effectiveness of learning is no more than the extent to which 'the truck which delivers groceries to the market contributes to the nutrition in a community' (Clark, 1985, p259).

The important factor which Clark identified as causing significant differences in instructional effectiveness was the instructional design. Of course, in any comparative research of the nature that he criticizes, the instructional design should be kept identical in the various modalities of lesson compared. Otherwise, this is a confounding factor. However, it is exactly in this aspect that there is the hidden promise of media in education. A given learning outcome may be achieved more effectively by a superior instructional design and, occasionally (though not always), the superior instructional design may require the use of specific media that have not been used in previous instructional designs.

We need to focus on questions of instructional design. What presentation or manipulation of available text and images makes most sense in terms of the desired learning outcomes? How do we structure a learning resource in such a way that it can serve the needs of a variety of students who access it for a variety of reasons and with a variety of prior learning abilities? In order to make multimedia instructional materials viable economically, it is necessary to achieve such flexibility in use. Also, there is a growing trend towards student-directed learning resources that are largely independent of specific curricula and course requirements. The design of these resources requires the ability to implement a flexible structure that could theoretically take learners from wherever they are at the moment to wherever they need to be within the domain of study. It is for this reason that the notion of hypermedia has become so completely intertwined with the multimedia movement. Therefore we need to look more closely at some aspects of hypermedia before we move on to aspects of instructional design related to multimedia.

Information databases or storytelling or what?

To what extent should we prepare interactive multimedia for education as *instructional* resources as opposed to *information* resources? This question requires a clear definition of what we mean by 'instruction'. In three of the four mini-scenarios of human interaction articulated earlier, I used the word 'instructor', whereas in one case I used the word 'resource' for the teacher element. Whenever the word 'instructor' was used, there was a clear implication that some fairly specific learning outcome was in the mind of both the learner and the instructor. Even in the so-called Socratic dialogue, the instructor clearly had some idea in mind of learning outcomes that should be achieved if the interactions were to be considered successful. Only in the student-driven third scenario, where the teacher was restricted to answering questions posed by the learner, could we postulate that the teacher had no clear objectives in mind for the outcome of the interactions. There might still have been objectives in the mind of the learner, of course, but the learner was not necessarily communicating these to the teacher or asking for help in their attainment.

This is the key difference between *instructional* IMM systems and *information dissemination* IMM systems. In an instructional system, the teacher element presents information, evaluates the learning and uses that evaluation to attempt to improve the learning process. In an information dissemination system, the emphasis is on the content, organization, structure and presentation. There is no mechanism built into the process to evaluate whether or not the learning has occurred or to take remedial action where learning has not occurred.

It is interesting to note that the majority of interactive multimedia products used within education are information dissemination systems rather than instructional systems. In contrast, in the area of training, the bulk of interactive multimedia programmes exhibit the elements of presentation, practice, evaluation and feedback. In the educational products, many of these functions are left to the teacher to build into the lesson plan as classroom activities, project work, etc. But the live teacher and the other support systems are not always available when a learner chooses to study a topic and future systems should be capable of adaptively varying between the instructional and the informational modalities. Using such systems, a student should be able to access a system-driven instructional presentation or to browse with a total information database and, in either modality, should be able to ask for evaluation, learning guidance or constructive feedback when needed.

How interactive multimedia technology is being applied in training and in education may be symptomatic of a deeper underlying problem. The training applications of interactive multimedia tend to be based on typical training objectives and algorithmically structured content. In such training programmes, the relatively shallow levels of interactivity of programmed instruction and current computer-assisted instruction are usually appropriate. By comparison, the majority of interactive multimedia products for the educational market focus on packaging a diversity of materials on a particular topic in such a way as to make them more easily available to the teacher or the learner in the classroom and the student in the library. The uses to which this information will be put and the specific learning outcomes which will be pursued have often intentionally been left undefined, this task being considered more the function of each teacher or each learner. As a result, the level of interactivity built into such material is quite shallow, typically restricted to selecting items from a menu that describes the content stored in particular nodes of a network. This content may be organized in several alternative ways, but as design methodology, this goes no further than typical practice in the organization of conventional library resources.

Very little progress seems to have been made in marrying these two modalities of utilization. Further, when one modality (or both) has been implemented in one system, the rationale by which the information has been organized, and by which presentation, practice, evaluation and feedback have been designed, has not always followed the theoretical and practical principles that are already well documented in the literature of instructional design.

It would be particularly interesting in IMM projects to pursue the fourth of the scenarios described earlier, the Socratic dialogue analogy. In this model, students may interrogate the system to find answers to questions they have in mind but may also be challenged by the system to demonstrate understanding and, in the light of their response to that challenge, may be directed to further information sources. Here the system and the user cooperate in working towards the achievement of agreed learning goals. Few commercially available

INTENT IS TO:	IMM potential	Design bases	Key design issues
ENTERTAIN	Slick presentations	Film design Graphic design	Linear, system controlled presentations are better
	User involvement	Game design Simulation design	Should be interactive, under user control
MOTIVATE	Gain attention through impact Show relevance to real life	ARCS model Motivation theories Needs analysis Audience analysis	Seek 'emotional engagement' in the task Many examples or contexts for a varied audience
INFORM	Structured knowledge base	Information science Content analysis	Use Information Mapping and other organizing tools
	Networking of information sources	Computer science Library science	Compatibility and access problems must be solved
TEACH	Multimedia 'instruction' Networked 'conversation'	Objectivism Instructional theory Constructivism Conversation theory	Provision of practice and feedback is essential Structural communication or 'ICAI' as design models
FACTUAL:	Quick reference knowledge bases Online performance support systems	Job-performance-aids design Expert systems design	Some 'intelligence' in the FEED-FORWARD function is desirable (a 'librarian' interface)
CONCEPTUAL	Visualization of abstract concepts Application to real examples	Message design Content analysis Audience analysis Situated cognition	Some 'intelligence' in the FEED-BACK function is desirable (a 'tutor' interface)
LOOSELY STRUCTURED	Multimedia encyclopedias Generic media banks/archives	Library sciences Audience analysis Content analysis Interface design	Possible use of multiple authors/sources for the separate components of the system
HIGHLY STRUCTURED	Hypermedia networks Specific user applications	Schema theory Subject expertise Content analysis Information Mapping	There must be a central team responsible for designing the structure and the components

Figure 3.2: *Summary of design issues*
(from Romiszowski and Abrahamson, 1992).

interactive multimedia packages have attempted this. There are, however, a number of experimental models and these are discussed later.

Instructional design issues

In the literature of instructional design, one can identify several models that appear to be highly applicable in the interactive multimedia arena. In some training applications of interactive video, models derived from the principles of programmed instruction continue to be applied with excellent results. In job-related training situations, the more conventional drill-and-practice and branching tutorial models achieve the learning results required. Computer-based simulations have been successful in promoting understanding of complex concepts or in developing heuristic decision-making skills.

As one proceeds into the area of learner-directed search of information resources, the focus switches from models for the design of specific objectives-based instruction to models for the design of knowledge bases. In a recent workshop I participated in on 'Hypertext and Hypermedia for Learning', I was surprised to find how few of the participants had any knowledge of the principles of design for such knowledge bases. Only a minority were at all interested in the predesign of a hypermedia environment that could serve as a reference resource within a particular domain of knowledge (Romiszowzki, 1990). This lack of interest in design issues for domain-specific knowledge bases is paradoxical, given that this is the major area of production by commercial organizations supplying the interactive multimedia market. It would seem that researchers in the field are not focused on major demands in the marketplace. It is not surprising, therefore, that few commercial products are exemplars of well-organized knowledge bases. It is certainly not the case that there is no research and development in this area. A powerful methodology that can be applied successfully to the design of hypermedia environments for free browsing or guided study is 'Information Mapping', a system developed in the late 1960s in the search for more effective technical writing and documentation methodologies (Horn et al, 1969; Horn, 1976; 1989). This particular methodology is most effective for structuring information for both initial learning and later reference purposes.

In deeper levels of interactivity, as illustrated by our Socratic dialogue scenario, it would appear that the area of machine-mediated instructional design is less powerful and less developed than in the cases we have just discussed. Such depth and complexity of dialogue would require significant progress in artificial intelligence (AI) applied to computer-based instruction. But the progress in the application of AI to education has, on the whole, been disappointing. When Sleeman and Brown published their classic book on intelligent tutoring systems (Sleeman and Brown, 1982), the general tone of the editorial and of many of the papers was that the millennium had arrived. The reader was left with the impression that, within a decade or so, progress would be such that many examples of intelligent tutoring systems would be in regular use in education and training. Six years on, the next seminal work on intelligent computer-assisted instruction (Self, 1988), was much more guarded in its expectations. Today, four years further on, a growing number of commentators are expressing doubts as to whether intelligent tutoring systems will ever become a significant feature in the day-to-day practice of education. We may indeed be attempting to exceed the theoretical limits of computability. There may be whole areas of human thinking that are not only dependent on the analysis, organization and manipulation of knowledge but are also highly dependent on personality and emotional traits that may be well beyond the capabilities of replication within computer software. Indeed, one prominent researcher in the field of machine instruction, Gordon Pask, refuses to allow his work to be classified as being within the field of artificial intelligence, on the grounds he has never seen a machine exhibit true intelligence and never will, given that he has never seen a machine with the capacity to exhibit emotions.

The question of emotion in education

Paulo Freire, author of *Pedagogy of the oppressed*, was recently asked a question on this issue by a young American mathematics teacher. She described herself as a 'passionate teacher', one who believed in the beauty and the inherent elegance of her subject and wished to communicate her passion for mathematics to her students. However, these attempts were typically rejected by her students. She asked Freire whether she should refrain from expressing her emotions in relation to her subject matter or whether she should continue to attempt to change the attitudes of her students towards mathematics and towards her teaching style. Freire's response was that teachers without passion and devotion to their subject are not teachers at all, and that students who do not develop a passionate interest in the subject will not remain true students. Here we have the opinion of a great humanist, an educational politician and, by his own self-description, a utopian. His comments are similar to those of Gordon Pask, who was responding from the field of research on machine-mediated instruction. On this question, educators from quite different starting points agree that an emotional element is essential in instructional systems.

If, as this account suggests, students (at least in some cultures) tend to reject emotional presentations of the content of education by their teachers, this may emphasize a particular and important role for media in education. After all, in the area of entertainment, media are used specifically to arouse emotions. The mass media communicate much more through the affective channel than through the cognitive channel. It is interesting to speculate whether interactive multimedia products are in any way more effective in this respect than well-designed linear media presentations such as films, television or radio programmes.

If we were to look at the field of instructional design and development from the viewpoint of emotion, we would probably focus on motivation for learning as one of the first practical indicators that an emotional set is present or that some emotional change has taken place. It is appropriate here to review some theoretical viewpoints that have been expressed in instructional design models.

Firstly, Thomas Gilbert (1962, pp12-13) in the preface to his influential treatise *Mathetics* wrote:

> Certain assumptions about motivation need examination, for they underlie the thesis developed here. The principles and procedures I describe will assume a motivated student, one that possesses a genuine educational objective. If the animal is not motivated, or to put it differently, if the teaching agent is not a clear instrument by which he can achieve a reinforcer, the animal will not perform and cannot learn. If a student is to learn, the consequences of the mastery of a knowledge or skill must be reinforcing. We must assume that the student possesses an educational objective, because by itself frequent and apparent success in the course of learning is not *intrinsically* reinforcing. Inherent in any well-designed set of teaching materials is an attempt to maintain the motivation of the student. No matter how well designed materials are, if mastery in a subject is not an objective of the student, or those who control him, the materials will fail because the student will not complete them. People are circumspect in what they choose to learn; the so-called programming principle that progress through the course of learning is inherently reinforcing is not only poor learning theory, but is, I think, an abandonment of common sense. We confuse the tendency to pay homage to education with a desire to learn. Only seven per cent of those who buy a well-known encyclopedia ever open its pages; this multivolume symbol of culture is placed on the altar of the home next to the even more infrequently used *Holy Bible*.

Gilbert seems to place the responsibility for achieving initial interest and motivation in the learning process on elements other than the instructional materials that we may develop. Perhaps this is where the passion of the teacher or the emotional content of media play a key role. On the other hand, Gilbert acknowledges that an essential role of the instructional process is to maintain and not to extinguish the initial motivation that the student brings to the learning. Within the behaviourist model, this maintenance of motivation is achieved through demonstrated success towards a goal that has already been emotionally accepted by the learner. Clearly, we should give greater attention to how motivation can first be sparked and then maintained.

A more recent model for systematically planning the development and maintenance of motivation in instructional systems is John Keller's Attention, Relevance, Confidence and Success (ARCS) model (Keller, 1983). According to Keller, the first stage of the teacher's task is to gain the student's attention and interest. The role of stimulating media and passionate presentations is important here. Once a student is engaged, the instructional process can commence. At this stage it is inevitable that, because of prerequisite sequencing, certain topics may have to be studied that are not clearly related to the ultimate goals or the reasons for the student's initial interest. Therefore, establishing the *relevance* of these topics to the reasons originally articulated for studying the topic is important at this stage. As the learner progresses into the body of the instructional process, any difficulties experienced with content or process may reduce the initial level of motivation. Therefore the instructional process needs to be planned in ways that enhance the student's *confidence* in an ability to succeed. Finally, this confidence should transform into real *success* in progressing towards, and ultimately achieving, the goals toward which the student was initially motivated.

In the context of interactive multimedia, one can possibly separate the aspect of emotional involvement from the aspect of effective learning by considering the implications of the four components of the ARCS model. The trend towards what I have described as 'surface-level interactivity' (which places control over vast bodies of subject matter in the hands of students and allows them to browse in a non-linear manner), is often justified by stating that students are therefore free to follow up their unique interests. Unlike the passionate mathematics teacher who is seeking to engage the students emotionally in the study of a specific area of content, we are seeking to empower each student to select areas of interest and follow them up by accessing relevant information. However, unless students have some goals, what will they choose to follow up? Surely, there is still a great need for the creation of motivation through engagement of the student's interest and passion for learning in the topic.

If we abandon the linear lock-step curriculum, in which classroom teachers are charged with infusing motivation and interest for the standard content in all the students who come through their classrooms, we must replace that lock-step 'machine for emotional involvement' by a series of smaller machines, each linked to a particular subset of content area. The encyclopaedic interactive multimedia environment may need to include 'passionate front-end introductions' to sub-topics to motivate students to become emotionally engaged. Once the student enters a particular domain of study, the nature of the interaction would be less related to emotional presentations and more dependent on the analysis of the structure of knowledge and methods by which the student can self-evaluate understanding and control progress so that confidence is built and ultimately success is achieved.

A language to describe the IMM experience

The emergence of information technology has brought with it a new set of technical terms and concepts that are now being integrated with those already current in the field of learning and instruction. In 1986, Kristina Hooper described how some practitioners used the language of information technology, focusing on such issues as processing speed, screen definition and production values, while others used the language of the social sciences, concentrating on such matters as the motivation and engagement of students, the development of creativity and the provision of new opportunities for thinking, interaction or entertainment (Hooper, 1988).

One recurring problem in interactive multimedia development projects is the establishment of a common set of understandings among team members who bring quite different perspectives and expertise to the common effort. For example, earlier in this chapter I described the two quite distinct and often opposed meanings that we ascribe to the term 'interactivity'; one primarily information technology-based and the other primarily learning technology-based. While we continue to use the term 'interactivity' without clarifying these two facets of its potential meaning, we will be doomed to misunderstandings with our collaborators or clients. The need for a unified philosophy and common-use terminology is seriously under-estimated in the field of IMM.

Interfaces and metaphors

It is not surprising that among the major areas for discussion in a newly developing technology are the tools themselves and the ways in which the users interact with them. The development of the Apple desktop interface and other user-friendly metaphors is achieving significant change in the acceptability of computer-mediated communication and computer-based education. I would like to add two further metaphors for interactive multimedia.

The first of these is the metaphor of the 'questions-driven environment.' The user of an information system typically decides to log on because of some question that requires an answer. This question may, however, be extremely general and not very well formulated. A human expert (for example, a skilled librarian), would receive such a question and analyse it further, reflecting it back to the questioner in order to clarify it or to break it down into a series of questions. This process would continue until the question was sufficiently precise for the librarian to direct the questioner to the appropriate book or shelf. This function of the librarian is critical to the library system and is not at all the same function as that performed by a card catalogue or other indexing system.

Whereas I may have been somewhat sceptical earlier in my comments about the likelihood of intelligent tutoring systems having much impact on day-to-day teaching in our schools and universities, I believe that the development of 'intelligent librarian systems', apart from being more tractable, is arguably a much more important task to claim our attention. I look forward to seeing such tools widely available within a few years. Of course, the real value of these intelligent librarians will be in the rapidly developing 'electronic libraries' that can be accessed through computer networks from home or office.

The second metaphor that I think is worth pursuing is that of the 'virtual learning community'. I am referring here to the increasing use of networking to enable individuals, separated by both time and distance, to form collaborative conversational groups on a variety of topics. I look forward to the day when computer-mediated communication is integrated with the other information resources and multimedia on networks to become part and parcel of a total *information and conversation* environment. As the transmission of multimedia over distance in real time becomes a reality, the possibilities for interaction among people utilizing the same information resources open many new opportunities for creative educational applications.

I see the personal computer becoming an integrated communication tool that allows one to work with materials and discuss those materials with a community of others interested in the same issues. Within these communities there will be experienced teachers who can serve in a tutorial role and indeed can be considered as the intelligent tutor element within the system. The versatility of this approach is superior to that promised by the AI-based intelligent tutoring system developments of the last few years. The costs may well be highly competitive with any other alternative forms of delivery in educational systems of the future. Current research, including some that I have engaged in, suggests that such electronically based distance education systems may be equal (and in some respects superior) to 'place-based' small-group discussion sessions. For example, we have researched the delivery of business cases over such networks and the quantity and quality of discussion and the outcomes are superior to the results when using the same case material in the traditional mode (Romiszowski, 1992).

Production and dissemination issues

In her summary of the 1986 conference, Hooper assessed the market penetration of interactive multimedia as very small (Hooper, 1988). In the years since that conference, the only real success story of optical disc technologies has been the music CD. Videodiscs, although growing in availability and acceptance, do not form a large part of the media used in training, education or even entertainment. The long-promised, cheaper and more practical CD-ROM interactive video systems, whatever their format, are yet to make any impact on the marketplace. There has been some progress in interactive multimedia acceptance since Hooper's analysis, but all in all we are still in the position of trying to create a significant market for these systems.

There are some signs, however, that an IMM explosion is likely to occur. A combination of growing numbers of enthusiasts, increased interest in the commercial potential, wider availability of development platforms and rapidly diminishing costs can almost guarantee that there will be an accelerated level of provision of interactive multimedia programming for educational and training purposes. As usual, the training field leads education in experimentation with new technologies. For example, one training materials supplier, Applied Learning International, which specializes in computer skills development and management development, is currently offering over 200 courses on interactive video or CD-ROM-based delivery platforms. This represents 16 per cent of Applied Learning's total course offerings. Almost all of this shift from conventional computer-based instruction and linear videotape training materials has occurred since 1987.

There has also been an increase in the number of videodiscs and the amount of accompanying software for computer control being offered to the education market. Among such programmes is the *Louvre Videodisc*, which presents just about all the significant works of art housed in that collection (ODA/Voyager Company, 1991). This videodisc is accompanied by software that enables the material to be accessed in a number of ways, making the package a versatile database on painting, sculpture, etc. This is typical of the non-instructional interactive multimedia products coming on to the market that are essentially information resources which someone, usually the classroom teacher, must decide how best to use. Another relatively successful product released in the US is the interactive videodisc *Martin Luther King Jr* (ABC News Interactive, 1989). This combines newsreel footage and photos with extensive textual information presenting the details of most of Martin Luther King's speeches and other documentation referring to key events in his life and work. These documents are interrelated in the form of hypertext and this product comes closer to the instructional paradigm although, once more, there are no self-tests or other ways by which a user may check whether specific learning objectives have been achieved. In the area of specific instructional materials, fewer programmes have been produced so far. Some, such as ODC's series, *Life Science* (Walker, McCormick *et al*, 1989), are quite elaborate IMM packages which involve texts and reference materials in addition to videodiscs and associated software. These products allow many alternative objectives to be pursued. Self-tests are incorporated in the material, allowing a student to evaluate progress and find quick routes for review of important basic concepts, etc. Interestingly, the tests and review guides are included in the supplementary texts and not in the computer-based components.

Experience in schools in the Central New York area where I currently work is showing that the more 'instructional' materials are not being accepted by the teachers as much as the more 'reference' materials such as the *Martin Luther King Jr* and *Louvre* discs. Whether this is due to their higher cost and greater complexity of use or a reaction by teachers to materials which take over the lesson planning is not clear. It is probable that both these factors play some part.

The real market breakthrough for interactive multimedia will come when the decisions of if, when, and how to use them rests with the learners. This will happen when IMM is available in reference libraries or for loan, or when both the video and computer program elements can be accessed at a distance through computer networks. Then we may see the real potential of interactive multimedia as self-study material realized in the educational and training context. Such use will involve both information dissemination systems and instructional systems, but where students have a clear goal that they wish to attain, the instructional function will be essential. It is therefore a matter of some concern that instructional IMM materials are not being widely produced and that, when they are produced, they are not often well designed.

Implementation and management issues

However promising and effective a new technology may be in small-scale pilot projects, it only ultimately survives and prospers if it is capable of being implemented and managed effectively on a relatively large scale. One of the major obstacles to large-scale implementation foreseen by Hooper in 1986 was the cost of IMM hardware. From today's vantage point, one can see a significant reduction in cost. Another stumbling block to large-scale implementation has been the bewildering range of standards in hardware delivery platforms and control software. Again, this is likely to become less of an issue as serious market forces begin to play their part.

A more serious problem may be the adjustments in teaching methods and organizational structures of schools that are needed to take advantage of interactive multimedia on any reasonable scale. There is always an enthusiastic group of innovators and early adopters who will try any new idea, but many teachers tend to be late adopters and are often resistant to innovation and change. These teachers will need to be persuaded of some very clear advantages to the school, the students or their own professional positions before they will agree to become involved in interactive multimedia instruction.

Unfortunately, within the conventional school structure, many teachers are likely to see extra work and difficulty in implementing these interactive instructional systems. Some teachers may actually feel threatened by them. It will be difficult to convince these teachers that the potential benefits outweigh any negative aspects. By and large, technology-based innovations in the educational systems of the last half-century or so have resulted in ultimate rejection and failure. This holds true not only of the much maligned programmed instruction movement but also of instructional and educational television, individualized resource-based learning in all its forms and even major curricular changes, such as the introduction of a modern mathematics curriculum. Why then should we expect the current interactive multimedia revolution to fare any better?

In answer to this question, I believe that a number of factors will contribute to the adoption of interactive multimedia. Firstly, there has been for some time, and in many countries, a growing dissatisfaction with the apparent lack of effectiveness and efficiency of conventional educational systems. Secondly, there has been an ever-increasing emphasis on distance education and open learning systems. These systems are becoming major providers and are no longer regarded as poor substitutes for conventional classroom-based instruction. It is quite possible that, by the turn of the century, distance and open learning systems may account for more students worldwide than conventional campus-based systems, especially in the areas of higher education and continuing education. In the information age, it will be increasingly recognized that the conventional training institution is no longer a model capable of reacting sensitively to the fast-changing and varied needs of job-related education and training.

In the not too distant future, it is probable that most job-related procedural training will be delivered by what is becoming known as 'computer-based performance support systems'. These encapsulate, in one system, all the materials necessary for initial training, on-job reference, performance evaluation and quality control. Many routine jobs, and those involving low-level intellectual tasks, will be taken over by expert systems. The more conceptual and heuristic decision-making activities will become major components of many people's work. Traditionally, these are best taught by small-group learning activities (seminar, case study and role play). It is in this area of instruction that *virtual groups* of individuals separated by time and distance may replace or complement *place-based groups*. If this is the case, then such virtual groups will utilize a variety of materials as a basis for their discussions. Many of these materials could well be in the form of interactive multimedia. How IMM may feature in a future scenario is discussed further in the next section.

The synergy of converging technologies

At the 1986 conference, Kristina Hooper asked what would happen when one combined the traditions of a dozen or more professions, all of which had had some part in the development of interactive multimedia. She asked whether the results would be something new. Could they possibly be boring? Would they be significant educationally? Would they be entertaining? Many such questions concerning technological synergy were asked at the conference, but few answers were given. We are probably still no closer to being able to point to a sufficient number of 'war stories' in the interactive multimedia 'revolution' to form any generalizable opinions about the future.

However, one important aspect of technological synergy not addressed by Hooper was the synergy of information technology, educational technology and telecommunications technology. The third partner, telecommunications, has joined this synergistic group comparatively recently. Computer technology and educational technology have been bedfellows since the beginning of computer-based instruction in the early 1960s. The more recent developments in telecommunications technology, the digitization of all data, the broadband transmission possibilities opened up by fibre optics, the worldwide satellite communication networks and ISDN have opened up a vast array of opportunities for the processing, storage and transmission of information. One interesting outcome of these advances in telecommunications is that the distance education delivery systems of the last decade have been substantially different from the earlier systems such as that of the Open University in the UK. Whereas the Open University was based on a correspondence course model and essentially conceived as a system broadcasting one message to many students, the modern distance education systems are small interactive discussion networks utilizing telecommunications with print as the support medium rather than the principal medium.

The networking of computers has created the opportunity for a completely new modality of communication. Unfortunately, because of the earlier tradition of teleconferencing, this modality was initially known as 'computer conferencing'. I say 'unfortunately' because, in many people's eyes, conferencing is synonomous with little more than chit-chat. The versatility of networks of computers as communication tools allows more variety in communication and instructional modes than mere conferencing. This is now widely realized and has led to the more generally accepted term, 'computer-mediated communication' (CMC).

The synergy of information technology and telecommunication technology is revolutionizing the world. Education and training are major enterprises that utilize information and are in the business of communication. They are well placed to exploit these new and revolutionary opportunities. The economic viability of networked education and training will inevitably increase as the relative costs of place-based education continue to rise. This is already happening in the area of human resource development (HRD) in the US and elsewhere, where the concept of networked training is rapidly being accepted by the business HRD community. As this trend continues, the first major mass market for interactive multimedia courseware will be established. Once the computer networks have been installed, the extra costs of equipping them with the hardware necessary for incorporating multimedia are not very high. In the medium term, as travel and subsistence costs continue to climb and as investment costs in interactive multimedia hardware and software continue to decline, the economic equation will increasingly favour the use of IMM in conjunction with computer-mediated communication.

As integrated systems of computer-based interactive instruction and conversational virtual groups become commonplace in the business setting, the model will be adopted by universities, further education institutions and, ultimately, school systems. In the long term, as the electronic transmission of multimedia over wide area networks becomes viable, both the educational power and the economic advantage of networked education and training will increase. At that time, the 'educational utility' concept (Gooler, 1986) may become a reality.

Conclusion: A research agenda

If, as I suggest, economics is going to be the major driving force for such trends, the chances are high that pressures will be put on trainers and educators to utilize these new technologies. These changes will generate many questions; we shall need to know whether such methods are reasonably equivalent to current methodologies of education and training or significantly inferior or superior to the best that we can currently do. At present, we have little research to guide us in answering these questions.

I have been particularly interested in this research agenda for a number of years because it is clear that, in the not too distant future, we are likely to be faced with a situation where technology is leading education and training in directions that may not be pedagogically ideal but which happen to be economically or politically expedient. As we are unlikely to be able to prevent such changes, it seems that we should be engaged in a programme of research and development that will render IMM/CMC systems more effective across a wide range of educational and training situations. We need to ask how we can get the best value out of the interactive multimedia component of such systems and how we can get the best value out of virtual group discussions.

Many current implementations tend to treat these two components relatively separately, as has typically been the case in conventional educational systems. For example, distance education students are sent assignments and, having carried them out, are invited to come 'online' to discuss their reactions or to respond to questions from remote instructors. The designers of the distance education courseware have usually given little thought to the role and structure of these interactive sessions and the instructors who lead the follow-up discussions have little idea of the design of the courseware unless they have made particular effort to review these materials. By comparison, I would suggest there needs to be a synergistic model in which the design and development of the interactive multimedia components of an instructional system occur alongside the design and development of the supporting discussion environments.

In one particular line of research and development, I have been developing environments for the study of case materials at a distance (Romiszowski, 1992). These involve the presentation of the 'facts of the case', either as conventional linear presentations or as some form of interactive simulation. Discussion of the case then commences in the interactive multimedia environment by means of an open-ended, conversational, tutorial form of computer-based instruction. At this stage, the surface-level interactions needed to check that the basic facts of the case have been understood by the student, and that some position, interpretation or decision has been taken by that student, occur within the multimedia package. The need for deep-level interactions with an intelligent tutor (or with other intelligent peers who may have opposing opinions) becomes greater as the focus moves to reflective analysis of the thought processes that occurred in individual students' minds during their analysis and interpretation of the case. When the discussion reaches this level of deep processing, network connections are automatically made to allow individual learners to share their ideas with other learners and tutors who form the geographically distributed 'virtual group' for the course.

This approach has been found to be both effective and efficient. It is effective in that it ensures that every participant not only considers the surface-level aspects of the case under consideration, but takes positions which require a considerable amount of deep processing of the underlying concepts and principles which govern the approach to take to the particular case. This deep processing results in conversational interactions that allow intelligent constructive feedback to be received by each participant, either from a distant tutor or from one or more peers. The overall effectiveness of this form of deep-level interaction is reflected in the ability to transfer the newly acquired heuristic problem-solving skills practised in one case to other, similar cases or even to real-life problem-solving situations. The efficiency of the system is reflected not only in the significant cost savings that can be achieved through the elimination of travel to group meetings but also through the efficient use of the time of the experienced tutors, who are only called in to interact with students at the deep processing level and are spared the relatively mundane task of evaluating and correcting basic surface-level misunderstandings of the facts of the case and their implications.

References

ABC News Interactive (1989). *Martin Luther King Jr*. Optical Disc Corporation, Warren, NJ.

Barker, J. and Tucker, R.N. (1990). *The interactive learning revolution: Multimedia in education and training*. Kogan Page, London/Nichols Publishing, New York.

Bush, V. (1945). As we may think. *Atlantic Monthly*, 176, 101-8.

Clark, R.E. (1985). Evidence for confounding in computer-based instruction studies: Analysing the meta-analyses. *Educational Communications and Technology Journal*, 33 (4), 249-62.

Gilbert, T.F. (1962). Mathetics: The technology of education. *Journal of Mathetics*, 1 (1), 7-73.

Gooler, D.D. (1986). *The educational utility: The power to revitalize education and society*. Educational Technology Publications, Englewood Cliffs, NJ.

Hooper, K. (1988). Multimedia in education. In S. Ambron and K. Hooper (eds), *Interactive multimedia*. Microsoft Press, Redmond, Wash, 316-30.

Horn, R.E. (1976). *How to write information mapping*. Information Resources Inc, Lexington, Mass.

Horn, R.E. (1989). *Mapping hypertext: The analysis, organization, and display of knowledge for the next generation of on-line text and graphics*. The Lexington Institute, Lexington, Mass.

Horn, R.E., Nichol, E., Kleinman, J. and Grace, M. (1969). *Information mapping for learning and reference*. Information Resources Inc, Lexington, Mass.

Keller, J.M. (1983). Motivational design of instruction. In C.M. Reigeluth (ed), *Instructional design theories and models: An overview of their current states*. Lawrence Erlbaum, Hillsdale, NJ, 383-484.

Nelson, T.H. (1967). Getting it out of our system. In G. Schechter (ed), *Information retrieval: A critical review*. Thompson, Washington, DC.

ODA/Voyager Company (1991). *Louvre Videodisc. Vol 1: Paintings and Drawings. Volume 2: Sculptures and objets d'art. Vol 3. Antiquities*.

Romiszowski, A.J. (1990) The hypertext/hypermedia solution – but what exactly is the problem? In D.H. Jonassen and H. Mande (eds) *Designing Hypermedia for Learning*. Proceedings of a NATO Advanced Research Workshop, Rottenburg, Germany. Springer-Verlag, Berlin, 321-54.

Romiszowski, A.J. (1992). Conversational systems for adult education and training. In *Proceedings of the International Interactive Multimedia Symposium*, Perth, 27-31 January, 495-523.

Romiszowski, A. and Abrahamson, A. (1992). Interactive multimedia for education, part 1: concepts/applications. In *Instructional Developments*, 3 (1), 1-10.

Self, J. (ed) (1988). *Artificial intelligence and human learning: Intelligent computer-aided instruction*. Chapman & Hall, London.

Sleeman, D.H. and Brown, J.S. (eds) (1982). *Intelligent tutoring systems*. Academic Press, New York.

Walker, T., McCormick, B. *et al* (1989). *Life science: The living textbook*. Optical Data Corporation, Warren, NJ.

4 Research support for interactive multimedia: Existing foundations and new directions

Thomas C. Reeves

Introduction

The 1990s are witnessing worldwide development and utilization of interactive multimedia. However, much of the development and most of the implementation of IMM seem to be guided by habit, intuition, prejudice, guesswork or politics. A solid research base seems largely absent in the rush to bring IMM products to market or to disseminate the technology throughout education and training. This chapter describes some research foundations upon which IMM should be based, and recommends directions for new research to guide the development and use of IMM.

Although the roots of IMM can be traced back to the 1940s, when Vannevar Bush gave the world a glimpse of the *memex*, a hypothetical mechanized system for organizing information via associations indexing (Bush, 1945), the current enthusiasm for IMM began in the late 1980s and continues to grow (Ambron and Hooper, 1990). International business interests are especially fervent in promoting the idea that IMM can provide students and trainees with learning environments of unparalleled effectiveness. For example, John Sculley, Chief Executive Officer of Apple Computer, asserts:

Teachers and students will command a rich learning [multimedia] environment that, had you described it to me when I was in school, would have seemed entirely magical. Imagine a classroom with a window on all the world's knowledge. Imagine a teacher with the capability to bring to life any image, any sound, any event. Imagine a student with the power to visit any place on earth at any time in history. Imagine a screen that can display in vivid color the inner

Learner's Knowledge,   **Design of the**
Experience, and Motivation   **Interactive Multimedia**

Figure 4.1: *Psychophysics of IMM* (based on Fischer and Mandl, 1990).

workings of a cell, the births and deaths of stars, the clashes of armies, and the triumphs of art. And then imagine that you have access to all of this and more by exerting little more effort than simply asking that it appear. It seems like magic even today. Yet the ability to provide this kind of learning environment is within our grasp. (Sculley, 1988, pvii)

James E. Dezell Jr, President of IBM's new education company, EduQuest Inc, is no less an enthusiastic promoter of IMM:

Multimedia brings to bear dynamic visual information in the form of full-motion video that gives you a direct pipeline into the brain. We, as human beings, process that data very efficiently. The power of full-motion video combined with interactivity allows every person to discover knowledge in the pattern that fits their paradigm for learning – the way they learn best, individualized. (Taylor, 1990, p27)

The assumption that IMM 'automatically' supports learning must be examined carefully. Some of the promotional advertisements and brochures for IMM technologies imply that if course content is presented to students in a multimedia format, both motivation and achievement will soar. This is simplistic and misleading. IMM cannot guarantee learning any more than a library in a school can.

Fischer and Mandl (1990, pxxiv), in describing what they call 'a psychophysics of hypermedia,' clarify the issue. They maintain that IMM programmes only come into existence when learners perceive and interpret them. The quality of interaction is determined by the skills and experience learners have with IMM and the degree to which the medium has been designed to support the interaction. Just as a library void of intelligent, skilled teachers and students capable of utilizing its resources is merely a warehouse, multimedia without the interpretative acts of learners is only a collection of textual, graphical and audio elements.

Locatis, Letourneau and Banvard (1989, p69) also comment on the issue of multimedia and learning. They compare the design of multimedia with many reference books, both formats often using a 'somewhat arbitrary alphabetical arrangement' for organizing content. Such arrangement schemes may work well with users who have the skills, motivation and experience to access information through free associative thinking. However, these informational structures may not be sufficient for tyros who are unable to provide the missing links. They conclude that 'linking information is a necessary, but insufficient, condition for learning' (p72).

However, in the same way that many people learn from texts without explicit instructional assistance being provided within the books themselves or by teachers or other structuring resources, people can learn from IMM without explicit pedagogy being incorporated into the programme. Such learning can be incidental or intentional, depending on the motives of the user, the accessibility of the information in the programme and the intellectual abilities and experiences of the learner.

On the other hand, when IMM programmes are designed intentionally to support learning, some level of pedagogy is required. Fischer and Mandl (1990, pxxiv) maintain that 'instructional hypermedia should contain a tutorial and/or pedagogical component . . .' Kinzie and Berdel (1990) describe instructional design features that can facilitate learning through IMM, including orientations, maps, help, hints and questions. Jonassen and Grabinger (1990) describe some of the problems involved in designing the learning interface (the features of multimedia that support learning) as opposed to the user interface (the features of multimedia that support exploration).

In short, a primary problem in designing IMM for learning is finding the balance between pedagogical support and exploration support (Rezabek and Ragan, 1989). The provision and integration of music, voice, still pictures, text, animation, motion video and a friendly interface on a computer screen do not directly support learning. These media elements are vehicles that enable learners to experience the instructional design and pedagogical support incorporated into the programme. In other words, these elements of IMM only become effective as they are activated within the context and interactions established by the pedagogical design of the programme.

Existing foundations of research support for IMM

The development of large-scale IMM learning environments has expanded greatly in recent years (Hannafin, 1992). For example,

IBM's two extensive IMM products, *Illuminated Books and Manuscripts*, and *Columbus Encounter: Discovery and Beyond*, are each advertised as providing more than 180 hours of interactive learning opportunities for middle and secondary school students (*MVM*, 1991). Unfortunately, the creators of these products prefer to emphasize the technical rather than the pedagogical aspects of their programmes. Consider, for instance, the words of Morgan Newman, one of the primary authors of IBM's *Illuminated Books and Manuscripts* series:

> We are convinced that things have to be damn slick to engage people. As brilliant as a one-bit HyperCard stack might be academically, the production values are incredibly disparate. It is our sole intention to grab people by the gut and turn them upside down. (Holsinger, 1991, p25)

bank or Some proponents of IMM even argue that, to be successful, IMM should be formatted like pop-music videos. Such treatment may grab the attention of learners and even sustain motivation; however, there is little evidence that this or similar approaches are adequate for other essential aspects of the instructional design, such as generating responses and receiving feedback.

Such disregard for pedagogy may reflect disappointment with earlier instructional technologies such as programmed instruction and computer-based training, which typically were based on behavioural learning theory (Hannafin and Rieber, 1989). Although there is some evidence that these programmes are effective for learning concepts and procedural knowledge, their ability to develop higher-order learning has been limited (Clark, 1992; Kulik and Kulik, 1986).

Many of these earlier technologies and the processes by which they were developed were based on what Duffy and Jonassen (1991) call the 'objectivist tradition', ie, the view that knowledge exists in its perfect form in the world outside the learner and that each learner possesses a more or less perfect understanding of that perfect form. Further, many of these earlier technologies used a behaviourist pedagogy (Skinner, 1968). Nix (1990) maintains that interactive instructional programmes designed from this perspective ignore, or even repress, human potential.

If learning how to learn and developing problem-solving skills are the primary goals of education and/or training, then new approaches to interactive learning, especially IMM, must be considered (Hannafin, 1992). The approach advocated in this chapter is to base the design of IMM for learning on sound pedagogical foundations that reflect contemporary cognitive psychology.

Effective pedagogy for IMM

What is the basis of an effective pedagogy for IMM? Certainly, the leading candidate today is the pedagogical philosophy known as 'constructivism' that has grown out of advances in cognitive science (Duffy and Jonassen, 1991; Nickerson, 1988; Papert, 1990).

According to Resnick (1989), there are three primary principles of contemporary cognitive theory, and each of these may be required to unlock the learning potential of IMM. Firstly, IMM should be designed to follow the principle that learning is a process of 'knowledge construction' as opposed to 'knowledge absorption'. Secondly, IMM should be structured to support the principle that learning is 'knowledge-dependent', ie, that people inevitably use existing knowledge upon which to build new knowledge. And thirdly, IMM should be designed to take advantage of the principle that learning is highly tuned to the 'situation' in which it takes place.

Knowledge construction

In traditional academic classroom instruction, knowledge is often perceived and treated as an end in itself rather than as a means to more important ends such as solving problems or understanding current events (Bransford *et al*, 1990). In mathematics, students struggle to 'learn' logarithms, geometric forms and statistics without perceiving their utility in fields as diverse as astronomy, architecture and agriculture. In science, these same students memorize definitions, tables and formulae without perceiving their enormous impact as tools in medicine, archaeology and criminology. In the humanities, students 'read' great works of literature without grasping their relevance to such contemporary issues as war, civil rights and the environment. In all these cases, new information is treated as isolated facts and discrete skills to be 'learnt' rather than as knowledge, skills and attitudes to be 'used'.

There are many contexts in which IMM can be designed to present a focal event or problem situation that will serve as an 'anchor' or focus for collaborative efforts among instructors and students to retrieve and construct knowledge (Brown, Collins and Duguid, 1989; Cognition and Technology Group at Vanderbilt, 1992). The knowledge construction process will in turn enable the instructors and students to understand the event or resolve the problem. Some cognitive psychologists call this type of instruction 'anchored instruction' (Bransford *et al*, 1990; Cognition and Technology Group at Vanderbilt, 1992) because the process of constructing new knowledge is situated or anchored in meaningful and relevant contexts. The events and problems presented in multimedia programmes should be purposively designed to be intrinsically interesting, problem-oriented and challenging. In response to these types of events and problems, students will construct useful (as opposed to inert) knowledge.

A well-designed and extensively researched implementation of the constructivist learning principle is the *Jasper Woodbury Problem Solving Series*, developed by the Cognition and Technology Group at Vanderbilt University (1992). Through these IMM programmes students discover the need to develop advanced mathematical problem-solving skills through simulated dilemmas in flying planes, operating motor boats and other high-interest video adventures. The *Jasper* series is an example of what Hannafin (1992) calls a 'generative' learning environment, ie, an IMM programme that requires students to construct or generate their own knowledge rather than select knowledge from prepackaged options. Knowledge acquired in such generative learning environments is more likely to generalize than the inert knowledge acquired in traditional passive learning environments (Cognition and Technology Group at Vanderbilt, 1992).

Knowledge-dependent learning

According to Glaser (1984) and other cognitive psychologists, knowledge begets knowledge. In other words, the ability to construct new knowledge is a function of both the amount and quality of one's existing knowledge as well as one's reasoning and other intellectual abilities. Educators at all levels have long wrestled with the question of whether instruction ought to concentrate on teaching content or on developing the general intellectual abilities of students. In the US there has been a surge of support for content, as evidenced by the calls for a return to 'cultural literacy' by Hirsch (1987), Bloom (1987), and others. On the other hand, some authorities continue to promote the development of critical thinking skills and creativity (Schank, 1988; Tuerck, 1987).

A reasonable approach to solving this dilemma is based on the recognition that it is as futile to teach thinking skills without knowledge as it is to teach knowledge without thinking skills. IMM can be designed to integrate both these goals. Such IMM programmes would recognize that learning depends heavily on what students already know and therefore provide 'cognitive bootstrapping' for the construction of knowledge and the development of intellectual skills (Resnick, 1989).

One way of 'bootstrapping' the development of new knowledge is to enable students to confront misconceptions they have about various ideas. For example, research in science education indicates that the construction of new knowledge in a field such as physics may be constrained by commonly held conceptions of natural phenomena that conflict with accepted scientific theories (Johsua and Dupin, 1987). When students are exposed to discrepant events such as seemingly identical tops that spin in wildly different ways, they are forced to confront their everyday conceptions of the phenomena. Then the students can be encouraged to resolve the discrepancies in collaboration with their peers and teachers, and ultimately construct new knowledge on the foundations of what they previously 'knew'.

Cates (1992) provides numerous examples of how IMM can be designed to support the 'metacognition' that students use when learning with IMM. For example, IMM can include advanced organizers, outlines, content maps, time estimates and other features that help learners develop accurate perceptions of the overall structure of the programme as well as aid them in focusing on the specific task at hand. Regrettably, no IMM programmes have yet incorporated more than a few of these metacognitive support strategies in a comprehensive manner. Important research and development efforts aimed at building IMM that support metacognitive processes are being led by Richard Mayer at the University of California, Santa Barbara (Mayer, 1989), and by Roger Schank at Northwestern University's Institute for the Learning Sciences (Schank and Jona, 1990). Researchers and developers at these and other institutions are building prototype IMM programmes that integrate two or more metacognitive support functions, but these functions are not included in commercially available IMM programmes at this time.

Situated learning

A major concern for educators and trainers alike is the degree to which classroom learning transfers to external situations in which the application of knowledge, skills and attitudes is appropriate. A major benefit of IMM is that knowledge constructed through interaction with multimedia programmes can become connected or conditionalized to goals and the appropriate actions required to attain goals (Collins, Brown and Newman, 1989). The cognitive theories of Newell and Simon (1972), Brown (1985) and others support the fundamental principle that the way in which knowledge, skills and attitudes are initially learned plays an important role in the degree to which these abilities can be used in other contexts. To put it simply, if knowledge is learned in a context of use, it will be used in that and similar contexts. This is especially important in training for the workplace, whether this be the construction site, hospital, bank or aircraft flightdeck.

In traditional instruction, information is presented in encapsulated formats, often via lectures and texts, and it is largely left up to the student to generate any possible connections between conditions (such as a problem) and actions (such as the use of knowledge as a tool to solve the problem). There is ample evidence that students who are quite adept at 'regurgitating' memorized information rarely retrieve that same information when confronted with novel conditions that warrant its application (Bransford et al, 1990).

One of the earliest IMM programmes to incorporate a 'situated learning' perspective was the Space Time Army Reconnaissance System (STARS) programme developed for the US Army (Reeves, Aggen and Held, 1982). STARS employed interactive videodisc to engage soldiers in learning literacy, mathematics and problem-solving skills within the context of simulated military environments. The soldiers signed up as members of an élite time-travel force and journeyed through time and space to highly motivating scenarios (such as the World War II Battle of the Bulge) where they had to apply or develop their functional literacy skills to accomplish military objectives. The simulated performance tasks served as pre-tests for diagnosing learner needs, contexts for instruction, and post-tests for assessment.

An important perspective on how multimedia can transform the conditions for teaching and learning through 'situated-learning' is provided by the research of John Seely Brown and his colleagues at Xerox PARC. Collins et al (1989) propose a 'cognitive apprenticeship' model of instruction as an effective alternative to traditional instruction. The researchers maintain that traditional instruction abstracts knowledge and skills from their uses in the world. In apprenticeship learning, on the other hand, knowledge and skills are seen as instrumental to the accomplishment of meaningful tasks. The apprenticeship model is based on modelling, coaching, scaffolding, articulation, reflection and exploration, as opposed to didactic teaching strategies such as telling and correcting. A critical characteristic of the cognitive apprenticeship is 'situated learning' described by Collins et al (p487) as follows:

A critical element in fostering learning is to have students carry out tasks and solve problems in an environment that reflects the multiple uses to which their knowledge will be put in the future. Situated learning serves several different purposes. First, students come to understand the purposes or uses of the knowledge they are learning. Second, they learn by actively using knowledge rather than passively receiving it. Third, they learn the different conditions under which their knowledge can be applied. Fourth, learning in multiple contexts induces the abstraction of knowledge, so that students acquire knowledge in a dual form, both tied to the contexts of its uses and independent of any particular context. This unbinding of knowledge from a specific context fosters its transfer to new problems and new domains.

An impressive IMM example of the principle of 'situated learning' is *Archaeotype*, developed at the New Laboratory for Teaching and Learning at the Dalton School in New York City (Moretti, Chou and McClintock, 1992). *Archaeotype* places sixth-grade students (11–12-year-olds) in the role of archaeologists exploring an IMM 'dig' filled with artifacts that they must discover, study and categorize with the overall goal of constructing a theory about the nature of the ancient site. Small teams of students work at the simulated site over a period of ten weeks, at the same time accessing a wealth of human, textual, museum and computerized resources to support their research. Researchers and developers at the innovative Dalton School, in a consortium with the Institute for Learning Technologies, Columbia University Teachers College and the Bank Street College, are also developing other IMM programmes that incorporate cognitive learning principles.

The three primary principles of cognitive learning theory described above in no way exhaust the pedagogical foundations for instructional IMM. Important research is occurring at a number of research and development institutions around the globe (Kearsley, 1991). Research already completed has been summarized in a number of journal articles and books (see, for example, Hannafin, 1992; Hannafin and Rieber, 1989; Jonassen and Mandl, 1990; Schank and Jona, 1990).

At the same time, not every authority is convinced that multimedia and constructivist theory represent major breakthroughs that go very far beyond existing approaches to computer-based instruction and learning theory (Merrill, 1991; Reigeluth, 1991). The next few years should provide a better basis for consideration of the theoretical and practical issues described in this chapter, especially as large-scale multimedia implementation efforts begin to occur in educational and training contexts. At the same, any large-scale implementation of IMM must be accompanied by more and better research. The next section describes some possible research directions.

How should IMM research be conducted?

One common way of conducting research in the field of instructional technology has been to compare the effectiveness of an innovation such as IMM with other instructional approaches – for example, a different medium such as linear video, or the ubiquitous 'traditional classroom instruction' (Clark, 1992). Research studies investigating the effectiveness of multimedia programmes in comparison with more traditionally structured computer-based instruction programmes have been reported (Lanza and Roselli, 1991) but, as is often the case with comparative research, the findings have often revealed no significant differences.

Another increasingly popular approach to research in this field is 'media replication' or 'attribute isolation' research (Ross and Morrison, 1989). Media replication studies attempt to isolate an attribute or dimension of computer-based instruction (CBI) – for example, learner control – and estimate its effectiveness in a variety of implementations (learner-control with advisement versus learner-control without advisement, for instance). Media replication studies have enjoyed little more success than the aforementioned media comparison studies. Ross and Morrison (p28) concluded that 'research findings regarding the effects of learner-control as an adaptive strategy have been inconsistent, but more frequently negative than positive'. Reeves (1992) described numerous theoretical and methodological flaws in existing media replication studies.

Media comparison and media replication research have been criticized in detail elsewhere (see, for example, Phillips, 1980; Reeves, 1986; 1989; 1990; 1992; Sanders, 1981) and are clearly inadequate as a scientific foundation for instructional design for IMM. The remainder of this chapter will consider and recommend research methods which, while they have rarely been utilized in this field, promise to yield useful results.

A multi-faceted approach to research is called for. This should include the conduct of intensive case studies (Stake, 1978) and the application of computer modelling (Pagels, 1988). Further, the aim of these studies should be the construction of prescriptive theory (Clark, 1989). Prescriptive theory has been ignored for too long in this field and greater skill in building and testing instructional prescriptions is required if research is to have meaningful impact on the design and use of IMM.

Investigations of IMM should include both observational and regression methods. These methods are recommended because of the exploratory nature of the research that must be done. Observational studies are needed to identify the salient variables in learning via IMM. Once these variables have been identified, multiple regression and computer modelling methods can be used to explore relationships among specified variables and to determine the extent to which criterion variables such as performance can be predicted.

Figure 4.2: *IMM qualitative research laboratory.*

Case studies

Guidelines for the conduct of case studies can be found in Flagg (1990) and Merriam (1988). Specific examples of IMM interface issues that should be investigated are described in Mayhew (1992). An important emphasis in this research might be the investigation of the mental models learners construct of the IMM interface and the content of the programmes (Jih and Reeves, 1992). Learners' mental models are not available for direct observation, but they can be measured via 'think aloud' protocols and 'teach back' methods. Kyllonen and Shute (1989) regard mental models as the most complex type of knowledge in a taxonomy that also includes propositional statements, schemata, rules, general rules, skills, general skills and automatic skills.

'Usability labs', as used by commercial software developers for formative evaluation of their products, may be required for intensive case studies. Evaluators and designers can observe and record users' interactions with, and comments on, the courseware as they work in an adjoining room observed through a one-way window and via closed-circuit TV cameras trained on such salient features as the users' faces, hands, controls and monitor screen. Using two-way audio, the evaluators may instruct the users to 'think aloud' or answer questions about choices made, confusion over the programme's interface, or actions taken. Videotapes of these sessions can be used for subsequent analysis and documentation.

The use of such research facilities does not eliminate the need for conducting case studies into IMM implementation in schools and training centres. Ideally, instructors and students would be recruited into ongoing IMM research. Ethnographic data collection strategies such as logs, anecdotal records, videotaping and observations may also be used to collect data that can be incorporated into computer modelling research.

Computer modelling

Pagels (1988) provides a general introduction to the concept of computer modelling as a research strategy. More specific guidelines can be found in Reeves (1992) and Jih and Reeves (1992). Computer modelling research with IMM would include the following steps:

- adapt or create a theoretical model of learning via IMM, including input, context, process and outcome dimensions;
- measure dimensions of the model in a practical education or training implementation context;
- analyse the data using multiple regression and computer modelling procedures such as LISREL (Byrne, 1989); and
- modify the model as indicated by the data analysis and derive prescriptive principles for design and use of IMM.

There are several methodological conditions that must be met for this approach. Firstly, the learners should be involved in purposeful learning, driven by either intrinsic or extrinsic motivation. Volunteer subjects learning materials unrelated to their education or training needs are inappropriate and limit the generalizability of the research (Reeves, 1992).

Secondly, the learners should spend many hours (rather than a few minutes) interacting with IMM. Clark (1989) estimated that most treatments used in research involving instructional technologies lasted no more than an hour. Reeves (1992) found that treatments in learner control research averaged 30 minutes. Important findings cannot be expected from studies in which students are exposed to trivial treatments for short periods of time. The creators of IMM learning environments stress the importance of sustained exploration by students and teachers (Cognition and Technology Group at Vanderbilt, 1992).

Thirdly, the population of learners should be diverse. Individual differences among learners with respect to aptitude, knowledge, skills, attitudes, personality characteristics, previous experience, motivation and so on, should be accounted for in any inquiry. The interactions among these individual differences, aspects of the IMM interface and other factors, such as the context of use and the programme's objectives, should be a major focus for the research.

Fourthly, if multiple regression and/or computer modelling studies are to be carried out, sample sizes of learners must be large, ideally running into the hundreds, to meet the requirements of the analytical techniques. The statistical background of most educational researchers is limited to methods used in experimental and quasi-experimental studies (eg, ANOVA), and thus professional consultation will be required to implement multiple regression and modelling statistical procedures (eg, LISREL).

Research examples

These new research directions are being pursued by faculty and graduate students in the College of Education at The University of Georgia. For example, Gustafson, Reeves and Laffey (1990) investigated trainee performance in Apple Computer's elaborate and extensive training course, *Macintosh Fundamentals*. Student paths through course modules and module sub-components, their selections among optional activities, time spent in various learning tasks, responses to practice exercises and test questions and a host of other aspects of their use of the course were collected via computer tracking. Subsequent analyses of this data yielded unexpected insights into the structure of course menus, students' understanding of instructional options and fluctuations in their interests and motivation levels over time. For example, the course includes sophisticated student services options such as the ability to take 'snapshots' of any screen in the program and 'bookmark' their path through the IMM, but the vast majority of trainees ignored these options. The findings indicate that trainees need much clearer orientation to the functions of the student services in the course and that the practical value of the student services should be enhanced.

Harmon (1991) observed 24 students interacting with the ABC News Interactive Programme *In the Holy Land*. His research design required the students to talk aloud as they searched through the programs, explaining what motivated their selections and paths. He found that the students generally did not look for new knowledge, but instead sought to confirm their existing knowledge, whether it was accurate or not. For the most part, the students actively searched the IMM for information that would confirm what they already thought they knew. In fact, in several cases, students continued to search for confirmatory information for many minutes despite coming face to face with a wealth of data that conflicted with their beliefs. The results support the need for metacognitive support structures in instructional IMM which aims to promote discovery learning.

Also at The University of Georgia, Jih (1991) conducted a study of the relationships among learners' individual differences, their mental models of an IMM programme, their navigational pathways through the IMM, and performance. Although methodological weaknesses in the study limited the generalizability of her findings, Jih found that learners construct very different mental models of the user interface of an IMM programme. She also found that the accuracy of students' mental models is related to their previous computer experience and preference for a graphical-style interface. Jih's research indicates that IMM developers should not assume that students will automatically construct mental models of the structure of the programmes that match the structure intended by the developers. Explicit assistance may be required.

The need for new research directions

The need for research of the kind described above is clearly critical. The power and complexity of IMM are increasing rapidly. For example, during the period that this chapter was being developed (1991–92), Philips launched their long-awaited CD-I system in the US, accompanied by scores of titles; IBM announced new computer systems designed for what they call 'Ultimedia'; and released the two largest multimedia titles ever created, *Illuminated Books and Manuscripts* and *Columbus Encounter: Discovery and Beyond*; and Apple released the most powerful Macintosh yet, the Quadra, as a workstation for multimedia and the QuickTime multimedia support software.

It has to be admitted that, at the time of writing, our knowledge of IMM design, especially in regard to user interface, is better described as an art than a science (Laurel, 1990). Studies of IMM implementation in schools and training sites are rare and few researchers in education and training have adopted the methodologies recommended above. This chapter calls for programmatic research in this area and provides initial guidelines for the conduct of such research.

Conclusion

What can we conclude about IMM design for learning? Although the IMM approach is sharply different from traditional instructional methods that require students to absorb messages prepackaged by others, multimedia does not, in itself, automatically guarantee more content learning or higher-order learning. In addition, while it is true that students can construct and appreciate the structure of a field of knowledge by actively exploring it, this does not automatically happen because information is presented via IMM. Multimedia for learning must be consciously designed to take full advantage of the advances in cognitive learning theory that have been made since the 1970s. Finally, the need for alternative approaches to research with IMM has been supported. Preliminary directions would include intensive case studies and large-scale applications of multiple regression and computer modelling techniques.

The difficulty of researching how people learn via IMM might be compared to the difficulty of measuring the development of black holes in space (Hawking, 1988). In both contexts, direct measurement is elusive. Astronomers use computer models to gradually improve their understanding of where the black holes are and what effect they have on surrounding celestial bodies. Similarly, instructional technologists are advised to construct models of the effective dimensions of IMM, collect relevant data, analyse the data with computer modelling methods and thus improve understanding of effective instructional dimensions 'bit by bit'. The uniquely powerful data collection capabilities of IMM lend themselves particularly well to the conduct of this type of research. Instead of sending probes into intergalactic space, we can programme accurate and tireless data collectors into the very phenomena we wish to investigate.

At the same time, we cannot afford to stand still until the research base is complete. We must envision new ways of creating multimedia and of enabling instructors and students to interact with the support of multimedia, bringing these ideas into being and risking the difficulties that inevitably accompany such experiments.

The process of theory construction and distillation into testable models is clearly more of a creative art than a hardened science. Perhaps we should adopt the motto of Michelangelo as we undertake to improve our understanding of the research foundations of IMM: *Ancora imparo* – 'I am still learning'.

References

Ambron, S. and Hooper, K. (eds) (1990). *Learning with interactive multimedia.* Microsoft Press, Redmond, Wash.

Bloom, A. (1987). *The closing of the American mind.* Simon and Schuster, New York.

Bransford, J.D., Sherwood, R.D., Hasselbring, T.S., Kinzer, C.K. and Williams, S.M. (1990). Anchored instruction: Why we need it and how technology can help. In D. Nix and R. Spiro (eds), *Cognition, education, and multimedia: Exploring ideas in high technology.* Lawrence Erlbaum, Hillsdale, NJ, 115–41.

Brown, J.S. (1985). Process versus product: A perspective on tools for communal and informal electronic learning. *Journal of Educational Computing Research*, 1, 179–201.

Brown, J.S., Collins, A. and Duguid, P. (1989). Situated cognition and the culture of learning. *Educational Researcher*, 18 (1), 32–41.

Bush, V. (1945). As we may think. *Atlantic Monthly*, 176, 101–8.

Byrne, B.M. (1989). *A primer of LISREL: Basic applications and programming for confirmatory factor analytic models.* Springer-Verlag, New York.

Cates, W.M. (1992). *Considerations in evaluating metacognition in interactive hypermedia/multimedia instruction.* Paper presented at the Annual Meeting of the American Educational Research Association, San Francisco, April.

Clark, R.E. (1989). Current progress and future directions for research in instructional technology. *Educational Technology Research and Development*, 37 (1), 57–66.

Clark, R.E. (1992). Media use in education. In M.C. Alkin (ed), *Encyclopedia of educational research.* Macmillan, New York, 805–14.

Cognition and Technology Group at Vanderbilt (1992). The Jasper experiment: An exploration of issues in learning and instructional design. *Educational Technology Research and Development*, 40 (1), 65–80.

Collins, A., Brown, J.S. and Newman, S.E. (1989). Cognitive apprenticeship: Teaching the crafts of reading, writing, and mathematics. In L.B. Resnick (ed), *Knowing, learning, and instruction: Essays in honor of Robert Glaser.* Lawrence Erlbaum, Hillsdale, NJ, 453–94.

Duffy, T.M. and Jonassen, D.H. (1991). Constructivism: New implications for instructional technology? *Educational Technology*, 31 (5), 7–12.

Fischer, P.M. and Mandl, H. (1990). Introduction: Toward a psychophysics of hypermedia. In Jonassen and Mandl (1990),

Flagg, B.N. (1990). *Formative evaluation for educational technologies.* Lawrence Erlbaum, Hillsdale, NJ.

Glaser, R. (1984). Education and thinking: The role of knowledge. *American Psychologist*, 39, 93–104.

Gustafson, K.L., Reeves, T.C. and Laffey, J.M. (1990). *The experience and outcomes of interactive videodisc orientation training for sales personnel.* Paper presented at Annual Meeting of the American Educational Research Association, Boston, April.

Hannafin, M.J. (1992). Emerging technologies, ISD, and learning environments: Critical perspectives. *Educational Technology Research and Development*, 40 (1), 49–63.

Hannafin, M.J. and Rieber, L.P. (1989). Psychological foundations of instructional design for emerging computer-based instructional technologies: Part I. *Educational Technology Research and Development*, 37 (2), 91–101.

Harmon, S.W. (1991). *On the nature of exploratory behavior in hypermedia environments for the design of hypermedia instructional systems.* Unpublished doctoral dissertation, University of Georgia, Athens, Ga.

Hawking, W.H. (1988). *A brief history of time: From the big bang to black holes.* Bantam, New York.

Hirsch, E.D. Jr (1987). *Cultural literacy: What every American needs to know.* Vantage, New York.

Holsinger, E. (1991) Ulysses: A new hope for education. *New Media Age*, 1 (4), 24–6.

Jih, H.J. (1991). *The relationship among the structure of interfaces, users' mental models, and performance in computer-based interactive courseware.* Unpublished doctoral dissertation, University of Georgia, Athens, Ga.

Jih, H.J. and Reeves, T.C. (1992). Mental models: A research focus for interactive learning systems. *Educational Technology Research and Development*, 40(3), 39–53.

Johsua, S. and Dupin, J.J. (1987). Taking into account student misconceptions in instructional strategy: An example in physics. *Cognition and Instruction*, 4, 117–25.

Jonassen, D.H. and Grabinger, R.S. (1990). Problems and issues in designing hypertext/hypermedia for learning. In Jonassen and Mandl (1990), 3–25.

Jonassen, D.H. and Mandl, H. (eds) (1990). *Designing hypermedia for learning*. Springer-Verlag, Heidelberg.

Kearsley, G. (1991). *Directory of interactive multimedia research centers*. Interactive Multimedia Program, The George Washington University, Washington, DC.

Kinzie, M.B. and Berdel, R.L. (1990). Design and use of hypermedia systems. *Educational Technology Research and Development*, 38 (3), 61–8.

Kulik, C.C. and Kulik, J.A. (1986). Effectiveness of computer-based education in colleges. *AEDS Journal*, 19, 81–108.

Kyllonen, P.C. and Shute, V.J. (1989). A taxonomy of learning skills. In P.L. Ackerman, R.H. Sternberg and R. Glaser (eds), *Learning and individual differences: Advances in theory and research*. W.H. Freeman, New York, 117–63.

Lanza, A. and Roselli, T. (1991). Effects of the hypertexual approach versus the structured approach on students' achievement. *Journal of Computer-Based Instruction*, 18, 48–50.

Laurel, B. (1990). *The art of human–computer interface design*. Addison-Wesley, Reading, Mass.

Locatis, C., Letourneau, G. and Banvard, R. (1989). Hypermedia and instruction. *Educational Technology Research and Development*, 37 (4), 65–77.

Mayer, R.E. (1989). Models of understanding. *Review of Educational Research*, 59, 43–64.

Mayhew, D.J. (1992). *Principles and guidelines in software user interface design*. Prentice-Hall, Englewood Cliffs, NJ.

Merriam, S.B. (1988). *Case study research in education*. Jossey-Bass, San Francisco.

Merrill, M.D. (1991). Constructivism and instructional design. *Educational Technology*, 31 (5), 45–53.

Moretti, F.A., Chou, L. and McClintock, R. (1992). The cumulative curriculum: Multimedia and the making of a new educational system. Paper presented at the Tenth Conference on Interactive Instruction Delivery, Society for Applied Learning Technology, Orlando, Fl. Society for Applied Learning Technology, Warrenton, Va,

MVM (1991) IBM presents Columbus and the Classics. *Multimedia and Videodisc Monitor*, 9 (5), 1,3.

Newell, A. and Simon, H. (1972). *Human problem-solving*. Prentice-Hall, Englewood Cliffs, NJ.

Nickerson, R.S. (1988). Technology in education in 2020: Thinking about the not-distant future. In R.S. Nickerson and P.P. Zodhiates (eds), *Technology in education: Looking toward 2020*. Lawrence Erlbaum, Hillsdale, NJ.

Nix, D. (1990). Should computers know what you can do with them? In D. Nix and R. Spiro (eds), *Cognition, education, and multimedia: Exploring ideas in high technology*. Lawrence Erlbaum, Hillsdale, NJ, 115–41.

Pagels, H.R. (1988). *The dreams of reason: The computer and the rise of the sciences of complexity*. Simon and Schuster, New York.

Papert, S. (1990). *Constructivism versus instructionism*. Paper presented at the Annual Meeting of the American Educational Research Association, Boston, April.

Phillips, D.C. (1980). What do the researcher and the practitioner have to offer each other? *Educational Researcher*, 9 (11), 17–24.

Reeves, T.C. (1986). Research and evaluation models for the study of interactive video. *Journal of Computer-Based Instruction*, 13, 102–6.

Reeves, T.C. (1989). New directions for the evaluation of interactive videodisc. *Interact Journal*, 2, 6–14.

Reeves, T.C. (1990). Redirecting evaluation of interactive video: The case for complexity. *Studies in Educational Evaluation*, 16, 115–31.

Reeves, T.C. (1992). Computer modelling: A research tool for computer-based instruction. *Interactive Learning International*, 8, 3–13.

Reeves, T.C., Aggen, W.D. and Held, T.H. (1982). The design, development, and evaluation of an intelligent videodisc simulation to teach functional literacy. In *Proceedings of the Fourth Annual Conference on Video Learning Systems*. Society for Applied Learning Technology, Warrenton, Va, 4–9.

Reigeluth, C.M. (1991). Reflections on the implications of constructivism for educational technology. *Educational Technology*, 30 (9), 34–7.

Resnick, L.B. (1989). Introduction. In L.B. Resnick (ed), *Knowing, learning, and instruction: Essays in honor of Robert Glaser*. Lawrence Erlbaum, Hillsdale, NJ, 1–24.

Rezabek, R.H. and Ragan, T.J. (1989). *Elaborated resources: An instructional design strategy for hypermedia*. Paper presented at the Annual Meeting of the Association for Educational Communications and Technology, Dallas, February.

Ross, S.M. and Morrison, G.R. (1989). In search of a happy medium in instructional technology research: Issues concerning external validity, media replications, and learner control. *Educational Technology Research and Development*, 37 (1), 19–33.

Sanders, D.P. (1981). Education inquiry as developmental research. *Educational Researcher*, 10 (3), 8–13.

Schank, R.C. (1988). *The creative attitude*. Macmillan, New York.

Schank, R.C. and Jona, M.Y. (1990). *Empowering the student: New perspectives on the design of teaching systems* (Technical Report No 4). The Institute for the Learning Sciences, Northwestern University, Evanston, Ill.

Sculley, J. (1988). Foreword. In S. Ambron and K. Hooper (eds), *Interactive multimedia*. Microsoft Press, Redmond, Wash, vii–ix.

Skinner, B.F. (1968). *Technology of teaching*. Meredith, New York.

Stake, R.E. (1978). The case study method in social inquiry. *Educational Researcher*, 7, 5–8.

Taylor, B.A. (1990). An agent for education change: Interview with Jim Dezell. *Human Capital*, 1 (2), 24–7.

Tuerck, D.G. (1987). *Creativity and liberal learning*. Ablex, Norwood, NJ.

5 Eyes on the horizon, feet on the ground?

Stephen Heppell

The development of educational computing

The rapid development of educational computing poses a straightforward challenge to education. How can education keep a watchful eye on the horizon for the new developments in technology that are appearing whilst keeping its feet on the ground? A mix of prognostication and pragmatism is a difficult, but necessary, balance for education to maintain.

Prognostication is particularly difficult because the development of computer systems continues to be characterized by frenetic change. The mid-1990s design life of a notebook or palmtop computer is now as brief as nine months, so a three-year period in educational development represents something in the order of four machine lives. In direct contrast, the rate of change in education remains slow. A cinema newsreel of the 1920s showing traffic, hospitals, cafeteria, sport, or indeed almost any aspect of our daily lives, will vividly remind us of the great technological changes that have characterized the twentieth century. However, show a short film of a group of 13-year-olds in a classroom and it is extraordinarily difficult to attribute its date accurately to any particular time between the 1920s and today without resorting to the clues of fashion and speech. Our classrooms have not yet been transformed by technology in the way that much of our everyday life has been.

This slowness of education to change, this intransigence of pedagogy and of institutionalized learning process, is not necessarily bad; the history of education is scarred with the wreckage of failed innovations, mechanical teaching machines providing an excellent example. However, in the mêlée of current technological change, there is a real danger that the seductive call of integrated media and of emergent 'edutainment' is so strong that the innate conservatism of education is in danger of being replaced by a hurried and unquestioning acceptance of new technology as being desirable in its own right. In this context, it is both appropriate and urgent that we should examine the ways in which educational computing has developed and the ways in which it might develop in the immediate future. We are at a critical crossroads in the development of our learning institutions. Education in general, and higher education in particular, is being forced to seek learner productivity solutions, to offer more for less without a diminution of the student experience resulting in less for more.

Some reflection and thoughtful prognostication might be appropriate at this time. Beginning with the way in which educational computing has developed, drawing on experience from the United Kingdom, it is possible to characterize the development of educational computing in four overlapping stages.

Stage One: initially the computer itself was seen as the focus of attention, the topic. As recently as the early 1980s plastic injection moulded keyboards (Acorn, BBC B and Sinclair Spectrum) were sold through educational distributors as a tangible and slightly absurd manifestation of the view that computer keyboard familiarity was a worthwhile end in itself:

> *'What did you do at school today Sarah?'*
> *'I used the computer.'*

'Using the computer' was regarded as a discrete and appropriate learning outcome on its own. Computer Studies as a subject was the logical extension of this 'computer as topic' phase.

Stage Two: here the computer was used to deliver those parts of the curriculum that were thought to benefit from the stimulus and interactivity offered by a computer screen. Tangible benefits logged by children in computer-resourced classrooms included the injection of interactivity into the learning environment and the use of the computer as a 'neutral arbiter', enabling children to take risks with their learning without fear of censorship or disapproval.

In Stage Two, teachers were asked for their own ideas about ways that the computer might enhance learning. Most teachers had no good idea about what the computer might be able to offer but they had much clearer ideas about topics that teachers did *not* want to offer; thus computers were called upon constantly to deliver 'difficult' topics through the development of task-specific computer programs. For example, there must have been dozens of programs written to 'teach' bearings:

'What did you do at school today Sarah?'
'I used a computer to learn about bearings and the compass.'

Much of the work at this stage saw the computer used as a kind of surrogate teacher, still containing a discrete and relatively small body of expertise which could be trickle-fed to the 'empty vessel' learner. This stage came about because few users could see what the potential of the computer might be for developing new pedagogies and learning environments, whilst most users could see that as a vehicle for delivering enhanced motivation, interactivity, rapid 'what if?' response and variety, it had a key role to play. Computers were thus called upon to offer significantly enhanced versions of current learning activities. But, as I commented at EURIT in 1986: 'the aims and objectives met by such computer-based learning typically do not focus directly on the acquisition of thought processes and organizational skills necessary to exploit the computer as a tool in the working environment of commerce and industry . . .' (Heppell, 1986).

Stage Three: this coincided with a dramatic change in software development. The 'useful little programs' (ULPs) that characterized early educational computing began to be outclassed by the dramatically sophisticated generic software tools that were becoming a normal part of the working world: spreadsheets, databases, word processors, desktop publishing, modelling, communications and graphics/design. Written by teams of scores of programmers, these generic software tools outclassed, outperformed and outsold education-specific software and the cottage industry of teachers coding ULPs in their back bedrooms all but disappeared in the face of this heightened sophistication. Indeed, with the exception of Logo, the current England and Wales National Curriculum (Technology, AT5) could be entirely delivered with such generic, open-ended, typically content-free tools, developed for business and adopted wholesale by education for the problem-solving environment that they offered. Observe–question–hypothesize–test was never so easy:

'What did you do at school today Sarah?'
'I tried to see if there was a link between my pulse rate and how long my arms were.'
'How did you do that?'
'I used a spreadsheet.'
'Was there a link?'

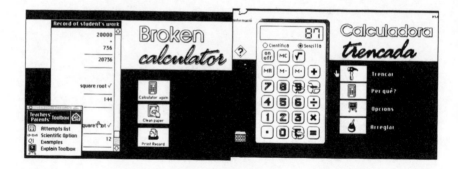

Figure 5.1: Broken Calculator, *English and Catalan versions.*

'No, but fitness turned out to be important from our data.'

There is, however, much that these tools do not offer that education needs, an obvious example being the ability to analyse drafts and developments to enable us to offer formative assessments. These generic tools tend to offer a 'snapshot' view of where learners are now rather than a dynamic view of the strategies and processes that they harnessed to arrive there. Because of these and other shortcomings, we have now only just begun to ask the questions that suggest we are nearing the beginning of Stage Four.

Stage Four: this will begin to take advantage of the trend towards modular software to allow us to 'plug in' the components that are specific to educational needs: better recording of achievement, local culture and language support, context-specific advice and help, appropriate tasks and so on. For example, even with simple task-specific programs, the particular needs of education need to be addressed. In the screens shown in Figure 5.1 a simple program, *Broken Calculator* (Xploratorium, 1991) poses the challenge for children of solving calculations with some of the keys on the calculator 'broken'. As the user tries various problem-solving strategies, the *Broken Calculator* keeps a log of attempts (which the user can delete if required – it is important not to threaten risk-taking in learning) which provide a developmental record for a teacher or parent wishing to offer formative process-based advice to the user.

These four stages of development seem encouraging enough, but in truth the impact that all this has had on education to date has been minimal. Our 1920s cameraman would still feel comfortably at home in a current school classroom, even with a computer tucked away in the corner. Figure 5.2 summarizes these four overlapping stages of development in educational computing.

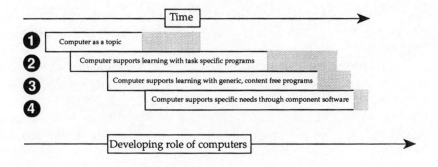

Figure 5.2 (a)

Figure 5.2(a) shows how the use of computers in the learning environment has changed, but none of these four stages shows a parallel which we might have reasonably anticipated, and which is illustrated in figure 5.2(b).

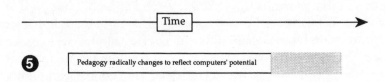

Figure 5.2 (b)

Computer manufacturers and software houses are fundamentally concerned with the way that people work and they have learned the lesson, from VisiCalc onwards, that offering new ways of working will sell. Eventually these new ways of working will impact on pedagogy and it is therefore important to ask: 'What new pedagogies will the technology support? What will the emergent Stage Five look like when it arrives?'

Thus far there has been neither a strong mechanistic nor a strong causal link between technological and pedagogical change but it is a not unreasonable contention that this link will need to be tighter rather than looser in the next five to ten years. If we can arrive at Stages One to Four through reflection and accumulated wisdom, then we need prognostication to anticipate Stage Five. To begin that prognostication we need to consider just what computers are going to be able to offer us in the immediate and predictable future. In the Xploratorium, our learning laboratory at Anglia Polytechnic University, we have a particular need to know about that future. The Xploratorium is based in a teacher training faculty. Students beginning their Bachelor of Education degrees today will not emerge into classrooms for another four years, a very long time in educational computing.

The following list summarizes the emerging technologies which we are able to predict with some real certainty. Everything on the list is either in trial use at the Xploratorium or has been tried by us in other laboratories around the world. There is no speculation here about 'what' but, as ever in computing, there is considerable doubt about 'when':

- Computer data will consist dominantly of fully integrated digital media – sound, video, graphics, animation, speech and text. We have this already with integrated media but it remains a special case in current computing. What will emerge is the embedding of multiple media types into every facet of computing activity. Users will have both an expectation of and (arguably) an entitlement to this. Of course, there will remain occasions when a particular element of digital media (for example, sound or text) is not present but these will be special cases; normally the computer will deliver fully integrated media and this, of course, means very broad bandwidths for communication. We can confidently predict that integrated media will be the bedrock of educational computing and we shall return to the implications of this below.
- Text to speech and speech to text algorithms are now improving quickly and clearly will enable such configurations as voice in/text out and text in/voice out to become normal.
- Networking is set to see dramatic advances in the short-term future. Radio cellular networking, virtual telephony and the like are all an assured part of our future, and with projects like the Xploratorium's *Virtual Village* already beginning to investigate the grammar and conventions associated with asynchronous distance collaborative learning, it is clear that the physical limits of the learning group and their learning environment extend beyond their immediate accommodation.
- Thankfully, interface design is once again at the beginning of a very rich period of rapid development. The two-dimensional graphical user interfaces (GUIs) that we currently enjoy will begin to offer much more specific support for the individual, cultural and institutional needs of the user/learner. This means that the learners' network identity will be much more than an access code for file storage or a set of preferences, and it will accompany them throughout their learning lives. The key change here is in enabling systems to support progression and continuity throughout multi-

ple phases of education, and national/regional authorities may have a key role in facilitating this. Significant advances in the direction of users specifying their own interface environment might also be anticipated.

- The Xploratorium is currently pressing CD-ROM for all teacher training colleges in the UK and we are using a digital video window to provide 'agents/guides' who offer both technical support ('Would you like to see how to build a formula now? Watch the demonstration window and I'll talk you through it.') and what we characterize as 'insights support' ('Here are some ways that you might like to think about using this software. Which would you like me to tell you about?'). It is reasonable to expect that the provision of guide support offering both technical and insights support will be a natural part of the standard 'help' environment expected by users.

- In terms of hardware developments, we can anticipate continued exponential developments in processor capability, in portable computing, in storage and in communication speed; but in some areas we are reaching limits of effective development. Current sound capability of many micros offers sampling at 22Khz (or better) and CD audio offers 44Khz. Most of us cannot hear much better than this and so an effective limit is reached. Similarly, 24-bit screens displaying better than 16 million colours already offer 'good enough' colour capability and another effective limit is reached. For monitor displays, pixel size and resolution may improve significantly but it is possible also to anticipate a 'good enough' limit of screen resolution.

- Software applications, too, have probably begun to reach an effective plateau in terms of the power that a single application might offer and the clear development path is towards modular software rather than towards adding ever-greater functionality to single monolithic applications. Modular software has significant implications for educational computing, as has already been suggested above.

Thus far, then, we have some critical components of an understanding of future educational computing in place: we have a structured view of the historical development of educational computing together with a set of confident predictions of the immediate technological change we might expect. The next component is a clear taxonomy of the possible uses that emergent technology, and in particular integrated media, might support. Once again, it is possible to offer a developmental taxonomy.

The narrative function

Much of our pre-computer experience of integrated media comes from television and cinema. The linear narrative structure of the documentary, adventure, news, soap, serial and other familiar forms has delivered both entertainment and information reliably throughout the history of television and cinema. Visual grammar, cues, clues, signs and signifiers have emerged and many standard genres may be observed through form, structure and style. Much of the early pioneer work in integrated media owed a considerable debt to the narrative function borrowed from TV and cinema. Videodiscs contained long narrative passages and often the computer driving a videodisc served only to act as a search and find engine with some indexing functionality built in.

The narrative function still retains an important place in the design of integrated media, however. Narrative structures serve well to introduce new material or to deliver an overview of contents. In cases where a didactic input is replicated, the narrative function can also deliver an accurate clone of the original speaker. For example, in the CD-ROM *The Business of Quality* (Bratt/Ceiba Geigy, 1992), the user is placed in the position of a newly recruited worker in a case study factory where the management has not yet developed any clear understanding of Total Quality Management. The supervisor delivers a short linear narrative describing the task facing new recruits to the shop floor. This spoken contribution, with its faults of one-way communication, a deficiency model of the listener and a power coercion relationship of the speaker with the listener and its strengths in reinforcing the storytelling tradition, is ideally suited to the narrative function of integrated media.

Interestingly, television has itself recently shown considerable dissatisfaction with the purely narrative form of whole screen motion video. A growing number of television programmes are now seeking to offer an impression of interactivity. A familiar current motif is the narrative screen viewed over the shoulder of the 'pseudoviewer' who is making choices from a menu of possibilities (see, for example, School's Out BBC, 1990).

We can summarize the narrative function as 'stop', 'start', 'watch' and 'listen'. All of these are dominantly passive roles for the user.

The interactive function

Clearly, as soon as a computer is connected to any integrated media source (videodisc, tape, CD-ROM, etc) the potential opens up for the computer to do far more than fulfil the stop–start role that character-

Figure 5.3: *Screen from* The Business of Quality (Bratt/Ceiba Geigy, 1992).

izes the narrative function: 'browse', 'investigate', 'explore', 'choose' and 'do' are the roles for the user with an interactive integrated media source. This is not as straightforward as it might sound. Integrated media is typically characterized by vast data storage. A CD-ROM can contain the equivalent of some four metres of books on library shelving if the material is text-based. In the light of this, it is worth considering whether the book metaphor is an adequate structure with which to organize and make interactive such a vast information resource. Many integrated media sources have indeed attempted to organize themselves as pseudobooks and there are countless CD encyclopaedias and 'reference books' available in the market. Books initially seem to be ideally suited as a metaphor for organizing information. They provide a familiar and comfortable structure: they typically have an index, a contents page, chapter structures, headlines and footnotes on pages and a physical structure that offers clear clues as to where a reader is placed relative to the material in the book (for example, through the use of a bookmark). Unfortunately, as anyone who has attempted to use a large, multi-volume, encyclopaedia will testify, it is not a good way of organizing large, non-linear, text works. For example, imagine the problem of trying to trace all women scientists between 1842 and 1992. There is no useful index entry that will help in this and no search facility in a book. Nor is there any representation of progress where the information is not narrative in form. A bookmark in an encyclopaedia is not indicative of progress; it only marks a single reference point.

If the book is an inadequate metaphor for a text-based CD-ROM or similar storage device, it is certainly less than adequate when that storage device is a rich visual, aural and graphical resource too. A particular challenge for the interactive media is to identify an appropriate metaphor to guide and structure the browse, investigate, explore, choose and do modes of operation that the interactive function supports.

In the CD-ROM *Twelfth Night or What You Will* (Howard,1992), designer Graham Howard used the metaphor of the 'Theatre of Memory' to structure the information on the disc. Each segment of seating represents a different area of the disc to explore (for example, 'guided tours'; Shakespeare's life and times; and the play itself). This physical metaphor stays with the user throughout, either as a large version dominating the screen and serving as a main menu or, more typically, as a miniature palette in the corner of the screen. Observed testing has suggested that the physical representation of information expressed by this concrete metaphor is powerful and effective as a guide to navigation and leaves users confident in their own ability to utilize the interactive function of an integrated media resource. Experience has shown clearly that users will quickly develop their own model of the information on an interactive product unless a clear and effective model is provided for them. Facilitating inquiry through good design becomes critically important as soon as we progress from the narrative function described above.

The participative function

In almost every activity in our classrooms, students participate by creating and doing. When they read stories, we encourage them to write; when they look at pictures, we encourage them to draw. However, somehow, when it comes to integrated media in the learning environment (perhaps because of that frenetic and unquestioning acceptance of the desirability of new technology referred to above) the simple philosophy of 'learning through doing' appears to have been forgotten. A great many videodiscs and CD-ROMs deliver a mixture of narrative and interactive functions. Few offer a genuinely participative function that is overt and supported through the original software, although many more discs can be made participative with the aid of third-party software solutions.

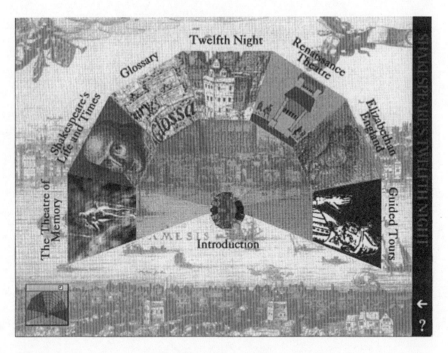

Figure 5.4: *Screen from* Twelfth Night or What You Will (Howard, 1992).

What form might participation take? It would be natural enough for students to be able to collect and re-present materials from the disc themselves and integrated media products are beginning to appear that encourage the user to place images, sounds, graphics and destinations into some form of electronic 'backpack' (for example, see BBC, 1989).

Other forms of participation are also important. Users creating their own images, text or movies and being able to 'put them back' into the screen would be straightforward if more software designers would take on board the need for embedding the participative function at the design stage. For example, in *Le Carnaval des Animaux* (Xploratorium, 1992), young users (target ages: 5 to 12 years) are given the opportunity to listen to the music of Saint-Saëns and explore his imagery (for example, the Swan or the Aquarium). They are then allowed to listen to the music whilst drawing, within the software that controls the audio CD, their own interpretation of each component of *Le Carnaval des Animaux*.

Participation does not stop here, because a presentation shell also structured into the software enables the users to 'tag' particular moments of sound in a 'hot text' field that will play selections in a peer presentation (for example, tagging the various animal sounds within

107

Figure 5.5: *Two screens from* Le Carnaval des Animaux (Xploratorium, 1992).

Figure 5.6: *Screen from* Le Carnaval des Animaux (Xploratorium, 1992).

the music, such as the donkey, cuckoo, etc). This simple piece of integrated media software enables children to contribute, create and present in a way that would be most natural in every other part of their curriculum but which seems to have been neglected in the rush to embed integrated media into the classroom.

We have then another of the critical components necessary for an understanding of future educational computing: together with a view of the historical development of educational computing and a set of confident predictions of technological change, we can put a clear taxonomy of the uses that integrated media should support: narrative, interactive and participative.

At the start of this chapter, it was suggested that pedagogy had been slow to change in response to technological innovation. Another component of our understanding of future educational computing is a grasp of the implications for our institutional learning environments of a particular change in pedagogy. To illustrate some of the possibilities of pedagogic change, two scenarios are offered below, not mutually exclusive but with enough philosophical distance between them to anticipate that one or the other – but not both – might become dominant in education over the next decade or two. The work being pioneered by the research team at Anglia's Xploratorium suggests a preference for the second option. However, either is plausible and both would have considerable implications for the way that our learning environment develops and is managed.

Pedagogic change

Scenario One

This first scenario assumes that computers actively change our current pedagogic practice by offering greater learning productivity. This productivity would be the result of delivering a really sophisticated level of learner support. If the tangible outcomes anticipated from a future education system are typified by competency statements and individualized certificated achievement, then within this scenario the computer might have a role to play in delivering and supporting the assessment of the results of that learner productivity.

We have seen considerable advances in interactive training environments and it is clear that context-specific 'smart' agents, integrated media, broadband networking and the rest could offer an environment that takes a learner from beginner to 'expert' (as assessed through check-box competency statements) through largely self-paced, self-assessed study and, probably, some distance learning techniques. This scenario would suggest that our current educational environments (with classrooms for 25–30 students, and some spaces, such as halls and gymnasia, for 300+ students) will be too inflexible to provide the kinds of individualized and small learning areas that might be needed. Large buildings of the kind housing our current schools would need extensive refitting, and replacement might be the cheaper option. Schools will be likely to resemble the best of current open-plan offices with their emphasis on the flexibility of the work group and variety in the day-to-day structure.

Scenario Two

If, on the other hand, the tangible outcomes we anticipate from our future education system are typified more by process outcomes, then two key emergent learning outcomes move to the fore alongside the individual endeavour of Scenario One: collaboration and presentation. At the Xploratorium, we are working at software environments that see peer presentation of work and work in progress as a key outcome. This requires some special facilities – the key element being projection facilities that enable learners to present their work on a large screen (ours is full colour, projected, 24 bit, 2m × 4m) with adequate connectivity infrastructure that enables most computers to be 'docked' into the presentation podium. A good sound system is essential too, for the aural environment is a key component of all future computer systems. Thus far, technology has conspicuously failed to deliver cheap solutions to the need for large, wall-sized, high-quality projection equipment for computer screens and this could prove to be a major constraint on the realization of this scenario.

Collaboration, too, needs some special support – again, at the Xploratorium we are working on collaborative environments that offer asynchronous working (ie, the learners do not have to be there all at the same time, or for that matter, all at the same place). Good asynchronous collaboration will always come back to the quality of networking and bandwidth. Digital video, sound and all the components of integrated media have heavy-duty networking requirements. Where collaboration is face to face the need is for smaller workspaces, probably adjacent to information resource areas. These information resource areas are interesting: information could be fully distributed (as it would be with Scenario One above) but Scenario Two would acknowledge the social element in discovery and learning and require small specialist information resource areas to ensure that the social element was not lost.

This second scenario would need a radical rethinking of the assessment model that we currently use to monitor our educational performance with its emphasis on individual endeavour and originality. Assessment is a key challenge for education. Computers have called our bluff on the myth that we could effectively police the originality of individual endeavour. With electronic text, the line between plagiarism and research is seriously blurred. It is not possible to unpack the individual efforts of specific contributors to a collaborative project where the output is electronic copy but is is possible to pay greater attention to collaborative skills, to the appropriateness of presentations, to the clarity and organization of meaning, to the quality (and efficiency) of research, and to a whole portfolio of other formative and summative assessment criteria. Computers in the learning environment have made us think hard about assessment and we should welcome that opportunity to review strategies. Integrated media present even greater challenges for the assessment process. What will students take away? What will be retained for future students to read or view? How do we moderate phrases such as '5,000 words or equivalent' when there is no simple currency of endeavour?

All the above places an emphasis on developments in the technology, on the role of teachers, on the infrastructure support for that technology and on elements of the learning environment such as pedagogy and assessment. What can easily pass unnoticed however, are the dramatic changes that are taking place in the learners themselves.

In today's world of mass media and multiple media types, children receive information via a broad portfolio of possibilities – even single-source media like television offer a complex sensory mix where traditional information structures (for example, narrative and linearity) exist alongside the fragmented and the multi-faceted (for example, in television commercials). Traditionally, research into children and the media has been weighted towards a view of their relationship with the media as problematic. It has dwelt on such issues as passivity, triviality, emphasis on raw appetites (such as avarice or violence) and the causal part of mass media in falling educational standards. Many research projects have surveyed the substance and process of children's viewing, seeking to uncover 'problem' factors and correlating them to behaviour with a view to media education solutions which will inoculate children against these harmful effects. Although children are active in synthesizing and making sense of their world, they are often portrayed as passive victims and concerns are expressed about the decline of their single media capabilities (for example, their textual literacy); they are characterized anecdotally and implicitly in much research as deficient learners.

However, a careful analysis of television programmes aimed at young children shows a rapidly changing perception of what is considered a normal viewing experience. In the 1950s and 1960s, typical children's programmes were paced gently, with steady narrative structures. The BBC's 1950s children's classic, *Andy Pandy*, starts with a lengthy introductory sequence interlinking titles with music and speech. This start-up sequence is strictly monomedia; the graphic title sequence animates, the commentary runs or the music plays. At no point does the delivery of two elements coincide. This gentle pace is in stark contrast with the visual, aural and graphical complexity of current child-focused media. If one analyses current advertisements aimed at children, it is quite common to discover video edits of less than one per second throughout the whole of a 20-second advertisement and preliminary observations suggest that young learners have no real difficulty in unpacking quite complex information – for example, detailed product awareness, a narrative thread and a vein of humour – from even the most rapidly paced and brief advertisement. This may, of course, reflect technological improvements in the construction of broadcast media, but it is significant that, anecdotally, parents report considerable difficulty in watching some programmes targeted at children. It is arguable (but untested) that they simply have not developed the ability to work comfortably with multiple media types simultaneously when the information flow from each media type is extremely rapid.

Increasingly, as has been suggested above, personal computers are able to deliver a rich integrated media environment that relies neither on the traditional passive delivery of television nor on the narrative tradition of literature. This dramatic stylistic change prompts a need to revisit traditional views of children's media interaction capability and to seek formal evidence of new information skills that they may have developed. In our work at the Xploratorium, we are suggesting (and seeking evidence to conclude) that children are active in synthezising and making sense of their world, including their media worlds, and that children as viewers (with television) or as navigators/participants (with integrated media) will construct personal meaning for 'media texts' through their response to a complex grammar of linguistic, visual and auditory conventions, cues and clues. We are seeking evidence that young learners bring an ability to handle this complex new grammar as a tangible asset to their learning environment. There is, of course, a parallel here with the process of the individualized reading of a literary text which highlights the act of reading as one of active cognitive processing. In both cases, the 'dialogue' between 'information author' and 'reader/viewer' has grammar, ground rules, cues and clues, which are used to signify meaning, to indicate generic structure and to reference the information web. The 'reader/viewer' recreates meaning, not by a mechanistic linear information output–information input model, but by bringing his or her own experience as 'reader/viewer' to the process. By an individual interpretation of the information, the 'reader/viewer' truly comes to 'own' the interpretation and is an active participant in the process.

In conclusion, it is possible to argue that computers have typically 'fitted in' with our current pedagogic practice and the impact of information technology on our learning environment has been surprisingly small. The task of keeping our eyes on the horizon largely has been a watching brief and thus keeping our feet on the ground has been but a small challenge. However, it is inevitable that pedagogy will change radically, given the rate of change in computer technology. This leaves education with a more interesting challenge than that of a watching brief. At a time when, as we are beginning to see with integrated media, the technology can deliver much of what we want, the problem of 'what do we want to do with our learning environments?' is a far more interesting, challenging and important focus for our concerns than the plethora of technical difficulties that have characterized the lives of educational computing practitioners so far.

Keeping our feet on the ground and holding on to a clear vision of learning objectives, the quality of process outcomes and the learning experience, is a big enough challenge to keep us occupied for a good many years to come. It is a challenge we should relish.

References

BBC (1989). *EcoDisc on CD-ROM*. BBC Interactive Television Unit, London.

BBC (1990). School's Out, from the series *Equinox*. British Broadcasting Corporation, London.

Bratt, P./Ceiba Geigy (1992). *The Business of Quality, CD-ROM*. Xploratorium, Anglia Polytechnic University.

Heppell, S. (1986). The use of business software as a content free teaching tool: Emulation or assimilation? In J. Moonen and T. Plomp (eds), *EURIT '86: Developments in educational software and courseware*. Proceedings of the First European Conference on Education and Information Technology, Twente University, Enschede, Netherlands. Pergamon, New York, 375–80.

Howard, G. (1992). *Twelfth Night or What You Will, CD-ROM*. Xploratorium, Anglia Polytechnic University.

Xploratorium (1991). *Broken Calculator*. From the suite of 'free to education' school software: *Xploratorium Workrooms*. Xploratorium, Anglia Polytechnic University.

Xploratorium (1992). *Le Carnaval des Animaux*. From *Insights for teachers as parents*. Xploratorium, Anglia Polytechnic University.

6 Interactive multimedia in education

Peter Olaf Looms

Introduction

This chapter explores the use of interactive multimedia in education. Its emphasis on schools, and to a lesser degree adult and vocational education and training, reflects my experience since 1969 with the development and evaluation of educational media in classroom instruction, distance learning and educational broadcasting.

My first exposure to an interactive multimedia product for educational use was in March 1985 at an in-service course about new information technology for language teachers. At that time, as an educational planning and evaluation officer with the educational broadcasting department of the Danish Broadcasting Corporation, my work included the off-air use of educational broadcasts and management issues related to the use of audiocassettes and videocassettes with other media in the classroom. The course gave participants the opportunity to work not only with drill and practice materials but with computer simulations and videodisc material based on the BBC course *Bid for Power*.

As Romiszowski (1992) points out, the term 'multimedia' is not new. Until a few years ago, multimedia was synonymous with educational broadcasting, in particular multimedia courses in foreign languages. One course in particular, the BBC's *Follow Me* – consisting of television and radio programmes, workbooks, audiocassettes and videocassettes – has been used by millions of learners worldwide. Although these multimedia courses used several different components ('multiple media'), many of the instructional design issues addressed at that time are still relevant today (see, for example, Innes, 1980; Rybak, 1980).

In this chapter I address a number of issues, the first of which is clarification of the terms 'multimedia' and 'interactive', and their use in the context of classroom instruction as well as in distance and open learning.

The term 'multimedia'

The multimedia language courses mentioned above were typically based on a package of materials. The textbook and television were usually the key components, and the others – radio, videocassettes and audiocassettes or even computer software – were options which could be used together at will. Television and radio were used as outreach media to 'recruit' users, to motivate, exemplify, provide context and instruct. The transmission times set the overall pace for work with course materials. The printed materials and cassettes provided examples for analysis and practice, both in the classroom and at home.

Although the various modalities – text, graphics, sound, pictures and video – were, in theory, available to the learner, the designers of such courses could not assume that learners had access to them all. Therefore, course guidelines were prepared to explain what was in each component and how best to use it.

From the user's point of view, one of the most significant differences between the multimedia courses of the past and present-day interactive multimedia was not the range of modalities available but rather their lack of integration and flexibility. Indeed, a number of the generic language courses on the market using interactive media – for example, *Hello Australia, España Viva* and *A vous la France* – are based on broadcast material. For this reason, I use the term 'multimedia' to describe any screen-based system where information in the form of text, figures, pictures, sounds or moving images is available to the user. In some cases these will be displayed on a computer screen, in others on a television monitor, but in this decade of digitization, the distinction between the two may well become superfluous. The fact that we are talking about screen-based systems does not exclude the use of other materials and media as an integral part of the interactive multimedia package. An example of this is the courseware produced for the oil company Norsk Hydro, in which learners work with large wallcharts displaying complex illustrations of oil rigs which could not be shown with the necessary resolution on monitors.

Interaction as learner control

While the term 'multimedia' offers relatively few difficulties, the term 'interactive' has several meanings, depending on the author and the context. One way of defining levels of interactive systems is the so-called 'Nebraska Scale', developed by the Nebraska Videodisc Design/Production Group in the early 1980s. The scale proposed was:

- *Level One:* a videodisc player with still/freeze frame, picture stop, chapter stop, frame address and dual-channel audio, but with limited memory and limited processing power;
- *Level Two:* a videodisc player with the capabilities of Level One, plus on-board programmable memory and improved access time;
- *Level Three:* Level One and Two players interfaced to an external computer and/or other peripheral processing devices. Digital audio, touch screens, etc might also be added to create new levels of interactivity but these all fall into this category.

It will be seen that this scale describes the technology used. It is of little use in describing the nature of the user–machine interactions taking place. For this reason I would like to examine the qualitative aspects of interactivity and then look at the issue of interactive media in the classroom.

Consider the example used earlier, the multimedia language course. Watching a television programme is essentially a real-time sequential process. Assuming that the viewer is actively involved in the process, his or her task is analogous to that of a detective trying to solve a crime. Rumelhart (1984) suggests that in both cases there is a set of clues. The viewer's job is to build a consistent interpretation of these clues. To do this, he or she draws on prior learning and experience to create the most plausible theory or working hypothesis. A major problem lies in the ephemeral nature and linearity of the broadcast medium. When the programme is 'live', the viewer or listener has no control over the organization or delivery of the content. However, by recording the programme, the user is independent of the transmission schedule and has the options of stopping the tape to make notes or repeating or omitting sections at will. Thus the issue of *who* is in control is central in interactivity.

An interactive medium allows increased user control over the learning process. However, while physical activities such as pressing a key, selecting an option or reviewing a sequence are important, it is not the quantitative increase in activity which should concern us but the qualitative improvement of the learner's cognitive processes. It follows that there is no direct relationship between the learner's use of the medium and the quality of the interaction. We may observe what the learner does, but can only indirectly evaluate the extent to which the interaction is considered and whether or not it leads to significant learning.

Another main issue in control in an interactive learning process is that of *who* is responsible for the outcomes? The authors of most works of fiction design them to be read from beginning to end. The compilers of manuals, directories and encyclopaedias, on the other hand, do not assume that their products will be read from A to Z. Where interaction is limited, the medium can only be a vehicle for instruction. The responsibility for the learning outcomes lies predominantly with the author, the producer or the instructional designer. As Færch *et al* (1984) point out in their empirical studies of classroom discourse, where there is no opportunity for immediate feedback, the message has to be complete and unambiguous for it to function effectively. Some interactive multimedia products may be organized in linear 'chunks' to serve as instructional resources with many of the narrative characteristics of conventional teaching.

At the other end of the continuum, interactive multimedia can be an electronic reference tool or what Romiszowski (1992) has termed an 'information dissemination system'. Here the learning task is formulated by the learner and not by the author or system.

To date, interactive multimedia as instructional resources are widespread in training, whereas interactive multimedia as information dissemination resources predominate in education. If the curriculum of an education system values learning and autonomy over teaching and content, there will be increased use of interactive dissemination resources as the student progresses towards these goals.

Karpatschof (1991) talks of interactive competence; that is to say 'the ability to solve tasks which could neither be solved by computers without people, nor by people without computers'. The ability to exploit interactive information dissemination systems may well be as important as the three Rs in education. If one supports this viewpoint, it is not simply a question of making multimedia as interactive as possible, but of providing the learners with the most appropriate kinds of interaction for any given stages in their development.

Interactions in the classroom

In addition to this issue of interactivity as a means of empowering the learner, there is the issue of interactive multimedia and classroom management.

Many of the products demonstrated at conferences and exhibitions imply either that the user will be working individually or that no other materials will be used in concert with them. In the real world of schools, however, there will be a classroom, a teacher, 20 to 30 students and perhaps only one interactive multimedia system. Interactive systems will most frequently be used by small groups of students, by the teacher when instructing the whole class or for independent study in the classroom or the library. Therefore, there are not only student–system interactions to consider, but also student–teacher and student–student interactions.

To ensure adoption in mainstream education, the development of interactive multimedia will have to embrace not only the system itself but the tools and guidelines for tailoring its use and integrating it with other learning resources.

Interactive multimedia in North America

Although the LaserVision videodisc was introduced in 1977, the CD-ROM in 1986 and consumer formats such as CD-I and CDTV in 1991, in global terms interactive multimedia using optical discs is still relatively uncommon. The US is by far the largest market. The most widely used format is the reflective optical videodisc, or laser disc. This was pioneered by such higher education institutions as the University of Nebraska and Brigham Young University in Utah, where in 1979 Larrie Gale and his colleagues transferred a Mexican film entitled *Macario* to disc to enable students to improve their listening and comprehension skills and to analyse the plot. Later that year they began work on *Montevidisco*, a computer-controlled videodisc which allowed students to simulate a visit to a small Mexican village (see Gale, 1983).

To judge from journals and conversations with developers, the use of interactive videodiscs grew slowly throughout the 1980s. Universities continued to play an important part in exploring applications. Interest spread to the K-12 sector where early titles were in biology, earth sciences and astronomy, primarily at junior-school level. After ten years of slow maturation, the videodisc entered a period of more rapid growth in 1990 when the number of players sold almost doubled. By the end of 1991, according to three different estimates (*THE Magazine*, Pioneer Electronics of America and *Multimedia and Videodisc Monitor*), there were videodisc players in 29 per cent of American schools. As cumulative sales were between 80,000 and 100,000 players, this corresponds to an average of three to four players per school. However, the distribution of videodiscs was by no means uniform. States such as Texas and Florida accounted for the major share of videodisc players in use.

It is important to note that most videodiscs are used without a computer, although software is usually supplied with the titles. The discs are commonly used as information dissemination resources in group work and as a reliable and cheap way of accessing stills, video and sound. At least 75 per cent of the videodisc players are used with a remote control unit or a bar-code reader. The bar-code system is an implementation of the interleaved 2 of 5 format, the patents of which are held by Pioneer, one of the major suppliers to the K-12 market. The introduction of a low-cost player produced by Panasonic for the Optical Data Corporation in connection with its agreement with educational authorities in Texas marked the turning point for the format at the beginning of 1991. Sales of this player passed the 15,000 mark in the course of 1991. Sony has also released a combination player or combi-player (a single player that can accommodate a variety of disc formats) with a bar-code reader using the Pioneer standard. By the end of 1992, low-cost combi-players with bar-code readers will be available for use with both videodiscs and compact discs, extending their use to music and language classes.

Until 1992, schools working with computer-controlled videodiscs mainly used two-screen configurations (a computer with its monitor beside a television screen connected to the player). Software has usually been delivered for Apple Macintosh using HyperCard but publishers and producers are now also releasing products for IBM compatibles using LinkWay, or in some cases ToolBook and Plus. For cost reasons, one-screen configurations using a video card are still not common in schools, although they are widespread in higher education and in training.

As of September 1992, there were just over 2,000 videodisc titles available for education in the USA, an increase of more than 78 per cent over 1990. Major producers include Optical Data Corporation and ABC News Interactive. Publishers of school books and television stations such as TV-Ontario and WGBH-Boston have also entered the educational market (Looms, 1991a). The trend is towards packages of educational materials (books, software, teachers' notes and lesson plans) of which the videodisc is a part. Prices for videodiscs and associated teachers' notes and software range from US$60–1,300, the average price being about US$500.

The availability of CD-ROM drives is lower but growing steadily. Some 17 per cent of schools had at least one drive at the end of 1991. Interactive multimedia products on CD-ROM are still the exception rather than the rule, but CD-ROM seems to be having significant impact in regard to reference works, particularly at college level. Students are now allowed to search CD-ROM versions of databases which in the past were only available online.

With the introduction of Apple's QuickTime, which allows for the transparent handling of compressed images, the Multimedia PC (MPC) specification from Microsoft and the appearance of a new generation of CD-ROM drives with improved data transfer and caching, multimedia products can be expected in greater numbers. Significant advances will be made by simply including digital audio help facilities in applications. The launch of Photo CD could also allow educational institutions to produce their own tailor-made CD-ROMs for use with a Photo CD or CD-I player in the classroom and later as a source of high-quality digital images for schools with access to a computer capable of handling the format.

The current situation in Europe

The use of interactive multimedia in Europe is nowhere near as widespread as in the USA. According to Anderson (1988), interactive multimedia in European education dates back to 1980, when interactive video systems were introduced in Holland. Hertkorn (1984) reports research carried out into the use of interactive videodiscs in schools in 1981–82, based on the work of 2,319 students in 55 classes selected from secondary and comprehensive schools as well as gymnasia. Although the project was well received by the teachers who took part, the initiative was shelved.

In Europe, unlike America, there is no commercially viable school market for educational multimedia, but there is a market for generic titles for vocational training. European universities are regular users of databases and bibliographies on CD-ROM, but otherwise interactive multimedia is used in a tiny minority of educational institutions, in spite of several national and European Community research and development programmes to promote these technologies.

In the UK, work with interactive multimedia dates back to microcomputers used to control videotapes and then videodiscs in the early 1980s. The first major project in education was the BBC *Domesday Project*, linked with the 900th anniversary of the Domesday Book in 1986. More than one million volunteers, including children from some 11,000 schools, collected information about their local communities and the two discs contained extensive national databases on all aspects of life in Britain in the 1980s.

The Department of Trade and Industry supported the sale of interactive video systems to schools, and later provided funding for the Interactive Video in Schools (IVIS) project and the Interactive Video in Industry and Further Education (IVIFE) project. Other significant initiatives in interactive video for teacher training and for the education of the deaf took place in Scotland and Northern Ireland. In 1991, funding was made available by the Department of Education and Science for teacher training and elementary mathematics projects.

At least 22 publicly financed interactive video titles have been produced in the UK (Mapp, 1991), and there are some 2,500 systems in schools, most of which are computer-based. However, it becomes clear when one visits schools in the UK that these initiatives have not been an unqualified success. A significant number of Domesday and IVIS systems are no longer in use. Teachers in eight schools that I visited in England in 1989 reported that they had had to spend many hours familiarizing themselves with their system, its user interface and its contents. They often felt unsure as to how the materials related to the national curriculum or might best be exploited in the classroom. Several teachers told me that they no longer used their systems because students had reconfigured the hardware and they were incapable of dealing with such problems. On the other hand, where teachers had good relationships with their students and had enough time and resources to adapt the materials to meet their own requirements, the systems were still in regular use and the school had significant support for the use of multimedia from the local community.

In a personal communication, Bruce Wright at the University of Exeter reports that the first generation of teachers who were involved with the Domesday Project or the IVIS titles has been joined by a new generation who prefer to work with simple delivery systems such as videodiscs with bar codes.

In France, the Direction des Lycées et Collèges (the management board for high schools and colleges at the Board of Education) conducted an experimental study in 200 schools which had videodisc players in the mid-1980s. The videodiscs in use were often from the CNDP (National Centre for Pedagogical Development) or from regional centres such as at Poitou, Charentes. The study has not led to the widespread use of videodiscs. At the beginning of 1989, the French Ministry of Education launched a CD-ROM initiative to promote the use of the format in education. There are now some 5,000 CD-ROM drives in French schools. Titles include literature, economics and history from the Second World War to the present day.

From a study for IBM by El Bacha *et al.* (1990), it appears that most teachers are reluctant to use interactive media for the same reasons that they are reluctant to use computers:

- it takes too much time to master these applications, especially when compared with books;

- the documentation is often poor, or in some cases non-existent. When it does exist, it only relates to the use of the software, ignoring the pedagogical content;
- the presentation of the courseware does not match expectations;
- the benefits of the courseware are negligible compared with the amount of time needed to learn how to exploit it effectively.

Some teachers are also not really convinced that children can learn from computers, believing that they only play with them.

Spain has been working with new information technology (NIT) including interactive multimedia at the regional as well as at the national level, as education is in some cases the responsibility of the autonomous regional government. Thus, for example, the Department of Education of the Generalitat of Catalonia has supported experimental interactive video projects in 20 centres, most of which are primary and secondary schools. One of the programmes is used in geography and is based on educational broadcast material. The Atenea project of the Spanish Ministry of Education and Science aims to introduce NIT to schools in its jurisdiction and this project has supported the use of CD-ROM and videodiscs on an experimental basis. As partner in the *500 Years After* project to mark Columbus' landing in the Americas in 1492, the Ministry evaluated the use of CD-I in its pilot centres during 1992. The Ministry has some 25 centres staffed by 'monitors'. The Ministry trains these monitors in the development and use of computer software and new information and communication technologies, and the monitors run in-service training programmes for their regions, thus acting as 'multipliers'.

In Denmark, with a population of 5.13 million, 3 per cent of primary and secondary schools have videodisc players, more than half of which are used with bar-code readers. The number of schools using interactive multimedia rose substantially in 1992, partly due to Ministry of Education funding for the local evaluation of generic materials. By mid-1992 there were approximately 120 videodisc titles available, 10 of which were Danish, the remainder being imported titles from the UK and other European countries, Canada, the US and Australia. The use of non-Danish materials is possible because there is no central approval of educational materials. This is ultimately the responsibility of each school board.

Well-designed resource discs in a range of subjects transcend national frontiers and cultural differences. After *Siulleq* (a videodisc/ CD-ROM resource about Greenland) and a videodisc about the Second World War, the most widely used titles in Denmark are the *Modules of Investigation in Science and Technology* (MIST) series from

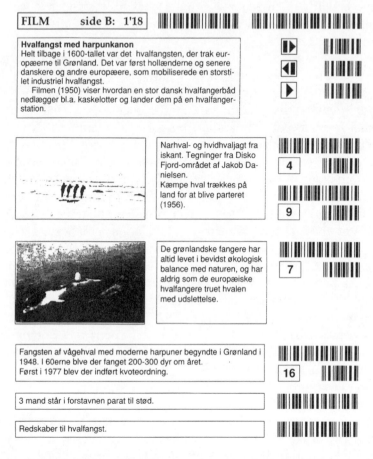

Hvalfangst

Hvalerne er rigt repræsenteret i havene omkring Grønland og har i flere hundrede år været et eftertragtet fangstbytte for både grønlændere og europæere.

| FILM | side B: 1'18 |

Hvalfangst med harpunkanon
Helt tilbage i 1600-tallet var det hvalfangsten, der trak europæerne til Grønland. Det var først hollænderne og senere danskere og andre europæere, som mobiliserede en storstilet industriel hvalfangst.
  Filmen (1950) viser hvordan en stor dansk hvalfangerbåd nedlægger bl.a. kaskelotter og lander dem på en hvalfangerstation.

Narhval- og hvidhvaljagt fra iskant. Tegninger fra Disko Fjord-området af Jakob Danielsen.
Kæmpe hval trækkes på land for at blive parteret (1956).

4

9

De grønlandske fangere har altid levet i bevidst økologisk balance med naturen, og har aldrig som de europæiske hvalfangere truet hvalen med udslettelse.

7

Fangsten af vågehval med moderne harpuner begyndte i Grønland i 1948. I 60erne blve der fanget 200-300 dyr om året. Først i 1977 blev der indført kvoteordning.

16

3 mand står i forstavnen parat til stød.

Redskaber til hvalfangst.

Figure 6.1: *Extract from* 'Grønland – med et pennestrøg' ('Greenland at the stroke of a pen') (reproduced by kind permission of the publishers, Danmarks Radios Forlag, Denmark).

the UK, and resource discs from France and Germany for use in the visual arts and history. Three of the four Australian titles available in Denmark are used in English as Foreign Language programmes. These are highly rated by their users and the underlying methodology is widely accepted in Denmark. Danmarks Radio Forlag and the author have developed bar-coded workbooks and worksheets to accompany LaserDisc programs such as ODC's *The Frog* and *Siulleq/ The Greenland Project* (see Figure 6.1).

With CD-ROM, the trend is much the same as in the USA. As hardware falls in price and the range of reference materials increases, the change from experimental to mainstream status may well take place in the United Kingdom, The Netherlands, Spain and Scandinavia (Looms, 1991b). Barker, in an article on the British CD-ROM in Schools scheme, lists 46 titles available to schools, most of them from the USA (Barker, 1991).

Interactive multimedia – obstacles to be overcome

I would like to analyse the reasons for the disappointing reception interactive multimedia has had in schools – with the exception of the USA – and to discuss how some of the obstacles to their introduction and adoption can be overcome. In doing so, I shall refer to our experience in Denmark.

Rowntree (1982, pp235ff) discusses at length the question of introducing change into education. He observes that schools, colleges and universities are constitutionally resistant to change. 'Yes, but . . .' is the automatic response to any would-be innovators. This stance may have some value as a survival technique but the instinct for self-preservation can swamp the need for self-renewal. Rowntree cites research by Paul Mort into the diffusion of innovation in the American education system. Mort (1964) suggested that up to 50 years could elapse between the identification of an educational need and the development of an acceptable way to meet that need and that therefore 'knowledge of the slowness of spread of an innovation – among the teachers in a school, among schools in a school system – is essential. Lack of such knowledge has resulted in the abandonment of many good innovations before they had a chance to put down roots.'

The Danish primary and lower secondary school system (or *folkeskole*) policy on innovation has been to encourage, evaluate and coordinate experimentation at local level. For several years, individual teachers and schools have been able to submit proposals for educational innovations to the Folkeskole Development Council and receive partial funding for extraordinary expenses in connection with their proposed projects. The Council monitors and evaluates the results (see for example Tufte *et al*, 1991), and the successful projects generate a body of experience which can lead to general changes in curricular guidelines or educational methodologies.

In 1992, the evaluation of interactive multimedia by schools and colleges was one of the six priority areas of the Ministry of Education Media Office. Schools wishing to evaluate the use of a given title in the

125

classroom could make a proposal to the Media Office and receive a grant of DKK20,000 (approximately US$3,500) to purchase the materials or cover additional staffing costs. The grant could not be used to buy hardware. In return for the grant, the school was required to submit a formal evaluation report. Innovation in this system spreads in a 'bottom-up' fashion. Teachers from pilot projects involving interactive multimedia present case studies and the rationale behind their work to peers through in-service courses. The second generation of teachers tends to emulate the work of those engaged in successful pilot projects and informal networks develop among teachers with common interests.

When computers were first introduced into Danish schools, they were used primarily in computer science classrooms. The current policy is to integrate the use of new information technology (NIT) into all subjects where this is relevant and effective. To aid this transition, curricular guidelines for each subject covering the integration of NIT (including interactive multimedia) have been prepared by curriculum committees. These committees typically include some of the most innovative teachers and the recommendations are based on their own first-hand experiences with NIT.

In the multimedia field, there are several interests at stake. At the political and industrial level, information and communication technologies already account for 5 per cent of gross national product on a global basis and 8 per cent for the industrialized countries (Commission of the European Community, 1991). As one of the major sources of technological development, these are of vital importance to the economy. This explains the emergence of sizeable research and development programmes and trade policies which influence the education system. Information technology advisors at Ministry level and computer science teachers see the need to expose schoolchildren to examples of NIT as a preparation for using it in later life. They do not question the need to use the technology. In their eyes, the major problems concern the practical issues of funding and standards. On the other hand, teachers have the feeling of history repeating itself. They recall the introduction of the overhead projector, language laboratories, video and, most recently, computers. Each innovation claimed to be a panacea, but each in turn failed to revolutionize education. Teachers therefore look upon NIT as no more than part of a set of tools available for their educational needs and also as a potential threat because of the resources that are being diverted from conventional materials to NIT.

One of the widely quoted models for systematically planning the development and maintenance of motivation in instructional systems is John Keller's ARCS model. This acronym stands for Attention, Relevance, Confidence and Success (Keller, 1983). I would suggest that the same model can be used to promote innovation in schools, but that it should be applied in two stages: first with the educational decision-makers and teachers and then, only when this first stage is satisfactorily completed, with the students. Some of the factors that need to be considered for the initial phase are:

- Establishing motivation
- Establishing interest
- Relevance
- Building confidence
- Indicators of success
- Hardware and software
- Costs

Establishing motivation – knowing what multimedia is and what titles are available

Relatively few teachers and decision-makers have first-hand knowledge of multimedia technology and a mere handful are familiar with the titles available for educational use. Until 1991, the only titles available were generic from elsewhere in Europe and the USA. The problem is aggravated by the decentralized nature of school purchasing. Decisions about materials acquisition are taken by individual schools rather than at the school board level. Getting the necessary information about multimedia across to the right people is a daunting task. In Denmark, interactive multimedia for education is currently available through two outlets: a specialist distributor and consultancy team which was formerly the subsidiary of a major Danish publishing group and the publishing wing of the Danish Broadcasting Corporation. Hardware manufacturers have promoted multimedia in a limited way by donating computers and peripherals to pilot schools and by supporting the production of Danish titles.

Establishing interest – reducing the gap between reading about multimedia and wanting to use it

Promoting a multimedia title can be a challenging task. Where multimedia is used for distributing well-known resources, such as data and software, end-users familiar with computers can be reached by conventional means. But where the design of the multimedia is not an extension of, but a radical departure from, existing educational practice, the gap between reading about the product and wanting to use it may be considerable. Also, it is surprisingly difficult to write about the design and effect of multimedia. Teachers and developers do not use the same terminology and do not find it easy to talk to and understand each other. Høirup (1989) describes a three-year project with interactive media and the strategies used to encourage colleagues at his own school to use it. His colleagues only began to use a particular multimedia simulation in their own classrooms when they had seen the product demonstrated, had grasped the underlying rationale and had successfully tried out the product for themselves.

There is no simple solution to the issue of experiencing multimedia first-hand rather than reading about it. In my own organization, we devote a lot of time and energy to presentations and courses, followed up by the loan of equipment and titles to energetic teachers around the country who want to experience multimedia themselves before committing their school. In the short term, by concentrating on and supporting these opinion leaders, we hope that they will discover for themselves the potential for some of these products in their classrooms. In the medium to long term, these are the people who will decide whether and how fast multimedia will be adopted by a majority of their colleagues.

Relevance – knowing when and how to use multimedia in the classroom

In industrial training, there is often a good case for individualized instruction requiring as many workstations as there are students. In Danish schools, this is felt to be both economically unrealistic and undesirable.

As schools have moved away from computer science as a separate subject to the integrated use of NIT in normal classes, there is typically one computer with one CD-ROM drive or videodisc player in the classroom. Its use requires the class of up to 25 students to be organized into groups of two to four students, each group working in turn with the multimedia and other materials.

With the notable exception of *The North Polar Expedition* – an interactive simulation requiring at least six participants who take on the roles of expedition members – most multimedia have been produced with individual users or small groups in mind. Considerable ingenuity is required on the part of the teacher to combine the use of multimedia with other individual and group activities. Timetabling a simulation like *The North Polar Expedition*, for example, requires a double period if students are to complete the simulation and have the opportunity to discuss the results.

The kind of classroom management issues which can arise are described in Looms (1989), writing about *The EcoDisc*. This material allows students to explore a nature reserve in the south of England by providing surrogate walks, sampling techniques, statistics and background information. Then, acting as reserve managers, the students draw up a draft plan for the area and the simulator generates reactions in the form of letters, newspaper articles and answerphone messages from the interest groups in the area. A final plan is then drawn up and feedback, in the form of environmental impact statements and interest group reactions, completes the activity. *The EcoDisc* exists in three versions, two based on videodisc and one on CD-ROM. The CD-ROM version allows users to work in any of nine European languages.

Although *The EcoDisc* is highly motivating, initially it could not be used in Danish classrooms in its original form. There were no suggestions as to how the material could be used in a typical class of more than 20 students. With the permission of the producer of *The EcoDisc*, Peter Bratt, teachers put together a series of additional materials, based on the BBC Schools Television programme and associated transcripts by Peter Bratt and the computer simulation program for the Acorn Model B microcomputer which originally accompanied the television programme. In its revised form, the students first saw the television programme, then split into groups, working in turn with the videodisc, worksheets and other background materials. The teacher's role was to set the scene, organize and support – and make the best use of the interactive multimedia as a dissemination resource.

The first generation of teachers to use multimedia will need, for a few years at least, considerable support to sustain their initial interest. They will need help to see the relevance of multimedia in relation to the curriculum and they will need to be given tools that ensure they can make a mark on 'their' multimedia. This is one of the attractive features of bar-coded worksheets. Although by no means a sophisticated solution, both teachers and students can put together their own bar-coded worksheets and reports with the aid of a photocopier or a computer and printer.

Building confidence

This is crucial for teachers. Our experience in Denmark shows that 'going it alone' is rarely a recipe for success. Wherever possible, we prefer to support groups of teachers from the same school or neighbouring schools and to make sure that they at least have a minimum of technical support available, particularly at the beginning of their work. Until the 'one-box' multimedia machine without cables and peripherals is invented, someone will always be required to check the system.

The use of team-teaching using interactive multimedia has also been found to be a useful confidence-builder, as teachers rarely have the opportunity to see or learn from what goes on behind the doors of other classrooms. Video recordings of classroom activities have proved valuable as bases for discussion of classroom management issues.

Indicators of success

There are several indicators of the success of a project. Satisfactory learning outcomes and examination results are but two. Success for a teacher using multimedia in Denmark rarely comes in the form of promotion or a salary increase but there may be other rewards, such as opportunities to take part in conferences and teacher training workshops, to write articles in teacher journals and to receive favourable press coverage or feedback from parents. Some of the people behind the most effective multimedia projects in Denmark have taken time to involve parents, school governors and school board officials from the start. If there is support of this kind, everyone gets involved and can share in the success of the project.

Hardware and software – resolving the chicken and the egg paradox

One of the classical problems facing multimedia (or just about any technological innovation) is the chicken and egg paradox. Users are reluctant to use a medium unless there is a plentiful collection of titles relevant to their needs and publishers are hesitant to invest in titles for a market that does not yet exist. The decentralized structure of the small Danish educational market has made the commercial production of multimedia a hazardous proposition. This is why the first commercially available videodisc titles in Danish only appeared in 1990, all of them subsidized productions (*Siulleq/The Greenland Project; Resistance and the German Occupation of Denmark 1940–45*, and the Nordic CD-ROM project with statistical data).

Added to the problem of a lack of titles is the fact that many of the titles released a few years ago required specific disc players, CD-ROM drives or hardware configurations. On top of this, marketing people prematurely heralded the appearance of 'edutainment' products on CD-I or CDTV, or on multimedia CD-ROM derivatives such as DVI and CD-ROM XA. It is easy to see why most teachers have adopted a 'wait and see' attitude. Technical standards play an important part in the understandably cautious schools environment. Until recently, educational aids used in schools were expected to last a lifetime. But in

Table 6.1: *Budget for educational resources at a typical Danish folkeskole.*

Year	No of pupils	Total budget (DKK)*	Budget per pupil per year
1989	600	600,000	1,000
1990	570	572,000	1,003
1991	550	553,000	1,005
1992	540	550,000	1,018

* 1 US dollar = approximately 6.3 Danish kroner as at June 1992.

the space of a decade we have seen the development and obsolescence of several generations of microcomputers.

The use of the small computer systems interface (SCSI) on drives and the appearance of an increasing number of DOS/Macintosh compatible titles have already improved confidence in the CD-ROM format. The availability of grants for evaluating existing interactive multimedia seems to have reduced the perceived risk of using multimedia in the classroom and in itself helps to resolve the chicken and egg paradox. Finally, if the Multimedia PC (MPC) specification based on Windows 3.1 and CD-ROM technology announced in 1991 becomes widespread and hardware costs continue to fall, this could represent a stable set of standards to further reduce fragmentation of the education market.

Costs

When laser disc players and CD-ROM drives first appeared in Denmark in 1986, they were relatively expensive: both cost at least US$2,300. Over the last six years, prices for both computers and drives have fallen, so a complete system with computer and CD-ROM drive (and cables) can now be had for much the same amount. A laser disc player with bar-code reader costs between US$800 and US$2,000 and titles in Denmark cost from US$250 to US$1,000. These prices may seem reasonable, but the figures should be considered in the context of school budgets in Denmark.

From Table 6.1 one can see that school budgets for educational resources (paper, photocopying, chalk, exercise books and computers) have fallen steadily in line with reduced enrolments, while spending per pupil has almost kept pace with inflation (2.4 per cent per annum). The purchase of one computer and CD-ROM drive in 1991 required 3 per cent of the school's total budget or the equivalent of the total budget per pupil for 17 pupils. The equivalent figures two years ago were 5.3 per cent and 32 pupils.

A developmental scenario for interactive multimedia in education

In conclusion, I would like to sketch a scenario for the development of interactive multimedia in education for the next two or three years, making specific reference to Europe and the US. To look beyond such a timeline is too uncertain.

Throughout most of Europe, school enrolments have been falling for more than a decade, due to the decline in the birth rates. This decline is bottoming out and by the end of the 1990s we should see a stabilization of school enrolments. In countries such as the UK, total spending per student per annum has stabilized or has even increased in real terms, although much of this increase has been needed to make up for the budget cuts of the 1970s and to improve teachers' salaries.

In countries such as Denmark and the UK, there is a trend towards the full decentralization of the running of schools. School governors are now assuming full financial responsibility for schools' activities. Pilot projects where decentralization has been fully implemented show that decentralized decision-making and the right to reallocate funds within the overall budget bring greater flexibility and broader cost-awareness. There are already instances of schools finding funds for interactive multimedia or other priority activities by making one-off cuts in the allocations for building maintenance.

Manpower and resources will be required to apply the Keller ARCS model to the decision-makers in schools. Without the necessary political and financial support, innovation in this field will not be consolidated. Most interactive multimedia products will still be designed primarily for use as information dissemination resources rather than as instructional resources. This will not change until the teaching profession comes to see interactive technologies as a supportive innovation and not as a threat to its livelihood.

Interactive multimedia will continue to develop in American schools. Combi-players with bar-code readers handling videodiscs, compact discs (and perhaps CD-I) will be with us at least until 1997, and conventional CD-ROM applications will become common in school libraries in the very near future. Outside the US, it is by no means clear whether the laser disc format will gain a foothold in schools before the next generation of digital optical discs (CD-X) based on compact disc technology begins to mature. Whether CD-X is

CD-I, Commodore's CDTV, Fujitsu's CD-ROM-based FM Towns, Photo CD or even CD-ROM XA, will be decided by the consumer and professional markets. Any delivery system which drops below the US$250 mark will probably find its way into schools.

CD-ROM will be seen as the preferred distribution medium for software and digital resources (bibliographies, dictionaries, illustrated reference materials such as newspapers on a subscription basis and annotated works such as the complete Hans Christian Andersen in several languages) from 40Mb upwards. The reasons will be affordable drives and reliability coupled with low replication and mailing costs. A series of visual resource discs produced by museums, archives and television stations will be released on several formats, including laser disc, CD-ROM and CD-X. This is the 'multiple-media' approach envisaged by the Jean Talon Project in Canada, described later in Chapter 12.

Computer science teachers will join forces with innovative teachers of other subjects to ensure the full integration of interactive multimedia in the classroom and the school library. Schools will begin to use Integrated Systems Digital Networks (ISDN) instead of modems and telefax for communication with other schools and services. The high-definition videodisc format announced in Tokyo in September 1991 will begin to appear, initially for professional applications but later in the 1990s as a consumer format, replacing the laser disc standard.

If work towards achieving a universal descriptor and an interformat exchange structure is successful, completely digital multimedia systems will become a reality. Jurgen (1992) provides a lucid account of standards being established under the auspices of the International Organization for Standardization (ISO), the Joint Photographers Expert Group (JPEG), the International Telegraph and Telephone Consultative Committee (CCITT), the Motion Picture Experts Group (MPEG) and the Society of Motion Picture and Television Engineers (SMPTE).

There is a strong case for interactive multimedia. Given support and encouragement, I feel sure that it will become one of the mainstays of education by the end of this century.

References

Anderson, J.S.A. (1988). *The European Commission seminar on the application of interactive video systems to support learning in schools.* Cultra, Co Down, Northern Ireland. 28 September – 1 October. *Vol 1: Final report, Vol 2: Reference report* (including state-of-the-art papers from eight member countries), Department of Education, Northern Ireland.

Barker, J.P. (1991). CD-ROM in schools: Special report, *Inside IT*, 56, 4–7.

Commission of the European Community (1991). *Information and communication technology in Europe*. Catalogue No CD-70-91-095-DA-C. Euratom, Brussels.

El Bacha, N., Fuchs, E., Lampe, B., Malige F., Monteiller, L., Riou, A. and Thiriez, M. (1990). *IBM: European marketing*. ESCP, Paris.

Færch, C., Haastrup, K. and Phillipson, R. (1984). *Learner language and language learning*. Multilingual Matters, Gyldendal, Copenhagen.

Gale, L.E. (1983). Montevidisco: An anecdotal history of an interactive videodisc. *CALICO Journal*, 1 (1), 42–6.

Hertkorn, O. (1984). The laser videodisc in the Federal Republic of Germany. *NALLD Journal*, 18 (2) 33–41.

Høirup, M. (1989). CD-ROM in schools – what is required? In *CD-ROM Europe '89 Conference Proceedings*, London.

Innes, S. (1980). The development of BBC involvement in multimedia language programmes. *British Journal of Language Teaching*, 18 (2 & 3), 163–9.

Jurgen, R.K. (1992). Digital video (Special report on consumer electronics). *IEEE Spectrum* 29 (3). The Institute of Electrical and Electronics Engineers, New York, 24–30.

Karpatschof, B. (1991). Det selvorganiserende menneske og den selvorganiserede fremtid [Autonomous man and the self-organized society]. *Uddannelse: The Journal of the Danish Ministry of Education*, 10 (11), 579–86.

Keller, J.M. (1983). Motivational design of instruction. In C.M. Reigeluth (ed). *Instructional design theories and models: An overview of their current states*. Lawrence Erlbaum, Hillsdale, NJ.

Looms, P.O. (1989). What does CD-ROM have to offer? In *CD-ROM Europe '89 Conference Proceedings*, London.

Looms, P.O. (1991a). *Optical storage media and television stations: A status report*. Danmarks Radio, Copenhagen.

Looms, P.O. (1991b). Economic and design issues of large-scale multimedia databases. In *Proceedings of Conference on Hypermedia in Museums*, Pittsburgh, 14–16.

Mapp, L. (1991). Multimedia in UK schools. In *The European multimedia yearbook 1992*. Interactive Media International, London, 101–2.

Mort, P. (1964). Studies in education innovation from the Institute of Administrative Research. In M.B. Miles (ed), *Innovation in education*. Bureau of Publications, Teachers' College, Columbia University, New York.

Romiszowski, A.J. (1992). Developing interactive multimedia courseware and networks. In *Proceedings of the International Interactive Multimedia Symposium*, Perth, 17–46.

Rowntree, D. (1982). *Educational technology in curriculum development* (2nd edn). Harper & Row, London.

Rumelhart, D.E. (1984). Understanding understanding. In J. Flood, (ed), *Understanding reading comprehension*. International Reading Association, Newark, Del, 1–21.

Rybak, S. (1980). *Learning languages from the BBC*. Monograph. BBC, London.

Tufte, B., Holm Sørensen, B., Schoubye, J., Løkkegaard, F., Cornelius, H. and Arbov, J. (1991). *Medieundervisning – Evalueringsrapport for Folkeskolens Udviklingsråd* [*Media education – an evaluation report for the Primary and Lower Secondary Education Development Council*]. Danmarks Lærerhøjskole, Copenhagen.

7 Hypermedia, multimedia and human factors

Jenny Preece

Introduction

From ancient times written works were intimately connected with other forms of artistic endeavour. Today with the aid of graphic displays, computer-aided technology and windowing technology we have returned to this desirable situation. We have corrected the technology driven separation forced upon us for centuries by conventional practices of mechanical printing and data encoding. (Fox, 1989, p195)

Fox paints an optimistic view. Technology is now available which enables designers to integrate graphic displays, animation, film and interesting uses of sound as well as text. Furthermore, it is possible to transmit this information as data over both local and wide area networks. The key question is 'how can this technology be harnessed to facilitate learning and human endeavour?'

The development of multimedia systems promises to enhance learning and to enable users to interact with information in new ways. Despite these promises, if such sophisticated systems are not well designed, they will create psychological problems for users, such as memory overload and divided attention, or they will fail to suit the variety of ways that people work together or alone.

Sound, direct manipulation of interface objects, visualization of processes and dynamic video images are all features of today's state-of-the-art multimedia systems. Increasingly powerful computer graphics enable designers to create sophisticated three-dimensional images. Using specialist devices, users have the illusion of manipulating these images in virtual space or even of walking around in a virtual world. What are the promises and problems of these technologies?

In this chapter we shall start by attempting to define some of the different kinds of multimedia systems that currently exist. We shall then briefly examine the components that contribute to the way people interact and learn with computer systems, the nature of that interaction and how hypertext systems can be designed to support learning. Then we shall examine some of the claims that are commonly made about hypermedia learning systems and end by drawing some conclusions. The discussion will focus on the structure and display of information and not on state-of-the-art devices.

Multimedia and hypermedia

Four types of multimedia system can be identified: *non-computerized multimedia*; *interactive multimedia*; *hypertext*; and *hypermedia*.

Non-computerized multimedia

Non-computerized multimedia systems are those in which a number of different media are integrated into a single learning package or module. This is a common approach for distance learning or self-instruction. For example, the Open University in the UK provides undergraduate and postgraduate degree-level courses for students to study at home in their own time and without the constant presence of a tutor (Davies and Preece, 1989). Typically, these courses comprise specially prepared self-instructional texts, television programmes (or videocassettes), a home experiment kit (for science courses), audiocassettes and often a computer with software. These packages have for many years been described as 'multimedia' as they are based on carefully *integrated* collections of material delivered via different media.

Multimedia

More recently, the term 'multimedia' has also been used to describe systems in which various media are presented and integrated via a single computer system or a network. These systems can vary along several dimensions. Technically, they range from specially prepared packages which run on a single-user computer system in which input and output are achieved using a screen, keyboard and/or mouse, through systems which use sophisticated virtual reality devices like datagloves, datasuits, etc to networks which carry a variety of different types of media which collectively provide electronic conferencing, electronic mail, access to large data banks of textual and visual material such as slides of famous works of art, computer-based learning and training materials and so on. Another dimension along which multimedia systems vary is the kind of learning experience that they provide. They can provide a variety of self-instruction styles ranging from a linear presentation of concepts similar to a linear text but with pictures, video, sound and animation to highly flexible *hyper* environments, which encourage users to develop their own pathways through the material. In this chapter we shall focus our discussion primarily on single-user multimedia and hypermedia systems.

Hypertext

'Hypertext' is a system for presenting active text. The key feature, from the learners' point of view, is that the text has many nodes and links which allow them to determine their own routes through the material. Hypertext may contain text and graphics and, if the latter are present, it too may be classified under the multimedia umbrella. Definitions of hypertext can, however, be confusing. Gygi (1990) defines two broad types of hypertext: broad spectrum and a more clinical variety. The broad-spectrum definition is characterized primarily by the recognition that hypertext is a format for non-sequential representation of ideas. It is dynamic and non-linear. The second type is more rigorous and specific, but at its crux is the notion of computer-supported links (Laurel, 1990, p283). Hypertext has many applications, including use as a presentation medium for information management and browsing, providing access to information that the public needs (such as tourism information) and for various learning activities.

Hypermedia

Hypermedia combines aspects of hypertext and a variety of multimedia (text, graphics, animation, video and sound) used in some combination. The branching structure of hypertext is used with multimedia in order to produce a system in which learners can determine their own paths through the medium. There is debate about the relationship between hypermedia and multimedia and a number of definitions are discussed by McKerlie and Preece (1992). For our present purposes, we shall accept the definition provided by Fischer and Mandl (1990, pxix):

> Hypermedia are virtual media. The prefix 'hyper' in the hypermedia distinguishes this type of media from multimedia. The difference is based upon the depth and richness of the information contained. Hypermedia are also different

from multimedia because the learner decides how much of this virtual richness he or she wants to use.

There is considerable discussion about the use of hypermedia for different tasks but at present attention seems to be concentrated on its use for public information systems (eg, Davies, Maurer and Preece, 1991) and for education and training.

One of the main concerns for designers of hypertext and hypermedia is the need to provide users with navigational support so that they do not get lost in the myriad of links, often referred to as 'hyperspace'. For designers of multimedia the main design issues are how to integrate the media and which media to use for presenting different kinds of information. Research in human–computer interaction (HCI) and human factors provides general theory, knowledge and techniques which can support and guide multimedia and hypermedia development. As yet, however, little of this work has been concerned specifically with hypermedia and multimedia, but this will change as experience with the technology increases.

Four components of human–computer interaction

Diaper (1989a, p3) describes the goals of HCI as being to 'develop or improve the safety, utility, effectiveness, efficiency and usability of systems that include computers'. These goals are extremely relevant in considering interactive multimedia systems to support learning. Knowledge of the interrelationships of four key components (the learner[s], the learning tasks, the characteristics of the environment in which learning is taking place and the technical limitations of the delivery system) is essential. Each of these components has, in turn, many characteristics and all four components interact in complex ways.

Learners

Learners have physiological, psychological and social needs. For example, physiological requirements determine such things as how long the learner can sit in one position or how easy it is to reach certain buttons, etc. Similarly, some people enjoy learning by themselves while others like to work in pairs and in groups. However, catering for learners' physiological and social needs is relatively easy compared with the problem of catering for psychological differences. There are many psychological factors to consider when designing hypermedia learning systems. Some factors, such as the limitations of human memory, affect everyone in more or less the same way, whereas others, collectively referred to as 'individual differences', vary from person to person. Humans' psychological limitations include:

- *Memory load:* For example, how many different control icons is it reasonable to expect learners to remember at any one time – that is, to hold in short-term memory? How can users be helped to navigate through hyperspace?
- *Perception:* For example, what colours provide best readability or contrast and what size of text or graphics is optimal? How are different sounds perceived?
- *Attention:* For example, how can we help to draw users' attention to information that is relevant at any particular time when there is a lot of different visual information on the screen? Similarly, how can media be integrated so that they support each other and do not cause users' attention to become divided? If there is a multimedia application in which information is presented by voice while at the same time showing a slightly shortened textual version of the same information, it is quite likely that the users of such a system will either not attend to the text or will be disturbed by receiving two slightly different messages at the same time via two different media. (These issues are discussed in more detail in McKerlie and Preece, 1992.)

The two most important individual differences that need to be considered are:

- *Previous experience with hypermedia systems:* It is well known that one of the factors that has most effect on how successfully people see a new computer system for the first time is their previous experience with other computer systems, particularly similar systems (see, for example, Egan, 1988). Software developers quite rightly capitalize on this fact by developing their own 'look and feel' for their product lines so that it is easy for users to learn a new application or to move among different applications. For example, Macintosh applications have a different look and feel from IBM applications, although some developers' products do have similar features.
- *Previously acquired knowledge of the learning domain:* There are now a number of studies that show that the context of the domain can greatly affect students' ability to learn new knowledge or apply existing knowledge correctly. For example, in a study by Preece and Janvier (in press), students were asked to do the same graph interpretation exercises with two syntactically matched graphs

representing two different domains. Many examples were recorded of ways in which the domains to which the graphs related influenced the students' interpretations. In particular, there was evidence of the powerful influence of concepts derived from 'everyday' beliefs (in other words concepts not taught in science). There do not appear to be any comparable studies involving learning with hypermedia but it would be surprising if domain knowledge did not influence learners in various ways. For example, students' motivation and ability to find and apply knowledge are likely to be influenced by the domain of the learning system.

Several authors discuss the range and effects of individual differences. Bloom (1976) is renowned for his studies into human characteristics and leaning, while Egan (1988) reviews the implications of individual differences for human-computer interaction design.

Learning tasks and motivation

Detailed knowledge of the kinds of tasks for which a proposed system will be used is essential and there are a number of task analysis techniques for acquiring this information (see, for example, Diaper, 1989b; Benyon, 1992). A thorough task and requirements analysis, followed by user-centred design in which a prototype or system passes through an iterative series of 'design-test with users/redesign' cycles, helps to produce usable systems. However, the exact way that this applies to hypermedia learning systems is less clear. The philosophy of hypermedia is quite unlike that of the more traditional mediated systems which are designed for a specific task or a range of tasks. Although teachers and learners can set goals such as: 'Investigate Shakespeare's *Twelfth Night* on CD-ROM and answer the question "What was a jester's life like when Shakespeare was alive?" ', it is equally within the design philosophy that users should be able to wander through hypermedia following paths that take their fancy. Such open-ended learning activity is both difficult to design for and difficult to evaluate in terms of effectiveness against other systems.

Furthermore, despite many years of study, there are no adequate learning theories on which to base the design of hypersystems (Wright, 1989). Jonassen and Grabinger (1989) have pointed out that three types of learning process seem to be supported by hypermedia – information-seeking, knowledge-acquisition and problem-solving. The goals of users appear to fall into the following categories (McKerlie and Preece, 1992):

- finding an answer to a particular question (a searching task);

- gaining a sense of scope for the information (a browsing task);
- exploring a particular concept in order to learn (a learning task); and
- collecting and tailoring information (organizing and synthesizing information).

The distinct advantage of hypermedia for *information-seeking* is that very large volumes of information can be presented and learners can examine it in different ways. There is also the potential advantage that information can be presented in different ways relatively cheaply. For example, trends in data may be presented graphically, numerically or even by using a combination of these display media. The role of hypermedia in supporting *knowledge-acquisition* is more difficult to define but broadly it follows the line that exploring hypermedia or learning by interacting within the context of a hypermedia system will help students to develop their own schemata. Advocates of discovery learning, for example as espoused by Bruner (1966), are likely to be enthusiastic about the concept of hypermedia, as it supports students in determining their own learning routes and making their own discoveries. However, it also suffers the same problem as many other forms of discovery learning: that the lack of structure may not suit all students, every domain or all concepts. Much work is being done and remains to be done in order to establish theories of learning that are sufficiently robust to support good hypermedia design. (See Jonassen and Mandl, 1989, for a valuable collection of papers on this subject.)

The learning environment

Where students learn is also an issue worth considering, in both the design and the use of hypermedia. Physical conditions, such as lighting, need to be taken into account in the design of any system but it is the social issues that are of particular concern for hypermedia design. Students and other users who are accustomed to using computers and who have experienced discovery learning situations are likely to enjoy and learn well with hypermedia, while those less accustomed to working in such environments may take longer to accept the medium. Designers should therefore consider ways of building in different levels of support and structure for different usage preferences.

Technical constraints

The characteristics of the hardware and software that are used in the development and delivery of the system can be important too. For example, it is well known that slow response time and small display size will, if these presentation features fall below a minimally acceptable threshold, annoy the users of any system. In many currently available systems, the size of video windows and length of video clips have to be reduced because of the excessive memory demands of this form of display.

Interaction and learning

The issue of learning to use a hypermedia system versus learning about something using a hypermedia system has already been raised. Since learning theory is parsimonious in this area, it is helpful to draw on Norman's (1986) high-level theory of how people interact with a computer system.

Interaction and learning to use a computer system

Norman's theory of interaction provides a general explanation of why some people may have problems learning to use certain computer systems while others do not. Norman describes how the user of a computer system starts off with goals which are expressed in psychological terms. The computer system, however, presents its current state in physical terms, known as 'the system's image'. Consequently, the user's goals and system state differ significantly in their form and content, creating two 'gulfs' which must be bridged if the system is to be used successfully by users to achieve their goals. One gulf arises from the need for users to map their psychological goals on to the system in terms of executable physical actions; this is 'the gulf of execution'. The other gulf arises from the users' need to evaluate the physical changes in the system that result from their actions; this is 'the gulf of evaluation'. Successful interaction with the system relies on these gulfs being bridged and this can occur in two ways. The system can be designed so that its input and output characteristics match well with the users' model of how the system works – 'the users' mental model'. Alternatively, the users can bridge the gulfs by creating plans, action sequences and interpretations that move the normal description of the users' goals closer to the description required by the physical system. In practice, both options need to be used. In particular, well-designed systems are those in which designers have been able to move the system closer to the user by capitalizing on users' knowledge from previous experience. One way of doing this is by selecting an appropriate metaphor so that users can draw on analogies from their everyday knowledge in order to use the system. Other aspects, such as consistency and transparency in the behaviour of the system, and meaningful feedback when things go wrong, can also help to bridge the gulfs and make the system straightforward to use.

Learning about something using a hypermedia system

When considering systems for learning and training, such as hypertext and hypermedia, we need to be particularly aware that learners differ in knowledge of the domain and learning style. Their needs for help and support to understand the relationships among domain concepts will also vary. Furthermore, learners change their requirements for domain support as they learn, just as they do for system support. The major problem for developers of hypermedia learning systems is how to avoid overwhelming users with a complexity of domain and system information while retaining scope for learners to find their own learning paths. The complexity needs to be managed in such a way that users do not get lost in vast amounts of information.

The navigation problem

In order to navigate through hypermedia systems successfully, learners need to be able to answer the following questions (Fischer and Mandl, 1990):

- Where am I?
- How did I get here?
- What can I do here?
- Where can I get to?
- How do I go there?

Two more questions are important to understand the scope of the domain knowledge presented in the hypermedia system (McKerlie and Preece, 1992):

- What have I seen so far?
- What else is there for me to see?

Users are likely to have difficulty in finding their way around *any* complex system, but the nature of hypermedia has the potential to make this problem acute. The combination of a highly flexible system in which learners find their own paths, and the complex integration of a variety of different media (with, for example, colour graphics, film and animation displayed on several screens or windows and interrelated with sound) can be confusing. Users have not only to make sense of the variety of different stimuli associated with different kinds of information but they have to make decisions about which links to follow and which to ignore. Alternatively, it is possible that, unlike the comparatively featureless landscape of hypertext with few or no graphics, the visual variation offered by the different media may actually provide 'landmarks' and facilitate 'way finding'. Although the literature on navigation and hypertext is now quite large, the issue has been less well addressed in regard to hypermedia. However, the actual way that media are used and integrated to present the information that they carry is likely to be an important factor and worthy of research (McKerlie and Preece, 1992).

Navigation strategies

The strategies that can be used by designers in order to facilitate users' navigation include metaphorical interfaces, guides, maps, overviews and other graphical techniques, tables of contents and indexes.

Metaphors

The development of metaphorical interfaces, direct manipulation, graphical user interfaces (GUIs) and recent advances in the field of virtual reality allow users to control the system by manipulating objects (to a greater or lesser extent) such as icons, windows, menus and scroll bars. In well-designed interfaces, these objects are so selected and represented that users can intuitively deduce their meaning and their function in the system from prior 'everyday knowledge' and experience. Thus the designers' aim is to reduce interface complexity by allowing users to capitalize on prior knowledge of the real world. The desktop metaphor of the Xerox Star system (see, for example, Smith et al, 1982) and the Macintosh have made this design concept known to millions of people. (Carroll, Mack and Kellog, 1988, provide a good review of interface metaphors and user interface design.)

Metaphors which have been used in the design of hypertext systems include maps and other forms of navigational aids. Hammond and Allison (1988; 1989) have further developed and exploited the notion of 'travelling through' hypertext. Their system enables students to 'get on a bus for a guided tour' through the information. Benest (1989) suggests a book metaphor in which users actually see an open book on the screen with a table of contents and pages to turn, showing how much of the book has been read. Petersen (1989) displays a library which is the metaphor for a database of library information. Henderson and Card (1986) cater for users' needs to organize collections of software tools and to switch rapidly among tasks in a hypermedia system by tying these multi-tasking functions to the tasks and structural elements of a graphic 'rooms' metaphor representation; for example, 'opening a door' maps on to returning to a workspace that might involve one or more software tools tailored for some overall task. The overall system is a composite metaphor and individual software tools may have their own specialized metaphors.

Well-chosen metaphors can help to organize the elements in a system or describe its function. A 'window', for example, is an organizational metaphor and 'cut-and-paste' is an example of a functional metaphor. Even though metaphors often offer a far from perfect solution to the problem of interface complexity, their use in interface design is a natural way to learn (Anderson, 1983). Lakoff and Johnson (1980) say that 'the metaphors we use both intentionally and unintentionally, contribute structure in terms of which we organize our understanding of what is going on'. Carroll and Thomas (1982) say that when people learn they develop new cognitive structures by metaphorically extending old ones. They do this by positioning the new concept in the framework of something else that they already know. The power of metaphors may also lie in their pervasiveness in our use of language and hence our culture (Lakoff and Johnson, 1980). Consequently, when users invoke metaphors they may influence the success with which they learn to use the system (Carroll and Thomas, 1982). However, metaphors must, by definition, provide imperfect mappings to their target domains (Carroll, Mack and Kellog, 1988).

Functional mismatches may occur in which the interface metaphor offers more or less functionality than the underlying target system or simply behaves differently. For example, ejecting a floppy disk from a Macintosh system by placing it in the trash icon is a surprise to most novice users. The interface may also be a composite of several metaphors (Carroll, Mack and Kellog, 1988). For example, in the world of the desktop there are various kinds of desktop accessories and there is also the physical metaphor of direct manipulation. These composites may have mismatches with each other if they are not part of the same organizing theme. Consequently, the more aspects that are taken into account by a single metaphor the better the system is likely to be for its users (Carroll and Thomas, 1982). Verplank and Kim (1986) and Verplank (1989) suggest that designers should find a good organizing metaphor to avoid this problem. If designers do not provide users with appropriate metaphors they may develop their own, less appropriate ones (Lakoff and Johnson 1980).

Guides

Laurel (1990, p355) points out that

> since the beginning of this century, people have dreamed about the new companions they might create with high technology . . . all the computer-based personae that weave through popular culture have one thing in common: they mediate a relationship between the labyrinthine precision of computers and the fuzzy complexity of man.

The notion of someone who mediates between a computer and its users is appealing, particularly in hypermedia, where the structure of the information may be complex and the quantity vast. Furthermore, from a designer's perspective, they help to solve the problem of how to make a seamless transition from one type of medium to another, which is particularly important when one of the media is time dependent (such as video) and the other is not (Blattner and Dannenberg, 1992).

According to Laurel (1990, p355), 'an interface agent can be defined as a character, enacted by the computer who acts on behalf of the user in a virtual (computer-based) environment'. The agent is, of course, a kind of metaphor, a person or an organism that can help the user to perform a variety of tasks, including managing scheduling, providing advice and help about the system or the domain, searching for things or taking the user somewhere such as on a tour or to a particular part of the system. Thus, an agent can have a powerful role in hypermedia navigation for giving overview tours or locating specific information.

There can, however, be drawbacks to having an agent. Just like human agents, computer agents may have appealing or unappealing personalities or traits, so care is needed in designing appropriate agents. Cultural and gender differences can, for example, be important in agent design. Interface designers have long been aware of the need to design different ways of doing the same thing in order to cater for users' differences in expertise and preferences. Similarly, it may be important to provide different types of agents or even to let users define their own agents to avoid the problem of annoying or unpopular agents! Another argument against agents is that they need some intelligence to work well with all the overheads of memory and problems of artificial intelligence (AI), but this is not true. Several systems have 'unintelligent' (in the AI sense) agents which work perfectly adequately. In hypermedia, they can take such useful roles as navigator, searcher, domain or system expert.

Maps and other aids

As has been remarked earlier in this section, maps can form part of a metaphor or they may be used simply to show the relative associations among different kinds of information or topics. The hypermedia navigation problem can also be eased by the traditional techniques which form an essential part of books: namely, tables of contents and indexes. Although work has already been done on online versions for accessing information in linear electronic documents, the potential usefulness of tables of contents and indexes for hypermedia navigation appears to have been largely ignored.

Does hypermedia fulfil the claims made for it?

Similar promises are heard for hypermedia as for hypertext. It is said that learners will:

* be excited and motivated by hypermedia;
* be able to determine their own learning paths; and, consequently,
* be actively engaged in learning which will be exploratory in nature.

Does hypermedia live up to these claims? Although the number of hypermedia systems is increasing rapidly, evidence of their success as learning environments is mostly anecdotal. This is perhaps not too surprising, as traditional evaluation methods in which tests are devised to determine whether learning fulfils stated learning objectives cannot be easily applied to hypermedia. Any test that restricts users' access to the full flexibility of hypermedia goes against the underlying philosophy of hypermedia and so changes the nature of the system being tested. However, unmotivated use of hypermedia, in which users do not have goals, does not provide a suitable evaluation scenario either. Evaluators need to establish users' goals at particular times and then try to understand how users go about achieving these goals and what kind of problems they encounter. Some direction can be given to students by specifying a general task at a high level, such as 'What was X's relationship with Y in *Twelfth Night?*' However, the really interesting information that is needed to evaluate the system concerns the particular sub-goals students have at any particular times. For example, are they:

* looking for an answer to a particular question (and if so, what is that question)?

- gaining a sense of the scope of the information?
- exploring a particular question (and if so, what and why)?
- collecting and tailoring information (and if so, what and why)?

Evaluators need to obtain this information without intervening in the students' learning activity in order to establish whether or not the students:

- achieve their own goals;
- learn;
- are motivated by the medium and enjoy using it;
- can find their way around the system;
- experience annoying features which inhibit or distract them from achieving their goals.

Hypermedia is expensive to produce and, although the technology will become cheaper, many of the development costs are likely to remain high. Labour is expensive and high standard, high production-value video production and copyright charges for existing materials can incur major costs. However, hypermedia offers exciting prospects compared with hypertext and conventional learning materials. Furthermore, the visual nature of hypermedia could well reduce the navigational problems that learners often experience when using hypertext. It will therefore be important for designers to have a good knowledge of HCI and human factors so that distracting stimuli do not annoy or disorient learners. This could become even more imperative with the continuing increase in computing power and the development of novel devices. Although virtual reality holds promises of making interaction even more direct, there are obstacles to overcome. At present, the lack of tactile feedback and perspective are two obvious problems.

If we believe that hypermedia offers new and exciting learning experiences, it is important to carry out research which will help us gain a better understanding of how to develop good hypermedia systems. In particular, further information is needed so that the different media can be integrated effectively and the learners' navigational problems be alleviated while still retaining the flexibility and excitement promised by well-designed hypermedia.

References

Anderson, J.R. (1983). *The architecture of cognition.* Harvard University Press, Cambridge, Mass.

Benest, I.D. (1989). A hypertext system with controlled hype. In *Proceedings of the Hypertext II Conference*, York, 29-30 June.

Benyon, D. (1992). *Task analysis: Technical report*. Computing Department, the Open University, Milton Keynes.

Blattner, M.M. and Dannenberg, R.B. (1992). *Multimedia interface design*. Addison-Wesley, Reading, Mass.

Bloom, B.S. (1976). *Human characteristics and school learning*. McGraw-Hill, New York.

Bruner, J.S. (1966). *Towards a theory of instruction*. Norton, New York.

Carroll, J.M., Mack, R.I. and Kellog, W.A. (1988). Inteface metaphors and user interface design. In M. Helander (ed), *Handbook of human–computer interaction*. North-Holland, Amsterdam, 67-85.

Carroll, J.M. and Thomas, J.C. (1982). Metaphor and the cognitive representation of computing systems. *IEEE Transactions on Systems, Man and Cybernetics*, 12 (2), 107-15.

Davies, G., Maurer, H. and Preece, J.J. (1991). Presentation metaphors for a very large hypermedia system. *Journal of Microcomputer Applications*, 14, 105-16.

Davies, G. and Preece J. (1989). *Home computing as an integral part of distance learning*. Paper presented at the IFIP, WG 3.4 Working Conference on Methodologies of Training Data Processing Professionals and Advanced End-users. Helsinki.

Diaper, D. (1989a). Editorial: The discipline of HCI. *Interacting with computers*, 1 (1), 3-5.

Diaper, D. (1989b). *Task analysis*. Ellis Horwood, Chichester.

Egan, D.E. (1988). Individual differences in human–computer interaction. In M. Helander (ed), *Handbook of human–computer interaction*. North-Holland, Amsterdam, 543-68.

Fischer, P.M. and Mandl, H. (1990). Towards a psychophysics of hypermedia. In Jonassen and Mandl (1989), ix-xxv.

Fox, E.A. (1989). The coming revolution in interactive digital video. *Communications of the ACM*, 32 (7), 794-801.

Gygi, K. (1990). Recognizing the symptoms of hypertext and what to do about it. In Laurel (1990), 279-87.

Hammond, N. and Allison, L. (1988). Travels around a learning support environment: Rambling, orienteering or touring? In *Human Factors in Computing Systems: CHI '88 Proceedings*. ACM Press, New York, 269-70.

Hammond, N. and Allison, L. (1989). Extending hypertext for learning: An investigation of access and guidance tools. In A. Sutcliffe and L. Macaulay (eds), *People and computers V: The British Computer Society workshop series*. Proceedings of the Fifth Conference of the British Computer Society Human Interaction Specialist Group, Cambridge University Press, Cambridge, 269-70.

Henderson, D.A. and Card, S.K. (1986). Rooms: The use of virtual multiple workspaces to reduce space contention in a window-based graphical user interface. *ACM Transactions on Graphics*, 5, 211-43.

Jonassen, D.H. and Grabinger, R.S. (1989). Problems and issues in designing hypertext/hypermedia for learning. In Jonassen and Mandl (1989), 3-26.

Jonassen, D.H. and Mandl, H. (eds) (1989). *Designing hypermedia for learning*. NATO ASI Series, Vol 67. Springer-Verlag, Berlin/New York.

Lakoff, G. and Johnson, M. (1980). *Metaphors we live by*. University of Chicago Press, Chicago.

Laurel, B. (ed) (1990). *The art of human–computer interface design*. Addison-Wesley, Reading, Mass.

McKerlie, D. and Preece, J. (1992). The hypermedia effect: More than just the sum of its parts. In *Proceedings of the St Petersburg HCI Conference*, St Petersburg, Russia, August, 115-27.

Norman, D.A. (1986). Cognitive engineering. In D.A. Norman and S.W. Draper (eds), *User-centred system design: New perspectives in human-computer interaction.* Lawrence Erlbaum, Hillsdale, NJ, 31–62.

Petersen, A.M. (1989). A library system for information retrieval based on a cognitive task analysis and supported by our icon-based interface. In *Proceedings of the 12th International Conference of the ACM SIGIR*, Cambridge, Mass, 40–7.

Preece, J.J. and Janvier, C. (in press). Interpreting trends in multiple curve graphs of ecological situations: The role of context. *International Journal of Science.*

Smith, D.C., Irby, C., Kimball, R., Verplank, B. and Harslem, E. (1982). Designing the Star User Interface. *Byte Magazine,* 7 (4), 242–82.

Verplank, W. (1989). *CHI '89 tutorial notes: Graphical invention for user interfaces.* ID Two, San Francisco.

Verplank, W. and Kim, S. (1986). Graphic invention for user interfaces: An experimental course in user interface design. *SIGCHI Bulletin,* 18 (3), 50–67.

Wright, P. (1989). Hypertexts as an interface for learners: Some human factors issues. In Jonassen and Mandl (1989), 169–84.

8 Lifecycle costing models for interactive multimedia systems

William Tan and Ann Nguyen

Introduction

It is widely claimed that IMM, with its remarkable capacities to capture, store, process and transmit information, has a great potential to increase the effectiveness, reduce the cost and improve the efficiency of education and training by making learning processes more stimulating, increasing rates and levels of learning and allowing the end-users to be more fully in control of their own learning. To date, much of the literature has focused on the technology, theory and practice of designing and implementing IMM systems. Far less attention has been given to actually costing IMM practice.

The costs of producing IMM courseware are determined by such lifecycle items as the technology employed, the complexity of the content and the instructional design of the programmes, the degree of interaction provided for the learners and the extent and production values of the media components, particularly where video is employed. So great are the variables that lifecycle costings for IMM can vary from thousands to hundreds of thousands of pounds or dollars.

This chapter seeks to analyse and quantify the costs incurred in setting up and operating IMM applications of varying levels of complexity. The lifecycle models are based on the typical processes involved in developing and implementing IMM courseware in the context of an Australian tertiary institution. While the specific costings, which are given in Australian dollars, may not apply in other countries, the costing method and the system classification should provide a useful guide for educators, trainers and administrators in a range of organizational settings.

Definition of terms

Computer-based instruction (CBI) courseware is educational or training software which may comprise any or all of text, graphics, music, speech, sound effects, still images, animation, motion video, etc. Such courseware is organized as a structure of interlinked information chunks or nodes which can be accessed and associated with a number of preplanned options by learners according to their learning styles and/or needs. The program provides interactive dialogue with the learner and, in its more sophisticated forms, can respond with appropriate feedback, remedial or instructional sequences, or additional options in a variety of media according to the learner's ability, interest, pace of learning and need for further detail or challenge. CBI courseware can be utilized in self-instructional contexts, as a resource to support instructor-led courses or in distance education or open learning applications.

Interactivity is two-way human–machine communication involving an end-user and a computer-based instructional system. Users actively direct the flow and direction of the instructional or information programmes which, in turn, exchange information with the viewers, processing their inputs in order to generate the appropriate response within the context of the programme.

Level of interactivity refers to the capability of hardware and software components to effect certain predetermined interactions between a learner and a CBI system. For the purpose of establishing a simple model for comparative costings, we have established a classification for CBI systems which takes into account level of interactivity, complexity of implementation and extent of the developmental costs. This definition of interactivity level differs from the Nebraska Videodisc Design/Production Group's three degrees of videodisc system interactivity, which were proposed in 1980 (details of this system are given by Peter Looms in Chapter 6 and in the Glossary). For the purpose of our financial models and costings, we shall refer to three computer-based interactivity levels, *CBIL-1*, *CBIL-2* and *CBIL-3*.

At *CBIL-1*, learner input is through a keyboard or pointing device such as a mouse; a VGA monitor provides the output; and the courseware, developed from basic code or through an authoring system, utilizes text, graphics and (possibly) some simple animation but does not include still or motion video. Its earlier learning strategies were typically instructional, employing a drill and practice approach but hypertext systems enable the user to 'browse' through information with greater freedom and seek greater depths of understanding. Many tertiary institutions start with the development of such CBIL-1 products because they can be developed and delivered using the kinds of personal computer that already exist in laboratories and on lecturers' desks. No additional computing or audiovisual equipment is required and no specialized audiovisual production services are involved, so this is the least expensive form of CBI courseware to develop and deliver.

With our *CBIL-2* system, the learners can access and use computer-based courseware in tandem with a re-purposed videotape or laser or compact disc. The video material is essentially linear and the programmable memory and processing power are such that control is limited to the ability to start, play or rewind in regard to particular segments. Input is via a keyboard, pointing device or remote control. Output is via a VGA monitor (for computer-generated text, graphics/animation and sound) and a TV (for the analogue video and audio). The lifecycle cost of a CBIL-2 system is higher than that of a CBIL-1 system, because of the more sophisticated hardware/software configuration and the more elaborate instructional design and computer-based courseware development.

With our *CBIL-3* system, the users have at their disposal complex controls and courseware that make the fullest possible uses of sound and still/motion video on a laser- or CD-based disc, the overlaying of computer-generated text and/or graphics on to the video, and text, graphics, audio, still images, animation, etc, on disk. CBIL-3 input devices include keyboard, mouse, touchscreen, microphone, etc, and the output devices include VGA monitor, TV or projection TV, amplified speakers or headphones, printer, etc. The user can access and navigate the programme with speed, accuracy and flexibility. Each of the objects may be manipulated independently or in combination with other objects within the courseware. Our CBIL-3 courseware is therefore capable of accommodating instructional, experimental, exploratory and informational elements and a range of media in its overall design (see Table 8.1).

CBIL-3 courseware is the most expensive form of CBI courseware to produce and deliver. It requires sophisticated hardware and software and complex content acquisition, instructional design and media creation processes, all of which can drive up the lifecycle costs. However, if the product design is well suited to particular applications, it may prove cost effective in the long run because of its ability to promote deep learning and problem-solving skills and provide models, simulations and surrogate experiences that save costs in staffing, equipment, consumables and travel, reduce risks to health and safety, provide valuable just-in-time training, etc.

Table 8.1: *Four possible models for CBI courseware.*

Model 1: Instructional

Type: Drill and practice approach.
Nature: The learner is given question-and-answer instruction. This process tends to be repetitive. The information is provided by course designers who have to assume that the material is suitable for the learners. The process is usually applied to reinforce concepts and principles. It offers the learner limited control over his/her learning experience.
Learner's role: The role of the learner is that of the student. The learning can be enhanced by varying questioning and feedback styles and by adding reference materials and/or illustrative graphics.

Model 2: Experimental

Type: Problem-solving approach.
Nature: The learner is encouraged to manipulate and test ideas or hypotheses and remain in control of his/her learning paths.
Learner's role: The role of the learner is that of the tester who is provided with tools to experiment with various 'what-if' solutions or that of an inventor with materials and tools to analyse, address and solve problems.

Model 3: Exploratory

Type: Exploration approach.
Nature: The learner first explores with the tools and the materials. After an event, facts and structure are gradually revealed. The learner can experiment with the variables within a fixed model but not with the model itself.
Learner's role: The learner acts as a role player and can be led to react more imaginatively. Some applications (for example, simulations), allow the learner to develop cognitive and psychomotor skills. Effective learning can be achieved by the use of realistic simulations or games.

Model 4: Informational

Type: Autonomic approach.
Nature: The learner is provided with tools to reduce time-consuming calculations or processes to enable concentration on individual interests and motivations.
Learner's role: The role of the learner is similar to that of the researcher who is given a wealth of information without structure and has to set personal objectives and create independent programmes of action.

Learning environments for CBI systems

Computer-based interactive applications can be utilized in two main types of learning environment. The first is totally computer-based. The course provider uses interactive courseware to deliver, test and manage the learning or training enterprise according to the course requirements and the end-users' preferred ways of learning. In this environment, the prime role of the human instructor is to provide motivation, administrative and technical guidance and individual counselling. The students access learning stations for study, practice and testing, and can choose the learning patterns or pathways that best suit their needs. The students' log-on/log-off times and performance are monitored by the system.

In the second environment, the CBI courseware is a component of a lesson or programme. The instructor teaches the lesson or programme but at certain points employs CBI to provide surrogate experiences, stimulate discussion or problem-solving or offer remedial or tutorial support.

Learning strategies for CBI

Many existing instructional design models can be applied to CBI courseware development (see, for example, Gagné and Briggs, 1974; Boud, 1988; Gagné and Merrill, 1990; Merrill, 1991). A fundamental aim of CBI courseware should be to enable the learners to take more responsibility for their learning and to develop their own cognitive learning strategies. Table 8.1 provides a summary of four possible learning strategies that can be incorporated into CBI courseware.

CBIL-1 courseware is essentially limited to text, graphics and, possibly, simple animation; the motivational level of such courseware may therefore be relatively low (see Table 8.2). In contrast, CBIL-2 and CBIL-3 may provide a wider range of media and stimuli, generate higher motivational levels, be more influenced by cognitive theory and principles of adult learning, involve more complex problem-solving and therefore foster deeper learning. The additional costs incurred in developing and delivering CBIL-2 or CBIL-3 systems may be entirely justifiable if it is necessary or desirable for the students to achieve these higher-order cognitive tasks. However, a caveat is necessary here. To create effective interactive courseware, the developers must have an understanding of, and a concern for, the ways in which information and knowledge may be accessed, perceived, organized and applied by the learners. If the stimuli and questions delivered through the multimedia courseware, the browsable structure, the content or the media treatments are irrelevant to the learning task or the needs of the learner, the interactive components and audiovisual sequences will be no more than distracting interruptions to the learning process.

Table 8.2: *The motivational levels of various learning strategies and computer-based interactivity levels.*

Learning strategy	Computer-based interactivity level		
	CBIL-1	CBIL-2	CBIL-3
Instructional	low	moderate	high
Experimental	low	moderate	high
Exploratory	low	moderate–high	high
Informational	low	moderate–high	high

Lifecycle costing for different CBI courseware and platforms

As discussed earlier, the costs of implementing and delivering CBI courseware depend on the degree of interactivity required and the learning strategies, types of media and platforms selected for the product. The purpose of this section is to demonstrate how these costs may be determined. Firstly, we show how to establish a working formula for calculating lifecycle costs for the implementation of different levels of CBI courseware. Secondly, we provide examples of lifecycle costing for these different levels, taking into account all of the production, operational and recurrent costs.

The lifecycle costing formula for different levels of CBI courseware implementation can be established as follows:

(1) Courseware development costs can be described as

$$D_i = m_i M_i + j_i J_i + g_i G_i + a_i A_i + s_i S_i + v_i V_i + p_i P_i + o_i O_i$$

where, for a given CBIL i (i = 1, 2, 3),

D_i = total CBI courseware development costs and the following costs are measured in terms of labour and/or physical production costs:

M_i = material preparation costs

J_i = instructional design costs

G_i = graphics design and production costs

A_i = authoring and testing costs

S_i = scripting costs for video and audio production

V_i = video and audio production costs

P_i = video and audio post-production costs

O_i = optical disc mastering and duplicating costs

and where m_i, j_i, g_i, a_i, s_i, v_i, p_i and o_i are cost parameters for, M_i, J_i, G_i, A_i, S_i, V_i, P_i and O_i respectively. Their values depend mainly on the types of hardware and software used, as well as the costs of personnel in different institutions or organizations.

It should be noted that for $i = 1$ (CBIL-1), the last four cost components S_1, V_1, P_1 and O_1 are equal to zero (refer to our earlier definition of CBIL-1).

(2) The recurring operational costs of CBI courseware can be described as:

$$R_i = F_i + w_i W_i$$

where, for a given CBIL i ($i = 1, 2, 3$),
R_i = total recurring costs
F_i = fixed recurring costs per year
W_i = average amortized cost for each workstation per year

and where
w_i = number of workstations

(3) The total lifecycle costing can be described as

$$L_i = D_i + R_i N$$

where, for a given CBIL i ($i = 1, 2, 3$),
L_i = total lifecycle costs
N = period of lifecycle (typically 3 to 5 years' useful life)

(4) Therefore, the average lifecycle cost per student per year for a given lifecycle period N can be calculated as

$$T_i = L_i/Q$$

where, for a given CBIL i ($i = 1, 2, 3$)
T_i = average lifecycle cost per student per year
Q = total number of students per year using the courseware

We should note that T_i can be optimized by varying some key parameters:

(a) N, the total period or number of years for which particular CBIL courseware is designed to be useful, can be extended by such measures as updating the courseware after its normal lifespan.
(b) D_i, the development costs, can be reduced, for example, by iterative undertakings and/or accepting a template for the development of courseware.
(c) R_i, the total recurring costs, are technology related and may reduce as technology improves.
(d) Q, the population size, can be increased by utilizing the courseware across institutional, state or national boundaries.

Table 8.3: *Estimated person-hours involved in, and saved by, courseware development for instructor-led, CBIL-1, CBIL-2 and CBIL-3 presentation (per hour of delivery).*

Activity	Instructor-led classroom presentation	CBIL-1	CBIL-2	CBIL-3
	Estimates in person-hours			
Average courseware development time (per hour of delivery)	6	18	60	180
Possible reduction in instructor's presentation time (per class)	0	30–50%	50–70%	70–100%
Possible reduction in instructor's marking time (per student)	0	10%	10%	10%
Possible reduction in instructor's assessment and performance evaluation time (per student)	0	10%	10%	10%

We shall now provide some illustrative calculations for different levels of CBI courseware development and delivery. Basing our calculations on the typical amounts of time required for courseware development, we can compute production costs and lifecycle costs for our three CBIL models and for an instructor-led classroom presentation. The typical lifecycle costs for various populations of students in the context of tertiary institutions can then be calculated. In the example below, the population sizes per year are given as 100, 300, 600 and 1,000. The lifecycle costs per student per year (T_i) are then calculated and compared with the instructor-led classroom model and across different CBIL models.

In these costings, we assume the pre-existence of content material appropriate to the subject or syllabus and that all of the needs assessments, task analyses, goals, sub-goals, objectives, tests, etc, have already been determined. We do not include these course development costs in our calculations because we assume that these are the same for all the models considered. Drawing on our experience in courseware development at Griffith University – Gold Coast, we can indicate the person-hours required for courseware development for each hour of instructor-led, CBIL-1, CBIL-2 and CBIL-3 classroom presentation. We can also estimate the possible reductions in time

Table 8.4: *A breakdown of the person-hours and production costs (in Australian dollars) typically incurred in developing CBIL-1, CBIL-2 and CBIL-3 courseware.*

		Estimated time in person-hours		
Item	Activity	CBIL-1	CBIL-2	CBIL-3
(1)	Material preparation	6	6	24
(2)	Instructional design	6	6	24
(3)	Graphic design	0	12	24
(4)	Graphics production	0	18	24
(5)	Authoring and testing	6	18	40
(6)	Scripting	0	0	24
(7)	Project management	0	0	20
(8)	Video production (6 minutes)	0	0	$3,000
(9)	Audio production (30 minutes)	0	0	$1,500
(10)	Post-production	0	0	$1,000
(11)	Disc mastering	0	0	$3,000

needed for instructor presentation, marking and assessment/evaluation (per student). These are given in Table 8.3. The courseware development time includes instructional design, coding, testing and implementation for Novell networking.

For the purposes of our calculations, we suggest that CBIL-1 courseware development requires three times more person-hours than preparation for instructor-led classroom presentation, and that CBIL-2 courseware takes about three times longer to prepare than CBIL-1 courseware because of its more complex and demanding instructional design requirements. We estimate that the development time for CBIL-3 courseware is at least ten times that needed for CBIL-1 courseware development. This is mainly due to the large amounts of time needed for storyboard and script development, video production and post-production work such as editing, mixing and generating special effects, and for mastering the compact or laser discs. The development time for CBIL-3 courseware can of course vary significantly according to the platform and the required production standards and production values.

In Table 8.3, we tabulate possible reductions in an instructor's presentation, marking and assessment times when using CBIL-1, CBIL-2 and CBIL-3 systems. However, we do not take account of these additional cost savings in our calculations of lifecycle costing because the actual cost savings will depend on the content matter, the courseware design and the learning strategies used. It should also be noted that the instructor's time can be further reduced by utilizing computer-managed learning (CML) as well as CBI.

Table 8.4 gives a breakdown of the person-hours and production costs entailed in the various tasks involved in developing CBIL-1, CBIL-2 and CBIL-3 courseware. We assume here that staff with equal competence and skill are involved in all three models even if they are using different authoring tools. Clearly, the times indicated for courseware development can only be estimates. Actual times taken will vary according to the content matter, authoring tools and the competence and experience of the courseware developers. In the case of CBIL-2, we assume the re-purposing of existing videotape or disc material.

The cost estimates for CBIL-3 assume audio/video production and post-production of near-professional standard. We assume that 10 per cent of the presentation is in the form of motion video, which we have costed at A$500 per completed minute. This is substantially lower than current commercial production costs which start at about A$1,200 per completed minute because we assume here that the video production is relatively simple, does not incur expensive location work or talent hire and is done in-house using typical university or college production facilities. We also assume that 50 per cent of the presentation is in the form of voice-over which we have costed at A$50 per completed minute. The costs of disc mastering will vary according to the disc system used, the number of discs produced and whether this is done in-house or by an outside commercial organization.

Table 8.5 gives the total lifecycle costs of a 20-hour unit for CBIL-1, CBIL-2 and CBIL-3 using the production costs given in Table 8.4. The salary costs of the courseware developers (for example, tutors, instructional and graphic designers and programmers) are given at a rate of A$30 per hour. For each hour of CBIL-3 courseware, there is an additional cost of approximately A$8,500 for audio/video production and post-production and disc mastering and replication (if video is to be specifically produced as part of the CBIL-2 courseware development process, similar production costs will need to be included in this level's lifecycle costing). The delivery medium assumed for CBIL-1 courseware is diskette, at a cost of A$1 per student; for CBIL-2 courseware, diskette and videotape or compact disc, at a cost of A$6 per student; and for CBIL-3 courseware diskette and laser discs or compact discs, at a cost of A$20 per student. A typical lifecycle of courseware is taken to be three years. However, if the lifecycle is extended to five years after an update at the end of three years, there will be additional cost-savings for all CBIL models compared with instructor-led classroom presentation.

We are deliberately non-specific in regard to the development and delivery hardware utilized in these models because of the varying

Table 8.5: *Total lifecycle costing in Australian dollars of a 20-hour unit for CBIL-1, CBIL-2 and CBIL-3 and instructor-led classroom presentation (assuming that each lab session operates with 10 workstations).*

	Activity	Instructor-led	CBIL-1	CBIL-2	CBIL-3
A	**Courseware production costs**				
A1	Design and development cost = person-hours × rate @ $30/hour	6 × 30	18 × 30	60 × 30	180 × 30
	Cost per 20-hour unit	$3,600	$10,800	$36,000	$108,000
A2	Video/audio production/ disc mastering cost = (8) + (9) + (10) + (11)	0	0	0	$8,500
	Cost per 20-hour unit	0	0	0	$170,000
A3	Sub-total (A1) + (A2)	$3,600	$10,800	$36,000	$278,000
B	**Operation costs per lab per 10 workstations for a 20-hour unit**				
B1	Classroom preparation and assessment cost = person-hours × rate	1 × $30	0	0	0
	Cost per 20-hour unit	$600	0	0	0
B2	Instruction cost = person-hours × rate	1 × $30	0	0	0
	Cost per 20-hour unit	$600	0	0	0
B3	Amortized machine rental cost per 10 workstations per hour	0	10 × $1	10 × $2	10 × $3
	Cost per 20-hour unit	0	$200	$400	$600
B4	Media material cost per 10 workstations	0	10 × $1 @ $1/diskette	10 × $6 @ $6/tape or disc	10 × $20 @ $20/ CD-ROM/ laserdisc
	Cost per 20-hour unit	0	$10	$60	$200
B5	Sub-total = (B1) + (B2) + (B3) + (B4)	$1,200	$210	$460	$800
C	**3-year lifecycle total recurring costs for four different population sizes.**				
C1	100 students per year	10 classes	10 lab-sessions	10 lab-sessions	10 lab-sessions
	3 years × 10 classes × (B5)	$36,000	$6,300	$13,800	$24,000
C2	300 student per year	30 classes	30 lab-sessions	30 lab-sessions	30 lab-sessions
	3 years × 30 classes × (B5)	$108,000	$18,900	$41,400	$72,000

(continued overleaf)

161

Table 8.5: *Continued*

	Activity	Instructor-led	CBIL-1	CBIL-2	CBIL-3
C3	600 students per year	60 classes	60 lab-sessions	60 lab-sessions	60 lab-sessions
	3 years × 60 classes × (B5)	$216,000	$37,800	$82,800	$144,000
C4	1000 students per year	100 classes	100 lab-sessions	100 lab-sessions	100 lab-sessions
	3 years × 100 classes × (B5)	$360,000	$63,000	$138,000	$240,000
D	**Total 3-year lifecycle costs (A) + (C)**				
D1	Population of 100 students per year	$39,600	$17,100	$49,800	$302,000
	Total lifecycle costs per student per year	$132	$57	$166	$1,007
D2	Population of 300 students per year	$111,600	$29,700	$77,400	$350,000
	Total lifecycle costs per student per year	$124	$33	$86	$389
D3	Population of 600 students per year	$219,600	$48,600	$118,800	$422,000
	Total lifecycle costs per student per year	$122	$27	$66	$234
D4	Population of 1000 students per year	$363,600	$73,800	$174,000	$518,000
	Total lifecycle costs per student per year	$121	$25	$58	$173

All costs given in A\$ = £0.41 or US\$75.38 as at June 1992.

prices for different types of hardware. However, we adopt the approach of bundling and amortizing the costs of development and delivery hardware and software into an hourly machine rental rate. We assume that the typical rental cost for CBIL-1 is A\$3,000 per student workstation, for CBIL-2 A\$6,000 and for CBIL-3 A\$9,000. If we distribute these costs over 3,000 hours, the respective lifecycle costs for CBIL-1, CBIL-2 and CBIL-3 machine rental are A\$1, A\$2 and A\$3 per hour per student-workstation.

Figure 8.1 presents a direct comparison of the costs of these models. The graph shows that, as might be expected, as the levels of interactivity and complexity increase, the costs of development and delivery increase accordingly. However, if the number of students were larger than 1,000, our CBIL-3 product could become an increasingly cost-effective proposition. Furthermore, if development costs could be reduced, for example, by using a template and a cheaper

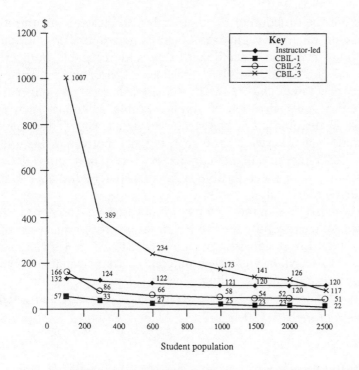

Figure 8.1: *Total three-year lifecycle costs per student per year.*

delivery platform such as CDTV, the CBIL-3 option would become extremely competitive against instructor-led presentation.

Conclusion

Lifecycle costing for CBI courseware development and delivery is a complex process dependent on many factors. However, by considering some simplified but realistically grounded models, we can derive some estimates for lifecycle costs per student for different levels of CBI courseware development and delivery and for given population sizes. CBIL-3 courseware entails higher initial development costs than CBIL-1 and CBIL-2 courseware because of the more complex and creative instructional and media design and the more sophisticated hardware requirements. However, the data show that CBIL-3 courseware can be a worthwhile option for a large student population and, of course, a quality product can generate income from sales to other organizations. Technical advances and falling hardware costs may help to reduce some of the development and delivery costs, although the developmental work will always be labour-intensive and therefore costly.

163

It is not the function of the cost analyst to measure all educational benefits or qualitative changes of an innovation. The adoption of IMM may result in such quantifiable and realizable outcomes as positions being freed, tasks being reallocated, cash expenditure saved, income generated and space or other resources no longer being required. It may also achieve immeasurable outcomes such as an increase in the amount of knowledge imparted, knowledge conveyed that could not otherwise have been taught, motivation heightened, deeper understanding, higher competency levels, or a course delivered in less time, or at more flexible times than before and thus creating time for further study or work.

In the current economic climate, innovators in IMM need to be able to examine carefully the full resource and cost implications of any new project. Lifecycle costing studies, conducted in association with studies into learning and other outcomes, are a valuable means of gaining a clearer understanding of what the process and the product actually entail, exposing the activity to public scrutiny and weighing its benefits against its costs.

References

Boud, D. (1988). *Developing student autonomy in learning* (2nd edn). Kogan Page, London/Nichols Publishing, New York.

Gagné, R.M. and Briggs, L.J. (1974). *Principles of instructional design.* Holt, Rinehart & Winston, Sydney.

Gagné, R.M. and Merrill, M.D. (1990). Integrative goals for instructional design. *Educational Research and Development,* 38 (1), 23–30.

Merrill, M.D. (1991). Constructivism and instructional design. *Educational Technology,* 31 (5), 45–54.

9 Interactive multimedia and culturally appropriate ways of learning

Lyn Henderson

Introduction

Interactive multimedia (IMM) courseware can never be culturally neutral. Therefore, minority indigenes such as Australian Torres Strait Islanders and Aborigines, or developing nations looking for technological solutions to their educational and training needs, will not be well served by packages designed for a majority Western culture and given superficial cosmetic changes in an attempt to serve these different markets. Cultural appropriateness has to be achieved through something far more than modifying text, voice-overs and music to localize the courseware. The total instructional design must go far beyond mere tokenism. The product must empower, extend and enrich the students' culturally specific knowledge and ways of thinking and achieve a nexus between these and the demands of the required academic culture.

The Queensland Remote Area Teacher Education Program (RATEP) is seeking to acknowledge these realities through an affirmative action programme that uses IMM to assist Aboriginal and Torres Strait Islander paraprofessional teachers to upgrade their qualifications and career aspirations through on-site provision in remote locations in the north of the state.

RATEP is a unique programme on three counts. Firstly, it is an inter-institutional community initiative undertaken by the James Cook University of North Queensland, the Cairns College of Technical and Further Education (TAFE), the Queensland Open Learning Centre Network, the Queensland Department of Education

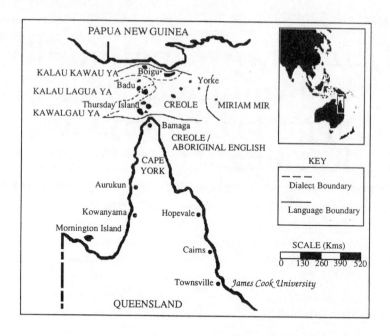

Figure 9.1: *RATEP sites and Torres Strait Islander linguistic boundaries* (adapted from Mitchell, forthcoming).

(Peninsula Region) and various Aboriginal and Torres Strait Islander committees and community councils at each of the off-campus RATEP sites. Secondly, it is the first instance of accreditation of a TAFE Associate Diploma towards a university award in Queensland. Thirdly, it is the only accredited programme in Australia comprising standard 13-week university units (and the TAFE equivalent) in which IMM has a central role.

In 1977, James Cook University of North Queensland (then the Townsville College of Advanced Education) introduced a special entry Aboriginal and Islander Teacher Education Program (AITEP). However, most of the AITEP students were from mainland urban backgrounds and the programme was criticized for not meeting the needs of the more traditional, remote communities. Homesickness, family obligations, the cost of living in Townsville with large families and fear of losing their culture were the main reasons for the low participation rates and non-graduation of students from the more remote areas (Henderson and Coombs, 1989). Loos and Miller (1989, pxvii), in an evaluation of AITEP, concluded that a radically different programme was needed to upgrade underqualified teachers' qualifications and produce Torres Strait Island and Aboriginal teachers whose unique cultural experience could be used to educate black and white Australian children. Thus was the concept of RATEP born.

Since 1991, the TAFE college at Cairns has offered an Associate Diploma in Education course to Aborigines at Aurukun, Hopevale, Mornington Island and Kowanyama, and to Torres Strait Islanders at Bamaga. The first group of Islander students completed the two-year Diploma of Teaching at the Badu and Yorke Island campuses of James Cook University in June 1992. In July 1992, a second cohort of students commenced their studies at Yorke Island, Boigu Island and Bamaga. Associate Diploma graduates are given one year's credit toward the three-year Diploma of Teaching. The RATEP students study the same subjects, with the same lecturers, and for the same Diploma of Teaching as all other James Cook students. Their qualification has currency throughout Australia and most countries overseas and the RATEP graduates can proceed to bachelors, masters and doctoral degree studies.

The historical, socio-cultural and political context

The Torres Strait Islands, settled by people from Melanesia some 4,000–7,000 years ago, were annexed by Queensland in 1879. Since then, the Torres Strait Islanders have lived under various forms of separatist legislation. The state government long held an isolationist and racist view of what constituted an appropriate education for the Torres Strait Islanders. The official view was that they could achieve little academically. Secondary education was withheld until 1964 and the Islanders' education did not come under the state's Department of Education until 1986. Loos (1982, p3) asserts that Torres Strait Islanders and Aborigines had 'an education imposed upon them which was designed to make them failures in a sophisticated society'. In 1992, less than 2 per cent of the Torres Strait Islanders had certified trade or professional qualifications.

Today, because of overcrowding and lack of employment in their home communities, more Torres Strait Islanders live on the mainland than on the islands. RATEP only caters for Torres Strait Islanders living in the Strait and the students for whom this programme is designed have limited experience of the world beyond. Except for Thursday Island, with its multicultural and small-town ethos and Bamaga, which comprises five small villages of Islanders and/or Aborigines, the population on each of the inhabited islands ranges from 150 to 300, few of whom are transitory, non-Torres Strait Islanders. Housing shortages force two or three families to share

167

three-bedroomed houses, making home study virtually impossible. One RATEP student was prepared to live for the first six months of his two-year course in a tiny galvanized iron shed with a dirt floor and a leaking roof because, as he said, he was 'hungry to be properly qualified'.

Each community is serviced fortnightly by barge from Cairns and more frequently by relatively expensive air services. Airports are often closed during wet weather. Inter-island travel is usually by private dinghy with outboard motor. Some RATEP students make two-hour crossings from their home islands to RATEP study centres, journeys which can take as much as six hours when the waves are running two metres high. Each community typically has two public telephones: one in the centre of the village and one at the airport. The RATEP study centre, based on the school, the medical centre (usually run by paraprofessional Islander nurses), the indigenous police officer and the community council have telephones and fax machines. However, atmospheric conditions, heavy rains, termites eating through the cables and other factors often render these systems unserviceable for weeks on end. The only electric power comes from generators that are so unreliable and limited in capacity that if the fans in the RATEP centres are not first turned off, the mere switching on of a photocopier or electric kettle can shut down the system. Satellite television first came to Torres Strait in 1990.

RATEP students from the Eastern and Western Islands still use their native language with Creole as their second language; students from the Central Islands have lost their mother tongue and Creole is their first language; most of those at Bamaga have either Creole or Aboriginal English as their first language. English is either the second or third language for all the students, a factor that RATEP has had to recognize, to ensure that academic discourse does not disempower the students.

Many traditional behavioural patterns have been retained in the communities. For example, any person has the right not to listen; peer pressure to conform is exerted on anyone perceived to be excelling beyond the group norm; and it is inappropriate for teenagers or young men and women to teach or demonstrate skills to older persons. There are also major gender differences; for example, eye contact between the sexes is largely avoided; a man is rarely contradicted in public by a woman, especially if she is younger; and females cannot be seated near or work with certain male relatives (Henderson and Foster, forthcoming).

In planning for RATEP, it was important to note that there were cultural, linguistic and individual differences across the student groups but the historical socio-cultural similarities were strong enough to speak in generalities in referring to Torres Strait Islander patterns of behaviour and ways of learning.

Assessment needs

Before the 1970s, no formal training in recognized teacher education institutions had been granted to Aborigines and Torres Strait Islanders. Teachers in these communities were local people with little formal education and limited English or literacy skills who were selected somewhat randomly from within the communities to perform this role. The subsequent AITEP programme, introduced in 1977, was criticized for not meeting the needs of remote communities. It was recognized that the problems of geographical remoteness, racial discrimination, economic exploitation, educational marginalization, land alienation and enforced dependency of the indigenous communities of Torres Strait and Cape York had to be addressed. RATEP was conceived as a programme that would seek to redress these social, economic and educational disadvantages.

Given the remoteness, dispersed nature and small size of the communities to be served and the relatively small numbers of students enrolled in the programme, it was decided to use specially developed IMM courseware as the main means of instruction, plus reading, workbooks, audiotapes and videotapes, radio, peer discussion, on-site tutorial support and teleconferences, facsimile and E-Mail. All these presentational and interactive modes had to be used in ways compatible with the Islanders' learning patterns (see Macindoe and Henderson, 1991).

IMM technology and software chosen for the project

RATEP commenced at James Cook University with two courseware programmers who had had no previous experience with the Macintosh platform, IMM or distance education. They prepared two 13-week subjects containing IMM courseware and associated print materials in five months. The model subsequently adopted by RATEP for IMM courseware development utilizes a competent courseware developer as the project coordinator. The coordinator liaises with lecturers who are given a two-day workshop on how they can effectively employ IMM in their subject areas. These lecturers/courseware developers then prepare material to be programmed by part-time university students and graduates, some of whom have become extremely adept at suggesting appropriate changes that account for cultural differences and using the more advanced programming functions of the authoring programme. This model's main weakness lies in the fact that in respecting the autonomy of the lecturers, it does not require them to submit their material to experienced courseware developers for IMM editing. As a result, with some of the lecturers not yet fully conversant with (or fully convinced of) the value of learning through IMM, a few of the programmes still make overuse of electronic page-turning or repetitive teach–test strategies.

Three Macintosh Plus Computers for word processing and desktop publishing and three Macintosh IIcx machines with 8Mb RAM and 40Mb hard disk were acquired, one of each for the Townsville coursewriter-programmers and the Yorke and Badu campuses, and a colour scanner and PLI drive. The more expensive Macintosh platform was chosen because the inaugural Director of RATEP was impressed by the authoring program, Authorware Professional (which appeared to have the capability to marry programming, pedagogy and cultural context), and the service, resources and support pledged to RATEP by local and state Apple distributors.

While RATEP continues to serve the needs of teacher education, the project has now extended to cover mathematics, physics, English and teachers' in-service programmes. As a consequence, the main centre at James Cook University is now known as the Remote Area Tertiary Education Centre (RATEC) and this centre incorporates RATEP. RATEC now has eight top-of-the range Macintosh computers for programming, five external 40Mb hard disk drives (one each for Boigu Island, Yorke Island and Bamaga), another six PLI drives, a Macintosh PowerBook, a CD-ROM player, two laser printers, a variety of software to process text and graphics and an IBM 486 PC compatible for translating the Macintosh-developed courseware to an IBM platform. QuickTime will allow video to be incorporated into subsequent and revised RATEP courseware.

Accommodating culturally appropriate ways of learning

As the RATEP project was in so many ways a trailblazer, there has been extensive monitoring of the IMM component (Logan and Sachs, 1991; Willett, 1991; Macindoe & Henderson, 1991; Henderson, 1992). The author's research has been concerned with student and on-site tutor feedback. Data were gathered from structured questionnaires, comments made during teleconferences, student progress through the IMM courseware, performance evaluations and interviews conducted by the author and a Torres Strait Islander enrolled in a higher degree. The use of two interviewers allowed for the complex cultural factors involved in the study. The RATEP students were asked to approve both researchers and all the interviews were conducted in ways compatible with the culture. The remainder of this chapter summarizes this research.

In their evaluation of RATEP, Logan and Sachs (1991) distinguish between *individualized programmes* and *personalized approaches*. They argue that individualized programmes create learning experiences and materials designed to assist a student in acquiring mastery of predetermined content and skills to common standards. Such programmes are confined to catering for quantifiable characteristics such as rates of progress and achievement levels based on group testing or criteria established for a particular task or subject. By comparison, personalized approaches include both quantitative learner characteristics (for example, competency and attainment levels) and qualitative learner characteristics (for example, individual and culturally appropriate ways of learning and motivational strategies). RATEP's curriculum and courseware were designed to provide personalized learning for individuals within integrated multiple cultural contexts.

RATEP has been shaped significantly by the interplay among various implicit and explicit cultural logics. Firstly, the courseware has had to recognize and incorporate Torres Strait Islander culture, including current-traditional ways of learning (Henderson and Foster, forthcoming). The term 'current-traditional' has been coined to emphasize the fact that Torres Strait Islanders' preferred ways of learning utilize both traditional and Western ways of learning and exchanging information. For example, some Western modes of interchange are utilized in schools, meetings and business procedures and these have impinged on the traditional methods which are still common in the home and community contexts. Secondly, RATEP has had to accommodate the specific requirements of an academic culture. This academic culture is expressed through the content to be taught and assessed, the written and oral genres and the culturally specific Western ways of promoting cognitive development through university study. Thirdly, RATEP courseware has had to incorporate design features that provide students with the means to control the matching of their academic learning tasks with their cultural and individual ways of learning. This interplay of cultural logics has been facilitated by means of random access and branching (Logan and Sachs, 1991). The principle of random access is embodied in the computer courseware packages, readings, workbooks, audiovisual materials, peer discussion and on-site and electronic tutorial support. The principle of branching is embodied in the provision of alternative pathways, presentation modes, sequences, sources and methods of assessment in the various aspects of the course. RATEP's IMM courseware also allows students to have random access to the various subjects and topics and then branch within each of these (see Figures 9.2 and 9.3). While the lecturers did not always find it easy to move outside their traditional pedagogical parameters in developing their subjects for optimal learning through random access and branching, the use of these strategies has allowed seemingly disparate cultural and pedagogical elements to be brought together coherently and cogently.

The current-traditional Torres Strait way of learning is through observation, demonstration, rehearsal/practice, immediate feedback and, when a task is not performed correctly, a repeat of this process. This learning methodology is similar to the behavioural model described by Joyce and Weil (1986). However, it differs in that demonstration and practice occur when the learner feels confident of success and not on demand from the teacher. The learner's scheduling decision also weighs possible performance outcomes against possible peer approval or ridicule. Indeed, the current-traditional model acknowledges that peer attitudes are a significant factor in an individual's achievement and that, in the traditional context, teaching and learning occur in environments where no shame can occur (Henderson and Foster, *op cit*).

Torres Strait Islanders are essentially visual–aural–oral learners and their teaching–learning model favours their cognitive strengths in visual and spatial information processing. Osborne (1982; 1986) asserts that text-based learning is not part of the Islanders' cultural methodology and that being a people-oriented rather than a task-oriented culture, intellectual development is essentially within the social context. Therefore, a comfortable relationship has to be established between teacher and learner for optimum learning to occur. Also, in current-traditional Torres Strait learning methodologies, the information given is limited to that needed for mastering a particular task. Torres Strait Islanders regard Western education as being based on a mass of extraneous information and questions designed to fail the learner or obtain worthless information already known to the teacher (Henderson and Foster, *op cit*).

The IMM courseware has been developed to accommodate these learning characteristics. A cyclic model has been developed which provides presentation and explanation of a particular concept (observation), followed by interaction, embedded in the theoretical discussion (demonstration of understanding, rehearsal or practice), and explanations as to why the student's answer was correct to reinforce the learning (immediate feedback). These explanations are clearly important in case the correct answer given was a guess. The explanations can also use different wording, a form of feedback common in both Islander and Western teaching methodologies. In the academic culture, this is an implicit way of showing students that ideas or problems can be correctly expressed in more than one way and that students do not need to memorize or plagiarize specific statements. The explanations can also build further information around the original concept. Such incremental learning ensures that the student is not overloaded with so much information that any demonstration of proficiency is impossible within a given time frame. This cyclic model is then repeated until the topic is completed. Interest is maintained and, more importantly for the academic culture, the validity of different ways of presenting and discussing concepts is emphasized through variations in screen presentation, type of interaction and form of feedback. Each part of a programme, as well as the whole cycle, can be practised/rehearsed (revised) until the performance (understanding) is deemed satisfactory by the learner. The cyclic model summarized in Figure 9.2 proved extremely acceptable to the students, who liked being able to work at their own pace, as one of the group put it, 'until it soaked in'.

The RATEP lecturer/courseware developer could of course have locked the learners into any cycle until their answers evidenced mastery. However, this would have been an imposition of a Western learning methodology and would have ignored Torres Strait Islander current-traditional ways of scheduling decisions about learning. Mastery can be ascertained through ways which allow the learner to set the rehearsal pace of mastering a task. A culturally appropriate way of ensuring that the learner has understood crucial concepts or reasoning processes is to rework these into subsequent cycles, particularly those that summarize or conclude a topic. One of the students insightfully described the cyclic model as 'spread out like a tree with roots' (Henderson, 1992).

This cyclic model contrasts a paradigm that favours large blocks of textual presentation or drill exercises with a summative test that gives feedback in the form of scores without explanation and then involves the learner in revision or new work according to these test results. Such a model does not allow learners independence to structure sequences that are individually and culturally appropriate for optimum learning. Some material was developed around a repetitive teach–test model and, in the words of one student,

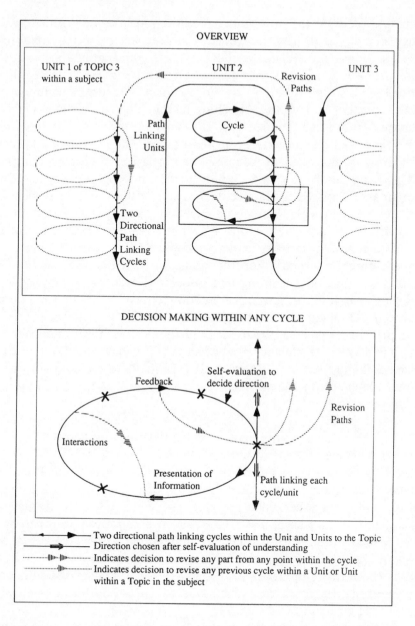

Figure 9.2: *Cyclic model of culturally appropriate ways of learning with IMM.*

'prevented us from becoming really involved in the subject and learning task'.

IMM has been found to be entirely appropriate for visual–aural–oral learners. The use of Authorware Professional-generated text, graphics, stills and diagrams with sound to illustrate or emphasize concepts or processes and simple animations such as moving arrows to link causal relationships provides a holistic, multi-sensory learning environment, which reflects the current-traditional informal learning patterns far more than any static display of text and graphics. Where extensive explanatory blocks of information are unavoidable, these are broken into smaller textual components and added sequentially to the screen, accompanied by graphics, animation and sound, to ensure that crucial concepts are considered by the student before the next concepts appear (Macindoe and Henderson, 1991). Click and drag interactions are used frequently. The students use the mouse to click on a word, sentence or image and drag it to an appropriate place to answer a question. If the answer is wrong, the words or images return to their original locations to await further attempts by the student. Time delays between segments of information, and explanations and feedback to students' responses have also been designed to provide implicit visual signals to promote increased understanding. Such an approach, unlike that of the typical textbook, ensures that the logic of expository and analytic discourse occurs visually and aurally.

Colours and typefaces (fonts) have also been found to be useful in enhancing understanding by these visual learners. Research has revealed that colour displays are not only more motivating than monochrome displays but can actually be used to improve and clarify the learning process. For example, one of the most successful RATEP subjects uses a particular colour and font (plus sound) for each topic and concluding sentence; a different colour and font (plus sound) in clarifying examples; and other colours and fonts for rebuttal points to the thesis being developed. The obvious danger of doing this is that it can produce a visually cluttered screen, particularly if there are value-added graphic images. However, the RATEP students have reported that this multi-sensory cluttered approach greatly increases their understanding of the content and the logic of the academic genre. They have indicated that they quickly lose the thread of an argument or need the help of an on-site tutor if they have to go back and forth between a series of screens bearing minimal information. Thus the developer's prime instructional objectives have had to be concerned with screen presentations that promote understanding and debate rather than with what might be judged by Western standards as clear, crisp, 'good' design. Presenting academic discourse without highlighting its logic or constructing its meaning simply disenfranchises learners for whom English is a second or third language. Nor is colour culturally neutral, so the courseware developer/designer had to be able to step aside from Western colour preferences and recognize that numerous bright colours on the screen help Torres Strait Islanders distinguish among key elements and cause them absolutely no aesthetic discomfort.

A multi-sensory approach which includes culturally specific music, language and images was also found to provide motivation to remain on-task. Utilizing the music, pictures and first language of the students' culture is not cosmetic or an act of tokenism. Pedagogically, such elements acknowledge the students' identity in the learning task (Macindoe and Henderson, 1991). In the words of one of the students, these features are 'familiar and relaxing; they lessen the tensions in learning'. The use of voice – in English and the students' first language – allows the lecturer to personalize explanations or express information in ways different from the text on the screen. One student said, 'It makes what is being presented real.'

Research reveals that computer-based learning can be effective among indigenous peoples (for example, Fleer, 1989; Jacobi, 1985; Sower, 1987). In extended families in small indigenous communities, individual physical space is virtually non-existent and mental space is highly valued (Henderson and Foster, forthcoming). The computer can grant such privacy to learners and allow them to work in a non-threatening environment at an individual pace without fear of peer ridicule and shame if their rate of progress is slow, if they get wrong answers or if they excel at the task. One RATEP student explained the benefits thus: 'On the computer I am not scared. I can get full marks or I can make a mistake and go back to see where I went wrong.'

The use of negative sound feedback such as buzzers to incorrect answers has been avoided, although recommended by the original instructional design consultants, to avoid causing the learners shame. Only correct answers have sound feedback and Torres Strait Islander music and Creole feedback have proved to be particularly effective in motivating students to work out thoughtful responses and obtain the right answers.

The Macintosh IIcx-based IMM systems are set up at each RATEP centre in the same room as the study carrels. This arrangement suits the people-oriented Islander culture and the Islanders' desire to learn and engage in tasks in group settings. Students may choose to work alone or with peers at the computer. In current-tradition teaching and learning, males and females are usually in same-sex groups but often in close proximity to members of the other sex, so there has been no problem with mixed groups working in such a setting. It is sometimes incorrectly assumed that the Torres Strait Islanders, particularly the males, lack independence in learning. However, this ignores the fact that individuals decide whether to listen and rehearse and hence to set their own pace of learning (*ibid*). Current-traditional age factors make it difficult for older female students to call on younger students to assist with courseware clarification when the on-site female tutor of the same age is unavailable. Sometimes, because of this cultural factor, IMM study was abandoned until the tutor was available. The male students had no problems with learning from the computer. There was no shame or loss of face in accepting directions, instructions and feedback on correct and incorrect responses in this human–machine interaction. It was seen as gender free and age free. Factors such as these highlight the need for course developers to ensure that their courseware is culturally appropriate and culturally accepted.

The students soon realized that the purpose of the question–answer interactions within the programmes was not continually to test and judge but to promote interrogation of the concepts being developed. When one student came to realize that a programme he was working through was not just questioning him for the sake of asking questions but to provide him with an incremental progression to mastery of the subject, he said, 'Learning becomes meaningful. It's not passing tests. If you learn meaningfully, you can pass it on.'

It was established that tries limits and time limits in question–answer interactions were important factors in catering for the multiple cultural context. The former is in accord with Islander ways of learning; the latter is in accord with the Western valuing of knowledge recall and application within short time constraints (examinations are a classic example of this). Time limits have been found to be useful for nurturing quicker thinking and the students enjoyed working against the clock – particularly in an environment where the activity is private, between the student and the computer. Tries limits promote thinking skills and independent learning and give the students opportunities to demonstrate their understanding without the fear of failure and in the knowledge that a correct answer will be given after they have made their own efforts (Macindoe and Henderson, 1991). The number of tries allowed depends on the degree of difficulty in a given activity. Students have criticized courseware that presents a correct answer after their first incorrect attempt at a problem. One student, for example, remarked that 'it did not allow practice'; another said that 'it indicates that the lecturer does not think we are capable of intellectually working it out for ourselves'. The tries and time limits prevent the possibility of students becoming entrapped in any one part of a course and have been found to provide a challenge and to reinforce current-traditional ways of learning in the academic context.

The RATEP students believe that the cyclic model and the other culturally appropriate techniques described above promote learning by making them feel that they are engaged in dialogue with a lecturer rather than with a machine. They believe that most of the lecturer/ developers have designed their courseware to personalize rather than to individualize the teaching–learning relationship.

The IMM courseware allows all question–answer and other interactions to be monitored, copied and delivered via modem or fax to the lecturer. Such monitoring indicates where clarification is called for with a particular student or where courseware revision is needed because most of the students are experiencing difficulty with concepts or processes. It also serves as a valuable research tool. The students are always told that their progress is being monitored and why. The students accept the reasons as valid and regard such auditing in much the same light as the monitoring by their Island 'teachers'. Within days, they forget that their answers are being monitored. This is an important factor in interpreting the students' commitment to learning.

Monitoring has revealed that the students do not take the expedient course of giving nonsense answers so that they can get speedy feedback and explanation and escape or proceed without truly testing their understanding. Indeed, monitoring has shown that the students often repeat interactions even after they have obtained correct answers because they are interested in the clarifications given in response to incorrect answers as well as to the correct answers. This behaviour suggests that the courseware supports a deep desire to learn, a behaviour in contrast to that cited in some other distance education research. Marlin et al (1990), for example, found that most distance education students only processed their texts in ways consistent with surface learning and wherever possible, avoided in-text activities and questions.

RATEP's navigation system allows student control over pathways, revision and access to data banks. It has been found that the students do not learn effectively if they have unlimited access within the programme, because they tend to skip about, often in panic, without consolidating understanding in any one segment. Most of the RATEP courseware therefore incorporates a blend of choice and programmed sequencing for optimal learning and empowerment and to ensure that the theoretical topics are worked through before the illustrative topics or the core studies. Pull-down menus (see Figure 9.3) allow the students to see the nature of the subject and the extent to which they have engaged with it. Bold as opposed to faint type in the menu indicates units that the students are free to access as opposed to units the student has covered. Each menu display is particular to individual students because when they log on, the program immediately places them at the point from which they previously exited. The navigation bar at the bottom of the screen indicates the student's progress and

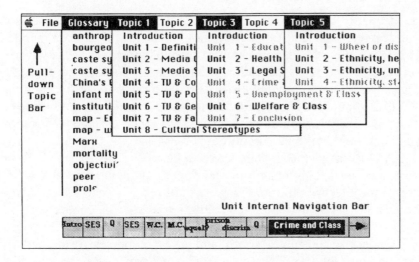

Figure 9.3: *Cognitive map of a subject* (from Henderson, 1990).

location within any unit and provides learner control over revision and quitting the subject. Each square of the navigation bar represents one or more screens and the words are a cryptic reminder of what is in that section for revision purposes. Together, the pull-down topic menu and the unit navigation bar provide a cognitive map of the subject. This schema has been found to support the preferred learning style of Torres Strait Islanders where the whole is broken down into the parts to be mastered as opposed to an approach which starts from the parts and builds to the whole.

Evaluation and conclusion

RATEP students have given much positive feedback on the IMM courseware described above. They report that the courseware enhances motivation and learning because it achieves an amalgam of Islander and Western ways of learning. One student claimed 'a feeling of expectancy each time I switch on the computer'. Another said that 'one can sit at the computer with good courseware until one's kidneys ache'. Others reported that IMM is so much better than text, which they 'hurried through because it was so boring'. A summary comment was: 'For the first time since the imposition of white education, RATEP is catering for our learning style.'

RATEP has a 100 per cent retention rate in the Diploma of Teaching. Logan and Sachs (1991, p41) concluded that 'the results are good quality courses showing evidence of integration, non-linearity, cultural relevance and experimentation'. Willett (1991) recommended that while the other six off-campus, technology-driven, state government-funded teacher education programmes operating through the Queensland Open Learning Project should receive no further funding, RATEP should be granted further funds to expand and he suggested that the model should be adopted by other distance education providers to Aboriginal communities.

RATEP has yielded a tentative checklist of issues that need to be addressed by IMM courseware developers, designers and authors in creating courseware for non-Western cultures. This checklist needs to be critically evaluated for implementation in specific contexts:

- Undertake consultation with, and have the courseware audited by, members of the client group. This acknowledges the expertise residing in such a group and attempts to some extent to equalize the control of knowledge and learning.
- Ascertain the preferred ways of learning of the client group.
- Model the ways and conventions of learning as closely as possible.
- Determine the extent to which the majority and the minority cultural ways of learning are to be promoted and reinforced.
- Implement a cyclic or other non-linear model that (a) avoids 'electronic page turning'; (b) maximizes branching for progress and revision; and (c) gives students control over the sequencing and pacing of the learning activities.
- Implement a multi-sensory approach that (a) combines text and interactions with time-waits, colour, sound, graphics, animations, skills and video; and (b) structures and restructures each concept to be learnt and makes the logic of the knowledge explicit.
- Use colours, sounds and images that are culturally relevant to the client group rather than to the aesthetic preferences of the courseware developer.
- Construct interactions that (a) largely avoid reductionist answers; (b) test higher-order thinking; (c) extend the learner; (d) afford the learner a number of tries to obtain the correct response or the option to choose and exit from an unlimited number of tries; and (e) are integral to an incremental learning approach rather than merely being tests (although summative tests can be most useful).
- Besides incorporating ways of learning, include knowledge specific to the client group in content and assessment.
- Incorporate cultural, age and gender differences in the instructional design.
- Avoid elements that can cause private or public shame.

- Include academic skills, such as the construction of academic genres in the screen design.

The aims of IMM incorporating culturally appropriate ways of learning are to empower minority culture students through an inclusive curriculum which validates their culture and achieves synergy between that culture and the academic requirements of the course, maximize learner control and choice and use methodologies which ensure interrogation of the knowledge presented as well as recall and application.

Note

Quotes from students in this chapter are from 1991 interviews with the following RATEP students at Yorke and Badu Islands: Barrier Henry, Mavis Joe, Edward Nai, Michael Nai, Manuel Nomoa, Denna Nona, Taum Nona and Mua Sailor.

References

Fleer, M. (1989). Is it hands-on or hands-off? Research into the availability and accessibility of micro-computers for Aboriginal school children. *Australian Aboriginal Studies*, 1, 31–6.

Henderson, L. (1990). *Contemporary Australian Society*. Interactive Multimedia Computer Courseware, James Cook University of North Queensland, Townsville.

Henderson, L. (1992). Concept theory, cultural difference and interactive multimedia. Paper presented at *Exploring Human Potential: Fifth International Conference on Thinking*, James Cook University of North Queensland, Townsville, 6–10.

Henderson, L. and Coombs, G. (1989). Confronting disadvantage: A demographic analysis of the first 53 graduates through AITEP. In N. Loos and G. Miller (eds), *Succeeding against the odds: The Townsville Aboriginal and Islander Teacher Education Program*. Allen & Unwin, Sydney, 17–34.

Henderson, L. and Foster, S. (forthcoming). *Interactive multimedia and Torres Strait Islander learning style*.

Jacobi, C. (1985). Project developing Indian software curriculum. *The Computing Teacher*, 12 (7), 12–17.

Joyce, B. and Weil, M. (1986). *Models of Teaching* (3rd edn). Prentice-Hall, Englewood Cliffs, NJ.

Logan, L. and Sachs, J. (1991). 'It opened my head': An evaluation of the first phase of the Remote Area Teacher Education Program. University of Queensland, St Lucia.

Loos, N. (1982). What is special about special education for Aborigines and Torres Strait Islanders? In P. Beinssen and J. Parker (eds), *Focus on Practice: Proceedings of the Third State Conference of the Queensland Special Education Association*, James Cook University, Townsville, 103–11.

Loos, N. and Miller, G. (1989). Introduction. In N. Loos and G. Miller (eds), *Succeeding against the odds: The Townsville Aboriginal and Islander Teacher Education Program*. Allen & Unwin, Sydney, xvi–xx.

Macindoe, M. and Henderson, L. (1991). Feedback to remote areas: Technology, the influencing factor. *Education Australia*, 15, 12–16.

Marlin, P., Patching, W., Putt, I. and Putt, R. (1990). Distance learners' interactions with text while studying. *Distance Education*, 11 (1), 71–91.

Mitchell, R. (forthcoming). *Historical linguistics in the Torres Strait*. Unpublished MA thesis, James Cook University of North Queensland, Townsville.

Osborne, A.B. (1982). Field dependence/independence of Torres Strait Islander and Aboriginal Pupils. *Journal of Intercultural Studies*, 3 (3), 5–18.

Osborne, A.B. (1986). *Torres Strait Islander styles of communication and learning*. Torres Strait Working Papers 1, James Cook University of North Queensland, Townsville.

Sower, R. (1987). Towards achieving an interactive educational model for special needs students: The computer writing project for native American students. *Journal of American Indian Education*, 27 (1), 30–8.

Willett, F.J. (1991). *Report to the Minister for Education, The Honourable Mr Paul Braddy, on the Queensland Open Learning Project*. Queensland Open Learning Project, Brisbane.

10 MAX – an Australian approach to audiographics in schools

Ian Conboy

Introduction

Victoria is one of Australia's smaller states. Unlike some of the other states, it has a uniformly distributed population but its small rural schools still tend to have lower retention rates than their urban counterparts. In 1986, the Department of School Education for the Ministry of Education and Training, Victoria, embarked on the use of audiographic telematics to improve these retention rates. Today, 25 groups of primary and secondary schools, learning centres and Technical and Further Education (TAFE) colleges are formed into clusters and linked by Macintosh computers, facsimile and loudspeaking telephones to provide a more comprehensive curriculum through an 'electronically extended classroom' infrastructure.

This was the first time that the state of Victoria had systematically applied electronics technology to a defined group of schools as a consequence of state government policy. Faced with the choice of an advanced technology central delivery system or a decentralized cluster-of-schools approach, the Ministry of Education chose the latter. The project has shown the importance of a well-researched and well-marketed policy for the successful implementation of technology-based change in education. The project has also shown what can be done with audiographics technology to create what Romiszowski (1992) terms a 'virtual learning community' and how teachers' concerns about technology can be accommodated in uses of electronic delivery systems to broaden curriculum options in rural schools. The material that follows is a summary of some key observations after six years. The project has been comprehensively evaluated in D'Cruz (1990).

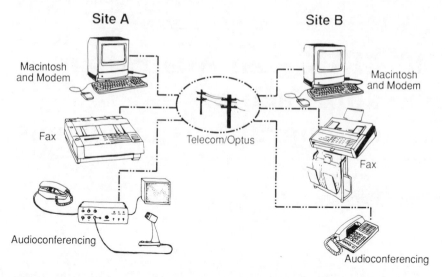

Figure 10.1: *The elements of the MAX network* (compiled from Elliott, 1991).

The policy setting

Australia's federal, state and territory governments are becoming increasingly interested in the nexus between educational policy and telecommunications policy. At the federal level, major reviews have been conducted into open and distance learning and the uses of alternative modes of delivery (see, for example, AEC, 1992; DEET, 1992) and networks of open learning centres are being developed at the state level (see for example, Queensland Board of Advanced Education, 1989; McGregor and Latchem, 1991).

The Victorian schools audiographics project had its genesis in the Ministry of Education, Victoria (1985) *Ministerial review of post-compulsory schooling* (The Blackburn Report). One of the aims in this report was to increase post-compulsory retention rates in government schools to 75 per cent by 1995. The audiographic telematics project also reflected economic policy outlined in *Victoria: The next decade* (Government of Victoria, 1987) and Victoria's social justice strategy which directs the operations of all state government departments. A social justice framework for schools (Ministry of Education and Training, Victoria, 1990) addresses such issues as school improvement plans, the organization of the schools' curriculum, the selection and treatment of content, the evaluation and reporting of student progress, professional development priorities and district and regional planning, including community resources.

Within these policy contexts, rural students were identified as requiring special attention. Like their counterparts throughout the world, small rural schools in Victoria have certain advantages and disadvantages. Greater opportunities for interpersonal communication are an obvious advantage while small classes, small numbers of teachers and a higher percentage of inexperienced teachers are their main disadvantages. Senior secondary students seeking a broader choice of subjects are usually forced into taking one or more print-based correspondence courses with little in the way of immediate feedback or personalized tuition to maintain their motivation and enhance their learning.

Telematics was identified as having a great potential for providing improved feedback for correspondence students and thus increasing participation rates. The technology was also seen as a means of sharing teaching and aggregating class numbers among schools and thus increasing retention rates. Telematics has been further influenced by the state government's District Provision Policy which encourages schools that are too far apart for any other form of reorganization to form into clusters, share scarce teaching resources and enable students to access other students and thus relate to a larger peer reference group.

Finally, it should be noted that implementation was based on an existing Country Education Policy (the Victorian component of the Commonwealth Country Areas Programme) which emphasizes local decision-making and community participation. Thus, although equipment standardization was agreed on at the state level, the educational applications were largely determined at the cluster or school level.

The MAX system

The 'home-grown' audiographics system developed to meet these needs was originally described as the 'Mac/Fax/Audio' system, soon abbreviated to 'MAX'. This audiographics technology was introduced into clusters of rural schools in order to consolidate small groups of students into larger 'virtual groups' and to obviate the need to move students or staff over large distances. Adoption of this innovation was achieved through a mix of 'top-down' and 'bottom-up' strategies.

The Victorian initiative relied heavily on practising teachers for advice about appropriate technology. Teachers in the Mallee Secondary College Cluster were invited to draw up a set of educational requirements for the technology. They indicated that their needs were for an audio link for voice contact, a document link to send handwritten and typed assignments to students and some form of substitute blackboard for visual display. In short, they wanted an

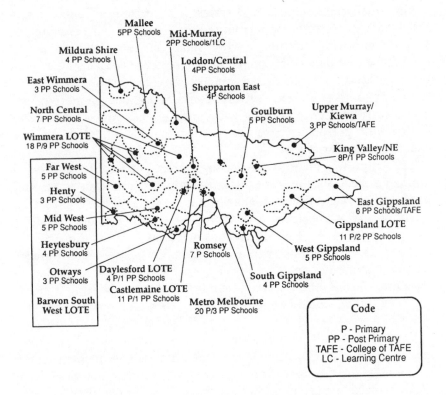

Figure 10.2: *Map of the clusters in the Victorian system.*

'extended classroom' mode of delivery which resembled as closely as possible their everyday teaching. While the Victorian telematics system might be open to criticism for not using the full potential of computers, it does allow the teachers to use the technology in accordance with their pre-existing patterns of pedagogy or operation. Indeed, one could argue that, in many instances, this is a precondition for the acceptance of any new technology in the classroom.

A large part of the success of this project is attributable to the active and ongoing participation of teachers in the developmental process. For example, although the project has been in operation since 1986, the software developer still involves small groups of teachers in teleconferences to discuss modifications to the software and new equipment is always field-tested in school clusters before final decisions are made to adopt it.

Victoria originally drew on pioneering work by the Educational Technology Centre in the South Australian Department of Education and adopted the DUCT (Diverse Use of Communication Technology) audio terminal to provide the audio link for MAX. This allows teachers or students to interact with classes at other sites and to work in a hands-free mode. The DUCT terminal is relatively easy to set up in a classroom and is reasonably portable. Multipoint links are possible using a Conferlink 6 audioconferencing bridge. Other audio conference units (Hybrid, Harvard Elite, NEC Voicepoint and Telecom Multivoice) have since been introduced into the system. Document links are provided by facsimile machines and as multipointing becomes more common, the ability to broadcast the same file to a number of locations may become desirable. Macintosh computers provide an acceptable visual link between two or more locations and overhead projectors with liquid crystal display units are used with larger groups. Point-to-point links are the most reliable but advances in the software and hardware allow for multipoint lessons (up to six sites at once). Scanners and printers are other optional peripherals.

At present, 205 sites are using the MAX system with *Electronic Classroom* software and NetComm 2400 baud auto modems. Using *Electronic Classroom* software, machines at up to six locations perform exactly the same computations as the teacher adds to a Paint document, types, or distributes preprepared screens. *Electronic Classroom* has been developed specifically for K-12 distance education by Revelation Computing Pty Ltd of Brisbane. This Australian software sells for A$600 per site (about US$450), which is cheaper than similar systems. *Electronic Classroom* software has the advantages of having been developed in close consultation with the teachers, being relatively easy to use and containing features which teachers employ in face-to-face teaching situations (Crago, 1991). This software provides a powerful interactive teaching tool using any number of computer programs (Elliott, 1991).

To use the *Electronic Classroom*, teachers simply dial all participating schools by clicking the schools names on a list. Once schools are linked by telephone, student machines already running the *Electronic Classroom* program are automatically recognized. When all schools have been connected, they are formed into a lesson before teaching commences.

Teachers may now draw freehand on the screen using mouse or pen, or utilize built-in tools for lines, rectangles and circles. If text is required, this can be typed anywhere on the screen in various fonts and styles. At any time in the lesson, text can be altered, moved or highlighted as required. Any preprepared graphics or text brought up on to the screen will automatically be distributed to the other site or sites.

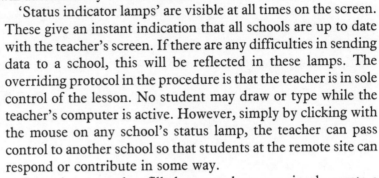 'Status indicator lamps' are visible at all times on the screen. These give an instant indication that all schools are up to date with the teacher's screen. If there are any difficulties in sending data to a school, this will be reflected in these lamps. The overriding protocol in the procedure is that the teacher is in sole control of the lesson. No student may draw or type while the teacher's computer is active. However, simply by clicking with the mouse on any school's status lamp, the teacher can pass control to another school so that students at the remote site can respond or contribute in some way.

 Once the screen has filled up, teachers can simply create a new one and continue teaching. Previous screens may be recalled at any time. After a lesson, students may print or save screens to disk as a record of their lesson. Teachers can reuse saved material in subsequent lessons. Multiple screens prepared before a lesson may be distributed to the other participants at any time during that lesson. Students' work can be similarly shared.

The *Electronic Classroom* software allows multimedia to be transferred among sites but it is not yet possible to send interactive multimedia materials with moving images over the network. Informal tests in transferring hypertext screens from the Distance Education Centre, Victoria (DECV) to remote country schools have established that the transmission rates are too slow. However, as technology improves and the costs of multimedia hardware and software decline relative to travel and subsistence costs, the economic equation will tip further toward the uses of interactive multimedia in conjunction with computer-mediated communication, (see also Romiszowski, 1992; Biggar and Scott, 1992).

The advantages of the MAX system

The Victorian audiographic telematics system has been found to have a number of very real advantages. These are summarized below.

Affordability

The MAX package is affordable. Initial establishment costs range from about A\$3,500 to A\$7,000 (about US\$2,600 to US\$5,250) per site, depending on the functions required. The concern for low start-up costs in part reflects the approach adopted by the original Management Committee, which not only envisaged the system as a rural network for delivering instruction but also as facilitating professional development, administrative meetings and other services for rural communities. Thus, rather than opting for high-cost technology and confining the project to a small number of trials and centres, the Management Committee chose to equip 79 of the rural schools with MAX. The relatively low capital costs of MAX encouraged other funding agencies to support the schools and expand the network to its present 205 sites. After several years of growing use, it appears that the technology is robust enough to stand up to a variety of applications.

Equipment, rental and line costs vary from cluster to cluster but, within the context of total education costs, these are relatively small items and the worldwide trend of falling communication costs, combined with inevitable technological developments, will help to make the system increasingly cost effective.

Versatility

It is important to note that the system is not only capable of multi-purpose delivery but comprises equipment which is in itself multi-purpose. Each of the three components can be separated and used individually for other tasks. For example, the loudspeaking voice terminals can be transferred to other telephone points and used for meetings; the facsimile machines can be used for administrative as well as teaching purposes; and the computers can be used for curriculum materials preparation and for classroom management tasks. This versatility makes the system even more cost effective, and increases the impact of the technology throughout each school. Some teachers were introduced to computers through telematics, and communities became aware of the system's potential through parents and community groups using it.

A further advantage of the three-part MAX configuration is that each component is capable of being independently upgraded. This is an important consideration in maintaining staff and student interest in the system. Also, there is a ready market for the resale of computers among teachers and rural communities. This provides each school with a financial base to upgrade its system.

The choice of a technology is always a trade-off among educational requirements, available budgets, ease of use, anticipated durability and so on. In adopting MAX, the lack of colour capability was originally traded off against the advantages given above. As technology advances and costs fall, more sophisticated features may be incorporated.

Teacher participation

The project's teacher-focused development process, supported by the software developer, not only ensures that the system meets the needs of teachers, but establishes a dynamic climate in which improvement is constantly being sought by the users. The project is not only improving the student retention rates but is providing a significant learning process for the teachers themselves.

Accommodating a variety of teaching styles and approaches

The system is flexible enough to accommodate a variety of teaching styles and approaches. The teachers can either use telematics in a responsive way with student-initiated contributions or preplan 'screens' of material for exposition. Irrespective of their teaching approaches, all the teachers have reported that telematics requires more preparation than traditional teaching, but most see this as being wholly beneficial for their teaching. The system also enables teachers to develop progressively their skills in telematics. Many have commenced with the audio and facsimile components and then, as they have gained confidence in their abilities, have progressed to the more challenging use of the computer link.

Suitability to the curriculum

The system has a broad range of curriculum applications. In the Far West Cluster, it has been used to link two schools to the DECV in Melbourne to teach music to second- to sixth-year secondary students who do not have direct access to qualified music teachers (Lipscombe, 1989). MAX also has an important role in implementing the Ministry's policy of providing all first-year secondary pupils with access to a language other than English (LOTE). The Wimmera Community Languages Programme uses audiographics to teach foreign languages to primary and secondary students. In 1986, only four government secondary schools in the district offered a foreign language and students from fourth year onwards had to rely on correspondence lessons. In June 1991, after nearly five years of using audiographics, 24 primary schools were teaching one of four foreign languages and six secondary schools were offering foreign languages, either by telematics or with a classroom teacher (Conboy, 1992). Rural primary clusters are also using telematics effectively to supplement a visiting

LOTE teacher service in the King River Valley Cluster in north-eastern Victoria (Conboy, 1991).

Improved learning

MAX has been found to improve the quality and the depth of learning. For example, in the East Gippsland Cluster, teaching mathematics via MAX has been found to be more effective than in the face-to-face situation (Wilson, 1989). It was found that when individual guidance with mathematics problems is withheld by a teacher within the classroom, some students tend to give up easily. However, when working through the same problem using the computer as an electronic blackboard and with only an audio link, the students at the other sites tend to forget that the teacher is watching and listening at the other end and proceed to work through the problem independently. Also, in such a situation, the visual link and audio system provide a 'window into the students' minds' and the remote teacher is often actually better placed to follow the students' mental reasoning than when they are physically present in the room. It is also interesting to note that, in reviewing the use of audiographic conferencing systems carried out by the International University Consortium in Maryland, Gilcher and Johnstone (1989, p107) observed that 'the lack of direct visual contact with their students has also forced instructors to improve their communication and listening skills'.

Computer awareness is a requirement for all pupils and the MAX applications have a key role in the state's policy of preparing its school population for a society fast becoming dependent on information technology (Australian Information Industry Association, undated).

Implementation

It is usual for new information technology to be introduced into education systems on a trial or pilot project basis. Such an adoption strategy may reflect administrators' or educators' uncertainties about the technology and its full implications. Sometimes the trial procedure is adopted through a desire to 'quarantine' the effects of the technology within a restricted area. Sometimes the trial or pilot project appears to be little more than an attempt to limit the capital and recurrent costs or spread the set-up costs over a longer period. While caution may often be justified in regard to new technology in the classroom, over-caution may deprive a whole student generation of

191

much-needed access. Another unfortunate effect of such trial or pilot projects is that they sometimes tend to overemphasize the hardware issues rather than the educational outcomes and systemic changes achieved through the adoption of the technology.

The Victorian initiative was a departure from the traditional trial procedure. There was official acknowledgement in the Ministry of Education's Blackburn Report (1985) that electronic delivery systems could expand the curricula for students in isolated schools. A Resource Agreement with the Commonwealth Government provided a budget of A$3.5m (US$2.6m) in 1987–88 to improve country student participation in 79 of Victoria's more remote schools (Ministry of Education, Victoria, 1987). The Ministry identified about 20 per cent of Victoria's schools as potential users of audiographic telematics and indicated that cost, flexibility and versatility were to be important criteria in resourcing these schools.

Clear goals for systems and clear articulation of such goals are important preconditions for the introduction of technology into schools (Hezel, 1991). Resource Agreement 3 made it clear that participating clusters were required to undertake thorough needs-assessment procedures and establish clearly defined educational goals and objectives. Clusters also had to prepare detailed educational specifications for their uses of the technology and were expected to develop system coordination and management structures and to seek cooperation with neighbouring institutions such as Technical and Further Education (TAFE) Colleges. Staff from the clusters were nominated to attend training workshops and the regionally focused approach ensured that a body of expertise and enthusiasm was established in the schools.

Key policy directions

Hezel (1991) argues that technology has to be implemented incrementally and that policies must exist to ensure its equitable distribution. Because most communications technology is developed for industrial or domestic applications, it is also imperative that it should be tested adequately in schools and that those who develop the policies should draw on this local, practitioner experience.

The Victorian MAX project has provided educational policymakers with a wide range of valuable information on key aspects of implementing communications technology for curriculum purposes: for example, in regard to the decision-making processes across the system and their effectiveness; the support for emerging school organizational structures such as school clusters; the relationship of telematics to Ministry policies; the reactions of the teachers involved; the nature of the teaching and learning process; the resource demands; the nature of staff development; and the appropriateness of the chosen technology for the needs of small rural secondary schools in Victoria. The schools telematics project was policy-driven. It is now becoming policy-influential.

School organization

As with similar education innovations involving technology, a number of second-order consequences have emerged. The enhanced communication among schools has encouraged the extension of the cluster form of school organization. Although various forms of cluster existed before 1986 (Education Department of Victoria, 1985), improved communications have encouraged schools to standardize their time-tables and share teacher expertise via telematics. The essential requirements of a cluster are that the educational provision should be enriched by joint action and by shared resources but that there should be no diminution of each school's distinct identity.

The Mallee Secondary College Cluster is, in many respects, at the forefront of developments in cluster administration. The cluster operates with a Coordination Committee and an Implementation Committee. The Coordination Committee is responsible for the conduct of cluster activities within Department of School Education guidelines. It has a broad representative supervisory role. The Implementation Committee is the operational body. Sub-groups of this Committee include curriculum programme teams, an equal opportunity working committee, an evaluation team and groups responsible for the newsletter, finances and careers and work experience (Ministry of Education and Training, Victoria, 1988). The Mallee Cluster is sophisticated and comprehensive in its operations. In addition to year-round operational matters such as professional development, the cluster is responsible for determining the curriculum provision for each school year (which in Australia commences in January or February). School representatives meet in the October/November period to identify courses which they will provide within their own schools and to negotiate courses which they will provide or require from neighbouring schools using MAX. This is a complex process and highly dependent on student choices, which are subject to change. When the representatives have determined what courses they can provide within the cluster, they then seek out any additional resources needed from beyond the cluster; for example, from the DECV or from a Regional Language Centre for LOTE.

While no two school clusters are identical, the work of the Mallee Secondary College Cluster has been valuable in addressing issues which are generic to all clusters; such as, the need to document adequately all stages of the clustering process, to involve the staff, the students and the community in the various stages of clustering, and to establish a sound management structure which ensures goodwill between the schools and the communities they serve (Lake, 1988).

Some rural secondary schools offer their MAX facilities to TAFE colleges and have become study centres for community-focused programmes such as adult literacy and return-to-study courses (Hill *et al*, 1991). The success of these cross-sectoral initiatives prompted the Ministry of Education to establish a Telematics Network Support Pilot Project in 1989 with a small staff to provide advice and training to all education sectors in Victoria. So far, 13 cross-sectoral projects have been funded under the aegis of this agency.

As a further development, school regions have been encouraged to form Regional Telematics Education Consortiums (RTECs) to coordinate cross-sector cooperation in providing education and training within their region. These bodies make decisions about the areas of coverage of communications technology and set priorities for installing equipment in their regions. The RTECs, like the Contact North/ Contact Nord Project in Northern Ontario (Arblaster, 1988), have the aim of moving institutions from the low risk/modest benefit end of the collaborative continuum (sharing information, experience, consultants, resources) to the high risk/major benefit end (collaborating in course and courseware development, credit transfer and creating a common open learning system). Clearly, the use of a technology networked among schools requires significant attitudinal changes in regard to relationships both among schools and between schools and other educational providers. Such changes take time because of the broader social factors involved.

The teachers' role

The nature of the innovation process in schools is determined partly by circumstances (eg, access to expertise, available finance, community support) and partly by the innovation's capacity to persuade teachers of its innate worth and practicality (Wright, 1987). Teachers also need to regard an innovation as ascribing to them acceptable roles and functions.

The MAX telematics project in Victoria has been characterized by a high degree of teacher loyalty. While not all rural teachers have engaged in audiographic telematics, those who have used the system are keen to continue to do so. Teachers cite a number of reasons for their initial involvement with the telematics technology – a concern to do more for their students; a wish to teach particular subjects or more senior students; a desire to acquire new skills; or the need to participate in meetings or professional development. The teachers involved with the telematics show high levels of motivation, competence and commitment. It is not easy to create a sense of 'a single class' when teaching students simultaneously on three or four sites but teachers have developed group-building strategies such as school student camps and billeting 'off-campus' students with their 'on-campus' students.

The teachers' support for the project and their involvement appear to be due to a number of factors. Firstly, the teachers are involved in key decision-making processes and act as group leaders for the statewide or regional MAX training programmes. Secondly, the teachers are not forced to teach via MAX. They are volunteers whose cooperation is sought by cluster committees and school principals. If they decide to use telematics they are provided with a two-day workshop to teach them how to use the MAX system and how to integrate telematics into existing lesson strategies. Thirdly, the teachers who choose to use telematics typically have at least ten years' teaching experience. These are competent teachers with a sound knowledge of their respective disciplines and they have status within their own schools. They are well placed to take up the innovation and promote it informally and formally in relevant school committees and forums.

One major difficulty with the project lies in the additional time and planning required to ensure the success of the MAX-delivered courses. Another problem is that the project is still at a stage where only a relatively small number of teachers are heavily engaged in the use of MAX, so it is still largely dependent on the skills and enthusiasm of key individuals. Growth in the uses of MAX will undoubtedly reduce this dependence over time and provide a broader base of support and expertise.

Telematics for professional development

There is growing awareness of the importance of professional development as a primary vehicle for educational change. However, limited attention has been paid to new strategies for its delivery (Hixson and Jones, 1991). This is somewhat surprising, given that alternative delivery methods are essential in geographically isolated areas and that declining budgets make it increasingly difficult to deliver adequate professional development by conventional face-to-face methods.

Since 1987, a small number of professional development activities have been delivered by audiographic telematics to country teachers in Victorian schools (for example, in connection with media studies and rural science teaching). MAX might not appear to be a medium that would allow for the richness of personal interaction needed for professional development; however, the technology appears to be acceptable for at least some forms of conference or seminar. It enables groups of teachers to take part in in-service activities within their own schools and these groups can discuss the issues among themselves as well as with the remote presenter, which tends to compensate for any lack of body language and visual interaction between the presenter and themselves.

In 1991, an initiative was undertaken in the Loddon, Campaspe-Mallee region to combine audiographics with interactive satellite television, print and face-to-face seminars to deliver two professional development programmes for teachers and two student support programmes (Conboy *et al*, 1992). At the beginning of each professional development seminar, four teachers in each school used MAX to link with their counterparts in other schools to discuss the subject matter of the unit. The teachers then tuned into the interactive satellite television broadcast by key speakers and two or three of the schools were rostered to question the speakers. Following the satellite broadcast, the teachers in each school used audiographic telematics to continue discussion. This mixed-mode delivery was found to be effective for expanding the teachers' knowledge base and developing new attitudes. The success of the Loddon, Campaspe-Mallee trial has encouraged the Victorian government to extend the satellite network in Victoria and to look to the RTECs to aggregate demands for training throughout their respective regions.

Conclusion

The Victorian audiographic telematics project, using MAX, has been a blend of 'top-down' and 'bottom-up' provision on a statewide basis. It has occurred within an education system which has a strong commitment to teacher autonomy and professionalism and which regards the role of technology as supplementary to the work of the good teacher. This approach to the MAX technology has strengthened the project because it has forced those planning and introducing the system to focus on what is acceptable within the context of the rural schools and what is practicable within the typical classroom.

The MAX system has been in use since 1986 and can be seen to have had a major impact in rural education. The introduction of the technology and the cluster system means that many senior students in small rural schools now have access to a more comprehensive curriculum; they can learn in 'virtual groups'; they can be stimulated and challenged by their peers in other schools; and they can receive more immediate feedback from their Correspondence School teachers. However, it may be in the second-order consequences that the project has had its biggest impact. The project has increased communication among schools, given rise to new forms of cooperation and empowered teachers and communities to engage in new self-help enterprises.

The MAX project has shown that the uses of technology in education must be for something more than a series of small-scale, independent trials in which the main beneficiaries are those who receive the grants. Technology must be used in ways that provide communication frameworks to the benefit of all learners and entire communities. It should be a simple extension for students who have learned via such technology to feel confident in accessing knowledge from global sources by satellite or other means. Educating students through such a system also means that they become the masters of the technology they use – a very productive side-effect for their future employment.

References

Arblaster, J.R. (1988). *Contact North: The concept, policy, development, and status of the Northern Ontario Distance Education Access Network.* Paper presented at the Annual Conference of the Association of Canadian Community Colleges.

Australian Education Council (1992). *Working party on a national education communications framework: Consultancies 1–6.* Adelaide.

Australian Information Industry Association (undated). *Towards a new approach to computing education in schools: A discussion paper.* Deakin, Australian Capital Territory.

Biggar, M.J. and Scott, C.J. (1992). Telecommunications networks for remote interactive multimedia. In *Proceedings of the International Interactive Multimedia Symposium,* Perth, 27–31 January, 313–20.

Conboy, I. (1991). *Evaluation of the LOTE telematics trial in the Ballarat Arch Cluster and the King River Valley Cluster.* Ministry of Education and Training, Victoria, Melbourne.

Conboy, I. (1992). The art of learning over long distances. *The Age* newspaper, Melbourne, 20 January.

Conboy, I., Elliott, N. and Martin, D. (1992). *Teachers train: Students at risk gain. Professional development using telematics.* Department of School Education, Victoria, Melbourne.

Crago, R. (1991). *Electronic classroom user's guide.* Revelation Computing, Brisbane.

D'Cruz, J.V. (1990). *Technology in education: A study of policy and practice in rural schools.* Ministry of Education, Victoria, Melbourne.

Department of Employment, Education and Training, (1992). *Review of modes of delivery in higher education.* Canberra.

Education Department of Victoria (1985). *Alternatives in school organisation, 4: Clustering, sharing, merging.* Melbourne.

Elliott, N. (1991). *Victorian telematics manual* (revised edn). Ministry of Education, Victoria, Melbourne.

Gilcher, K.W. and Johnstone, S.M. (1989). *A critical review of the use of audiographic conferencing systems by selected educational institutions.* University of Maryland University College, Md.

Government of Victoria (1987). *Victoria: The next decade.* Melbourne.

Hezel, R.T. (1991). Statewide planning for telecommunications in education: Some trends and issues. *Tech Trends*, 36 (5), 17–20.

Hill, R., Meulenberg, P., McNamara, S. and Dewildt, J. (1991). *It doesn't just happen!*, Report of the Ministry Telematics Network Support Project. Ministry of Education and Training, Victoria, Melbourne.

Hixson, J. and Jones, B.F. (1991). Using technology to support professional development for teachers and administrators (implications for state-level policy and planning). In A.D. Sheekey (ed), *Education policy and telecommunications.* Office of Educational Research and Improvement, Washington, DC, 36–50.

Lake, R. (1988). *Clustering: From conception to birth.* Paper delivered to the SPERA Conference, Launceston, Tasmania.

Lipscombe, B. (1989). The Bal-Cas music program: Making music in the Far West Cluster. In I. Margitta (ed), *Curriculum and technology in schools: Expanding alternatives in rural schools.* Ministry of Education, Victoria, Melbourne, 25–9.

McGregor, A.L. and Latchem, C.R. (1991). *Networks for learning: A review of access and equity in post-compulsory education in rural and remote areas of the state of Western Australia.* Western Australian Office of Higher Education, Perth.

Ministry of Education, Victoria (1985). *Ministerial review of post-compulsory schooling* (The Blackburn Report). Melbourne.

Ministry of Education, Victoria (1987). *Memorandum to Schools No 111. Commonwealth Resource Agreement: Using technology to improve retention in Years 11 and 12 in rural schools.* Melbourne.

Ministry of Education and Training, Victoria (1988) *Mallee Secondary College Cluster evaluation.* Melbourne.

Ministry of Education and Training, Victoria (1990). *The social justice framework.* Melbourne.

Queensland Board of Advanced Education (1989). *Queensland access to higher education: On the road to open learning.* Brisbane.

Romiszowski, A.J. (1992). Developing interactive multimedia courseware and networks. In *Proceedings of the International Interactive Multimedia Symposium*, Perth, 27–31 January, 17–46.

Wilson, J. (1989). Interview in *Telecom Report*, Television Programme 13. Cyril Jones and Associates, Melbourne.

Wright, A. (1987). The process of innovation in two primary schools: A case study of teachers' thinking. *Educational Review*, 39 (2), 107–15.

11 Librarians catch the multimedia wave

John Frylinck and David Raitt

Innovation in libraries

Driven by the desire to provide their clients with the best possible information services, librarians have involved themselves with networking, communications, document imaging, the electronic transfer of information and so forth since the onset of these new information technologies and have adopted microform technologies, the computerization of internal library functions and the now widely available Online Public Access Catalogues (OPACS). Information and entertainment stored in widely differing media have long been accepted into the mainstream of library activities. Many libraries already have substantial investments in non-print material and associated hardware. Librarians have worked out innovative methods of housing, indexing and making these materials available for use. Within the profession there is a substantial sub-group specializing in so-called 'non-book' librarianship. These groups organize regular meetings, seminars, etc and have built up a substantial corpus of knowledge through research and publication in newsletters and journals devoted to audiovisual librarianship.

Barriers and impediments to the adoption of IMM

While the library world can claim a few outstanding innovators, generally speaking there has been relatively slow acceptance of interactive multimedia (IMM) technology by librarians as well as the public (Raitt, 1991). On the whole, IMM is currently regarded with some ambivalence. Many library professionals look upon it as an interesting technology, but one that will require significant investment and change if its potential is to be fully realized. Possible barriers to the effective adoption of IMM by librarians may be cited as financial constraints and a lack of requisite resources resulting in a lack of opportunity to become familiar with the new and emergent systems; ingrained traditional resistance to change; a degree of uncertainty regarding the appropriateness of the technology to various applications; an inability to grasp the significance of IMM; a lack of experience, knowledge and skills in regard to IMM among library professionals; and the scale of some units (smaller libraries are generally slower to adopt new technologies). Other impediments to the use of electronic documents in library environments might include: researchers' and scholars' general reluctance to accept electronic information as an acceptable substitute for the printed word and their lack of easy access to systems providing this information; the variety of formatting standards; and such issues as licensing, the protection of intellectual property and the safeguarding of the integrity of data.

A further constraint on the growth of IMM raised by some is the lack of a consistent user interface. However, in our experience, library users have adapted to a variety of compact disc-read only memory (CD-ROM) interfaces without too much difficulty. The ready acceptance of CD-ROM technology by librarians, irrespective of interfaces, is worth a closer look as a potentially useful predictor of acceptance of IMM by this group.

CD-ROM

In the late 1980s, librarians found themselves, perhaps unwittingly, at the forefront of a technology that was due to change dramatically the way they provided information to their clients. This was the start of the CD-ROM era – an IMM-related field in which librarians led the way. The uptake of this optical disc technology by libraries was remarkable. The first databases on CD-ROM were largely textual and appeared in 1985. Within five years it was estimated that 80 per cent of all CD-ROM readers were located in libraries, mainly those with academic and professional specialisms (Feldman, 1990). The enthusiastic embracing of CD-ROM technology by librarians has been a worldwide phenomenon that shows no signs of abating. A variety of seminars, workshops and conferences have been held on this theme and the topic of CD-ROMs in libraries is the focus of a number of journals.

Since the late 1960s, the more progressive libraries have been searching remote bibliographical and other information databases on behalf of their users. This access is relatively expensive due to communication costs, database access charges and outlays on hardware, and the command-driven interfaces generally do not make for easy access to this information by neophytes. The arrival of CD-ROMs has changed all this dramatically. They provide an effective means of distributing some of the vast amount of information previously held at remote locations. They also come with reasonably easy-to-use interfaces. Because the databases already exist in digital form, they easily transfer to CD-ROM. Most of the early products were aimed at the library market and librarians eagerly implemented them. Workstations and networks intended solely for CD-ROM access have proliferated in libraries. With minor adaptations, these workstations can handle CD-ROM-based IMM products. CD-ROMs fit neatly into traditional library thinking. Sources can be 'acquired' and made available in the library and users can freely access the information they contain. Remote access through organizational networks is also possible. These developments are significant as we can see distinct similarities between the eager uptake of CD-ROM technology by librarians and that of IMM.

Libraries as a logical home for IMM

We would argue strongly that libraries, whether they be public, special or educational, are logical homes for IMM. Libraries typically are located centrally within the communities, organizations or institutions which they serve and they already hold extensive collections of information products which will attract users and support their work with IMM. The IMM products that are going to succeed initially in the marketplace will probably be those that can run on existing equipment or on equipment that needs little enhancement, and many libraries already have substantial investment in the hardware required to run IMM products. Libraries provide secure environments for IMM hardware and software and they are open for long periods and outside normal working hours. Centralizing resources into libraries avoids unnecessary duplication and there are established mechanisms for acquiring, housing and making available IMM, CD-ROM, computer-managed learning and other electronic systems. Library staff are knowledgeable information professionals who are user-oriented rather than information technology driven. They have developed considerable expertise in introducing the new information technologies to their clients and enabling learners and researchers to utilize these systems to maximum effect.

Free access

A further point favouring libraries as the setting for IMM is that for many years they have run their operations on the equitable basis of free access to information. As our society moves towards becoming an information-based one there is an ever-present danger of creating two classes – the information rich (who are well attuned to searching for knowledge in library and other environments and who have access to all the expensive hardware and software associated with information technology) and the information poor (socially marginalized by not being educated to use, or able to afford, such sophisticated tools). Some 'big ticket' IMM items may even be too expensive for the information rich. Furthermore, there will always be a large percentage of consumers who really only require occasional or short-term access to IMM. For these reasons, there will be pressure on libraries to provide IMM-based services for specialist clients and for wider community use.

The marketplace

It falls entirely within the traditional role of libraries as repositories for print and non-print media to acquire, stock and loan compact disc interactive (CD-I), Digital Video Interactive (DVI), multimedia CD-ROM and videodisc products. IMM products may be categorized as home entertainment, education and training, and information and reference. The last two categories are of concern to most libraries and many progressive public libraries provide non-print entertainment packages. Librarians will readily accept IMM titles in the 'reference' category and applications spanning learning and information, such as interactive encyclopaedias, should prove particularly successful in the library marketplace. At present, many of the CD-ROM-based IMM products appear to be aimed at the school market, whereas the early CD-ROM titles appealed particularly to specialist and tertiary libraries. No doubt an increasing range of IMM products will be developed for these sectors. Librarians have shown that, as a consumer group, they are fairly astute at conveying their needs to the producers of CD-ROM applications, both in terms of desired content and in regard to preferred price levels.

In 1986, there were about 50 CD-ROM products for sale. In 1991, according to the Ohio-based Optical Publishing Association, more than 3,350 CD-ROM titles were available; Hill and Mace (1991) predicted that this number would double in 1992. The quality of the CD-ROM products has also improved over this time. Superior and more sophisticated interfaces have become available, as have multimedia products. The initial IMM offerings have varied in quality as did the early text-only CD-ROMs. However, these products generally offer better information retrieval than their printed counterparts and they certainly provide innovative learning alternatives.

By 1992 there were some 2,600 companies involved in CD-ROM production, almost half of these based in Europe (Finlay and Mitchell, 1992). The most popular CD-ROM subjects have proved to be in biomedicine and health, science and technology, banking, finance, economics and government information, but there has been a noticeable increase in titles related to leisure and recreation, art and the humanities, computer applications and education and training. There has also been a significant increase in multimedia titles in, for example, CDTV, DVI and CD-I. This is an area where traditional online information services cannot presently compete because of limitations in data compression, storage, data transfer bandwidths and rates, and display possibilities (Raitt, 1992).

Traditional textbook publishers are taking their first steps into the IMM market. Maguire (1991) suggests that if these publishers wish to counteract the new arrivals such as ABC News Interactive, The Voyager Company and Warner New Media they will need to move quickly. However, we should not forget that many of the traditional textbook suppliers have a long tradition of stocking and promoting such 'multimedia' products as sound-filmstrips, slide-tape programmes and various forms of learning package.

There is a growing number of IMM and CD-ROM-based periodicals. Home-based demand for such interactive electronic journals is not likely to be large at present because of price and technological factors, and low domestic sales could deter the advertisers who can provide the revenue that helps to keep down the costs of such electronic publications. On the other hand, the utilization of such interactive journals in libraries, especially in a networked environment, could do much to avoid the current problems of storing and circulating periodicals.

The IMM industry is always looking for attractive and inexpensive applications that will fire the enthusiasm of potential domestic users. The price of CD-ROM drives has dropped significantly as CD-ROMs have gained in popularity. If the trend continues it is possible that they may achieve a major impact in the consumer electronics market. The ability to use CD-ROM players for a variety of purposes will also make them more attractive to price-sensitive consumers. CD-ROMs can already play audio CDs. Video is following the digitalization road pioneered by audio, opening a whole new field for the producers of IMM entertainment and information products. If the chosen medium is CD-ROM, the range of titles will increase and libraries and consumers will gain from a wider choice. A larger market will also result in lower prices. Related to this is the crucial issue of standardization.

Standardization

There is widespread concern over the computer industry's inability to agree on IMM standards, which has been a major contributory factor in the slower-than-expected acceptance of IMM. Fortunately, there are now moves towards the establishment of some common standards. The American Multimedia PC Marketing Council has specified minimum requirements for IMM hardware and the MPC logo is increasingly seen on equipment and products. The Joint Photographic Expert Group (JPEG) and the Motion Picture Experts Group (MPEG) are two committees working under the auspices of the International Standards Organization to define a proposed universal standard for the digital compression and decompression of still images and motion video/audio for use in computer systems.

A major factor in the rapid acceptance of compact discs, both in the audio format and in the ROM format which rode on the back of the compact audio disc, was early agreement by manufacturers on a single standard. One would have hoped that the manufacturers had learnt a hard lesson from the video standard wars. Unfortunately, history seems to be repeating itself with IMM and the user is confronted with a bewildering choice of standards and formats – for example, laser disc, DVI, CD-I and CDTV and varying multimedia platforms such as Amiga, NeXT, Apple and IBM. Multimedia may take off with the introduction of the Multimedia PC from Microsoft – although many feel that this platform relies on too slow a machine with facilities that are too basic for real applications (Jacsó, 1992).

There must be many potential buyers who are waiting for cheaper and standardized equipment, and for developments to stop evolving. One way of dealing with the issue of continually having to buy upgraded equipment is to make the new hardware and software downwards or backwards compatible. However, this would mean that users would not have the latest features and facilities.

Information professionals and consumers will tread warily in the IMM marketplace until a clear standard emerges. There is no room in today's market for incompatible and competitive systems. Librarians are unlikely to spend heavily in this area until a substantial degree of compatibility emerges, both in IMM product formats and in the requisite hardware. When this occurs, libraries will no doubt offer a full range of multimedia titles just as they currently do with audiovisual materials and computer software.

Library applications

The new magnetic and laser-encoded optical memory storage media will need to be carefully catalogued and stored and will need specialized and possibly dedicated equipment for their playback, like the other types of audiovisual material traditionally provided by libraries. The costs of providing such equipment will not be insurmountable for the larger libraries and may be in part recoverable by libraries requiring users to carry out their own desktop publishing, photo archiving, sound mixing, authoring, etc on a fee-for-service basis. Libraries may also need to explore issues such as whether or not to be in the business of hiring out equipment to users who only need to use it on an occasional basis or who are unable or unwilling to purchase such systems. It also seems likely that libraries will play a valuable role as transitional repositories for IMM items until appropriate learning stations can be made more widely available across the institutions or within the communities they serve. As a promotional strategy to encourage acceptance of these newer media, innovative libraries may wish to stock a wide range of IMM programmes and equipment in anticipation of demand. In this way, libraries will extend their role as proactive centres for learning and inquiry and will assist in the promotion of IMM. Hardware and software producers may need to cooperate in such ventures.

IMM holds countless possibilities for increasing the efficiency, enjoyment and speed with which users can assimilate information on library systems and services. Most libraries provide guidance for their clients in regard to the services provided and the physical layouts. To date, this has been done through print, guided tours, tutorials, face-to-face inquiry services, and more latterly, computer-based information terminals and products such as HyperCard. IMM can provide even more dynamic and appealing visitor/user information systems with animation, stills, video clips and voice-overs offering guided tours of the various facilities and tutorial support in their use.

Libraries and archives with large collections of pictorial matter (slides, photographs, maps, drawings, etc), will also have much to gain from utilizing IMM production and imaging technologies. Such visual material is extremely hard to preserve and control. For example, 35mm slide collections are notoriously difficult to keep in order and require detailed checking before and after loan, fragile materials need to be preserved, and audiovisual collections in libraries need a plethora of facilities for storage and replay. IMM offers the opportunity to reduce the security risks, the mass of equipment needed for audiovisual materials, and the space needed to store them.

Given the advantages of IMM, such as computerized indexing, fast access, good security and file integrity, and the ease of information sharing and distribution, many libraries may wish to install in-house desktop CD write-once recording systems for converting material to CD-ROM and other formats, and to acquire computer-based systems to reduce the long-term costs of storing paper documents, create training and reference materials and provide efficient retrieval and dissemination mechanisms. Flat-bed or hand-held scanners or other image-capturing devices offer the opportunity to take text and images from, for example, journals, and transfer these to hard disk for incorporation into electronic bulletin boards or printed notices or other files. Such methods also provide better ways of storing and providing access to items such as newspaper cuttings and photographic archives. Scanned images can also be transferred to users at other sites via local and other networks.

IMM can prove a powerful ally in the educational arena in the public library sector. For example, in the children's sections, where story hours are held during which books are read aloud or there is storytelling, multimedia electronic books (of which there is a growing number) can provide an interactive environment in which children can explore the stories. Such electronic fictional, reference and information materials would provide children with the opportunity to experience technology that they might not necessarily have access to in their homes and to learn in an interactive, informative and entertaining manner.

Libraries can also utilize IMM to develop and deliver in-house instructional and informational programmes for their staff and clients. Purpose-made storyboards and question and answer learning systems could be developed for use in the children's sections, and local and customized material (for example, related to local history collections) could also be prepared by the library staff, teachers or community groups.

Innovative technologies

Newer technologies that fuse computer-based interactive tablets, 8cm or 12cm CD-ROMs and/or smart magnetic and optical cards are becoming available in the shape of hand-held electronic books incorporating varying degrees of interaction. Details of products and developments of interest to the library and information community are outlined below, together with an indication of possible implications. Products discussed include the Data Discman, RED, Active Book, smart cards, Compact Reader, Book House, interactive tablets, Newton technology and voice applications (Raitt, 1991; Ducker, 1991; Feldman, 1990).

Data Discman

Sony, inventor of the Walkman and the Discman, has developed the Data Discman – a hand-held electronic book capable of reading information recorded on 8cm optical discs, as opposed to the more common 12cm format. A wide variety of electronic book titles, manuals, encyclopaedias, travel guides etc is currently available, ranging in price from US$18 to US$130 and the product has become a major success in Japan and the US (Herther, 1992). The latest version of the Discman is capable of handling audio output and is sold in the US bundled with three electronic titles, *Grolier's Electronic Encyclopedia/Concise Edition* (which includes 30 minutes of audio as well as some graphics), *Passport's World Travel Translator* (an obvious choice for an audio book) and a novel, *Sliver*, featuring multivoice playback ('Electronic book player reads aloud', 1992). The Data Discman concept is continually evolving and in future all discs will be produced in a format based on CD-ROM XA. Many believe that a breakthrough for IMM into the mass market could result from the arrival of portable players like the Discman. Clearly, libraries could provide optical copies of the applications software, games, tools, books, dictionaries, etc for use with such portable devices.

RED

Reddy Information Systems' RED is a wearable, hands-free CD-ROM delivery system with a head-up display, a real-time text-to-speech capability in English, French or Spanish, a zero-motion mouse and a memory card for instant updates of the CD-ROM information. RED is a combination of the Walkman, CD-ROM and Reflex Technology's Private Eye. RED provides interactive, multimedia and hypermedia presentations and allows the user to review text, graphics, animation and audio information. The CD-ROM is worn on the belt or wrist while the display is worn on the head.

Active Book

The Active Book Company in the UK is developing a range of slim portable pocket computers based on the book. To maintain the illusion of traditional pencil and paper, the user writes on electronic paper (an LCD screen plus transparent graphics tablet) with an electronic stylus. An optional keyboard for high-volume data entry and voice input is also possible. Active Books allow the user to cross-reference data dynamically, to build chains of association linking items of information such as text, speech or sound, fax or video images, bit mapped images and line drawings, etc. The multimedia pages, organized into chapters and parts, complete with indexes, further replicate the book concept.

Active Books store information on pages (between 100 and 300 at present), each of which has its own number. Several techniques are available to search the book, including a stylus to turn the pages until the required information appears. Chapters may be either basic divisions of information types (eg, fax, sound, photos) or some user-created division. Dynamic and static bookmarks help the user remember where information is stored.

Smart cards

Another form of compact, updatable, portable storage is the so-called 'smart card' (containing some kind of microchip) which comes in both optical and magnetic forms and can store considerable amounts of data. The optical Drexon LaserCard, for example, which is suitable for both writable and read-only applications, can hold some 2Mb of user data – equivalent to approximately 1,000 pages. On the other hand, the OptiCard, which is also the size of a credit card, is theoretically capable of storing over 200Mb of information on each side, but the current prototype's capacity is 50Mb of user data (equivalent to about 20,000 typewritten pages).

Such optical memory WORM (write-once/read many times) cards have the capabilities of being able to access an image instantly, transmitting it to remote users electronically or allowing several people to view the same image at different locations simultaneously. The high data density and capacity offered by the card allow the recording of text and numerical data as well as photos, dynamic video and audio information in digital form. The first applications of the OptiCard are being developed in such areas as personal health records, identification and security, electronic professional book publishing, and electronic storage of business correspondence. As the card is a write-once medium (an erasable, rewritable medium is under feasibility study) it can be customized by the end-user to become a personalized information source with a data integrity of ten years.

The OptiCard is accessible through a SCSI port on a personal computer and is able to work with any software retrieval package, given a suitable driver. Since the optical card drive can accept and return data to and from a PC, the large capacity OptiCard offers the possibility of putting on and storing in-house documentation, user manual, catalogues, directories and the like.

Smart cards exhibit considerable potential value to the library, information and publishing industries. Carefully constructed card sets could be available to library users to provide instruction or problem-solving in many subject areas such as electrical repairs, plumbing, cookery, gardening and sports. They thus could become an inexpensive alternative to books – projected costs are US$1 per card.

Compact Reader

The Enpros Compact Reader is a hand-held device that permits access to data stored in a credit card format that holds up to 20Mb. The optical cards can theoretically store 50Mb of data. However, Enpros, a Dutch company, found that for many applications (for example, telephone directories, dictionaries, flight schedules, bus and train timetables, hotel, restaurant and museum information) 20Mb (the equivalent of 10,000 pages) was sufficient.

Each card contains the software necessary to run the application contained on that card. The Reader uses the same techniques as CD-ROM, with the card rotating like a CD-ROM. The Reader can also take the 8cm 200Mb CD-ROMs for those needing greater capacity, eg, for image and audio applications.

The prototype Compact Reader is the size of a largish book. The touch of a button enlarges the text and the backlighting enables it to be read in the dark. The device connects to a television set or monitor for viewing by several people. Other features include sound output, eg, for pronunciation from language dictionaries or from music, and a Braille reader replaces the LCD screen for the visually impaired. Utility functions (clock, alarm, agenda, memo) will be added and, since the Compact Reader is a small computer, it includes inherent DOS capabilities such as file transfer and fax communication.

In The Netherlands, Enpros has signed up customers such as KLM, Shell, PTT, VVV (tourist offices), ANWB (the motoring organization) and Spectrum (a publisher). Infocards bearing the Dutch telephone directories and the State Railway timetables are also being created.

Book House

The Book House is a library system using hypertext techniques to help users find books without the limitations of traditional information retrieval. The project was field tested at Hjortespring Library in Denmark, with good results. The user interface of the Book House is based on a building like a real library with the user being able to enter rooms filled with children's books, adult books, etc. The system supports four basic search strategies, using icons and pictures to enable location of the books or topic sought (Nielsen, 1990).

A number of hypertext novels have also been developed where the reader can follow different threads, but a true hypermedia film would be a real challenge, with its infinite range of options, flashbacks, jumps into the future, overlays of scenes and so on. (Peter Greenaway's *Prospero's Books* begins to give us a glimpse of the possibilities here.) It is envisaged that libraries could make available copies of such hypermedia novels and films.

Interactive tablets

Computer-based interactive tablets such as the GridPad or Wang Freestyle could have applications in libraries and information centres. Users could write down details of books borrowed on the tablets if the library staff were absent (eg, in a small library) or if the computer system was down. Mobile libraries could also use the tablets, transferring locally stored data to the main library computer for updating. Similarly, since forms are a practical application for such tools, an input sheet could give users in the field collecting information for a centralized system (such as the Agricultural Research Information Service or the International Nuclear Information System) an easy and quick method of data input, without the need for voluminous paperwork or immediate access to a computer. Data could be directly transferred to a central or local computer over telephone lines or sent on floppy disks or small RAM cards by mail. During stock-taking and revision (where it is necessary to walk around book shelves and stacks) library staff could use such devices to note down, in longhand, the number of copies of individual titles or titles which are missing, damaged, to be withdrawn or replaced, etc. Alternatively, a stock list could be provided so that titles and boxes could be checked. Library user surveys employing this technology, with interviewers using electronic clipboards, will also benefit from this form of data collection (Martin *et al*, 1990; Watt, 1991).

Newton technology

Apple Computer Inc recently announced a new product line of Personal Digital Assistants (PDAs) – hand-held devices, based on a powerful RISC processor, that use digital technology to bridge the gap between personal computers and consumer electronics. Based on an entirely new intelligent technology which Apple calls Newton, the first products will be small, portable electronic notepads which intelligently assist the user in capturing, organizing and communicating ideas and information. The technology will permit free form notetaking and drawings and as the devices are used they will learn more about their users and propose solutions to help them work, plan and schedule more efficiently. Besides providing handwriting recognition, the Newton technology incorporates object-oriented data structures for organizing and accessing information as well as built-in wired and wireless communications capabilities. Intelligent cards will also be made available to enable greater amounts of information to be stored and retrieved. The Apple Newton PDA is expected to be ready in early 1993.

Voice-activated applications

The most frequent use of interactive voice interfaces is to control a computer (for example, where the use of hands may be inappropriate or inconvenient or in hazardous environments where wearing gloves makes keyboard entry difficult). Such a system accepts voice commands and translates them into a sequence of keyboard commands. In a library situation, this could mean that merely speaking a unique book identifier or name could trigger the system into automatically filling in the remainder of the bibliographic or personal details relating to that item or person. Reports generated with such a system (Kurzweil Applied Intelligence, Inc. has developed a system called VoiceReport) can be printed immediately or stored as ASCII files for further use and processing by database management systems or expert systems – for instance, to issue a recall or reserve notice or to generate an order form. Lange (1991) reviewed voice response and voice recognition technologies as well as several voice applications in libraries and information environments (including systems for the visually impaired, talking books, voice input and output in online systems, etc.) and showed what can be done given the right interest, support and incentive. For example, voice macros could replace conventional log on command strings and OPACS could be voice directed so that the user has only to say a subject term or an author's name to get a list of references relating to the chosen topic. Scherr

(1989) describes a voice-operated document delivery system in which documents are ordered verbally, retrieved from the file store, compressed and faxed automatically to the user.

Impact

At present, many of the above devices are having a relatively minor impact on the library scene but a growing number of publishers are turning to CD-ROM and optical cards to publish reference works such as encyclopaedias and dictionaries, tax guides, maintenance manuals, literary works and transportation timetables. The possibility exists to customize such media so that users can obtain their own personalized choice of literature, images or music. Smart cards, using write-once or erasable technology, could allow the production of new versions of books or manuals away from the printing press environment (eg, at point of sale outlets), thus revolutionizing printing and distribution. Furthermore, for books held in electronic or optical form, there is a reduced likelihood of them ever going out of print. There is also the intriguing possibility that these electronic versions may even supplant books and libraries in areas where lack of funding or low levels of political commitment mean that certain services or certain books are not being provided. If books on cards or CD-ROMs really do become so cheap, the next generation of children might find themselves growing up with electronic books and miss out altogether on the conventional book. (This would not be dissimilar to the experience of some developing countries which have bypassed developed countries and immediately progressed to the latest all-digital telephone exchanges and television systems because cheap, proven technology was available to them.)

Smart libraries

If electronic books are with us, electronic libraries cannot be too far behind. The Canadian Smart Library Project aims to provide users with virtually all the tools they need to gain access to electronically formatted information in all media (except print) no matter where the data may be in the world. The Smart Library is seen as an information supermarket with many terminals and it uses optical card technology (OptiCard) for security.

Similarly, the idea of IMM information sources stored in a central electronic library and called up as required by subscribers is already with us. In New Jersey, Bell Atlantic and AT & T have started a project that allows the transfer of information (including voice and full-motion video) via telephone lines. The system, based on 'asymmetrical digital subscriber line' (ADSL) technology, uses compressed video signals. A company, educational institution or community can use ADSL and similar communication-enabling technologies (eg, broadband optical fibre) to share centrally stored information and entertainment sources (EDGE, 1991). The library and information service of the group involved is the logical unit to maintain the electronic library and provide equitable access.

Virtual reality

The domain of virtual reality, which utilizes new user interfaces, offers an exciting potential. This medium lends itself to the creation of interactive pathways and links through the increasingly complex information maze. The differences in accessing information from IMM sources (including virtual reality) as opposed to printed material or even machine readable textual material will be of interest to librarians. Virtual libraries could quite successfully mimic real libraries. Users, wearing the requisite virtual reality paraphernalia such as helmet, goggles, data gloves, etc, or working within a desktop environment, could be guided through the intricacies of info-space as if it was a 'real', comfortable, old-style nineteenth-century private library, a modern resource centre containing a variety of media or some other form of collection. Virtual reality also has many possibilities for training library staff and users. At present, the downside of this exciting new technology is the high cost.

Information sharing

Librarians have a fine record of inter-library cooperation and materials transfer. The ability to move electronic images, sound and text around national and international library networks raises a host of interesting questions for inter-library loan operations, not the least of which is 'Who owns the information?' Librarians are sensitive to copyright issues and will no doubt be willing participants in the debate that is sure to arise over, for example, the ownership of the copyright of digital images that are easily downloaded and recycled.

Telecommunication facilities such as ISDN and telefacsimile machines have greatly improved some aspects of document delivery.

Bulick (1990) gives a useful overview of the problems and possibilities of multimedia transmission. ISDN offers great opportunities in the IMM field, as shown by a cooperative venture between Telecom Australia and the State Library of New South Wales entitled the ISDN Multimedia Library Link. This project has demonstrated the feasibility of transferring multimedia images scanned from collections held in one library to another (Wright, 1991).

Another Australian project, dubbed the 'Telelibrary', is developing a system for the electronic scanning, storage, retrieval and delivery of full text documents and images. Developed jointly by the Royal Melbourne Institute of Technology (RMIT) libraries, Telecom Australia, the Collective Information Technology Research Institute, Kodak and the RMIT Department of Communication and Electrical Engineering, the Telelibrary project is testing the practicability of using Telecom's ISDN and other networks to obtain documents and images in electronic form from virtually anywhere in the world. Organizations currently participating in the project are the National Library of Australia, Library of Congress, British Library Lending Division, State Library of New South Wales, University of Western Sydney, Telecom Research Laboratories, San Diego State University, University of Southern California, Blackwells, Delft University of Technology and the National University of Singapore (Brent and Alessio, 1991). Developments such as these open up a whole new 'document' delivery field for librarians, with technology offering the opportunity of much greater sharing of information than ever before. Agreement on common standards will again be crucial if experiments such as these are to take off on any scale.

For completeness, we should also mention schemes such as Project Gutenberg, in which computer-searchable collections can be transmitted by discs, telephone lines or other media. Such electronic books will not have to be reserved and restricted to use by one patron at a time – all materials will be available to all patrons at all locations all of the time (Hart, 1990). Project Gutenberg is but one attempt to support and coordinate the creation and distribution of electronic texts (Basch, 1991), although at the time of writing none of these projects embraces multimedia.

Conclusion

Libraries play a pivotal role in information, education, training and lifelong learning. Librarians and libraries are in the business of acquiring information and organizing this information for use by their clients. Librarians are adept at helping clients find their way through the mass of information sources now available. The format of this information is irrelevant. The acceptance and the utilization of multimedia has been a reality in libraries for many years. However, what is new is that computers now can handle non-textual formats effectively and efficiently. We can confidently predict that within a few years a wide variety of multimedia products will be commonplace in libraries. Libraries provide an ideal focal point to raise awareness of IMM and its possible applications. Many librarians will be capable and enthusiastic agents for IMM promotion and will collaborate happily with other groups in this exciting new field.

References

Basch, R. (1991). Books online: Visions, plans, and perspectives for electronic text. *Online*, 15 (4), 13–23.

Brent, W. and Alessio, R. (1991). The Telelibrary and AARNet. Paper presented at Networkshop '91 – Expanding Network Services, Hobart, Tasmania, 2–4 December.

Bulick, S. (1990). Future prospects for networked-based multimedia information retrieval. *The Electronic Library*, 8 (2), 88–99.

Ducker, J. (1991). The electronic reference book. In D. Raitt (ed), *Proceedings of Online '91: 15th International Online Information Meeting*, London, 10–12 December, 467–75.

EDGE (1991). Information services: Bell Atlantic and AT & T offer multimedia information services to schools – over copper wire. In *EDGE: Work-Group Computing Report*, 4 November, 2 (76), 7.

Electronic book player reads aloud (1992). *Information Retrieval and Library Automation*, 27 (12), 3.

Feldman, T. (1990). *The emergence of the electronic book*. British National Research Fund Report No 46. British Library, London.

Finlay, M. and Mitchell, J. (eds) (1992). *The CD-ROM Directory, 7th edition*. TFPL Publishing, London.

Hart, M.S. (1990). Project Gutenberg: Access to electronic texts. *Database*, 13 (6), 6–9.

Herther, N.K. (1992). Sony's Data Discman springboards consumers into optical's future. *CD-ROM Professional*, 5 (2), 10–12.

Hill, A. and Mace, T. (1991). Optical explosion. *PC Sources*, 2 (10), 389–96.

Jacsó, P. (1992). What is wrong with the MPC specification and logo? *The Electronic Library*, 10 (1), 3–4.

Lange, H.R. (1991). The voice as computer interface: A look at tomorrow's technologies. *The Electronic Library*, 9 (1), 7–11.

Maguire, J.G. (1991). Interactive magazines. *Computer Graphics World*, 14 (8), 33–40.

Martin, G., Pittman, J., Wittenberg, K., Cohen, R. and Parish, T. (1990). Sign here, please. *Byte*, 15 (7), 243–52.

Nielsen, J. (1990). *Hypertext and hypermedia*. Academic Press, London.

Raitt, D. (1991). Technologies and applications for tomorrow's information society. *Proceedings of the 5th Australasian Information Online and On Disc Conference*, Sydney, 30 January–1 February, 1–38.

Raitt, D. (1992). A review of some advances in electronic and optical publishing. In

12 The Jean Talon Project

Eric Lugtigheid

Introduction

The Jean Talon Project aims to create and distribute educational and informational IMM materials intended to increase knowledge and understanding of Canada in the twentieth century, and, by so doing, to create an environment conducive to the electronic publishing of products that will have an important place in the classrooms and living rooms of the nation.

The first section of this chapter describes the project. The second presents the findings from the research studies conducted to test the viability of the project and to develop an understanding of the Canadian educational market for interactive multimedia products.

Project description

The project is named after Jean Talon who, in 1666, as Intendant of New France commissioned the first census to be undertaken in Canada. Talon's census data on the basic needs and resources of the young colony with its 3,225 inhabitants of European stock continues to be a valuable resource on the early Canadian settlement. The Jean Talon Project is based in part on the British Broadcasting Corporation's *Domesday Project* (see for example, Barker, 1989). This interactive videodisc marked the 900th anniversary of William the Conqueror's Domesday Book, which provided a record and assessment of the wealth and resources of eleventh-century England. The project used interactive videodisc technology to present a detailed portrait of the United Kingdom, its economy, culture, society and environment, in the 1980s. The Domesday Project took two years to complete and the database contains the equivalent of 300 volumes of text, more than 54,000 photographs, 24,000 maps, 10,000 data sets and moving images with sound.

The concept

The Jean Talon Project proposes the creation of state-of-the art computer-operated products that will make an important contribution to the advancement of Canadian Studies by increasing Canadians' knowledge and awareness of their country. Seizing the potential of newly emerging information technology, Jean Talon will take Canada – the beauty and splendour of the land and the arts and culture of its peoples – into the schools, libraries and homes of the nation. It will help ensure that Canadians' sense of citizenship and national identity are strengthened through knowledge of how their culture, society, and environment evolved throughout the twentieth century. As a record of Canada's experiences in the twentieth century, Jean Talon will be a gift to Canadians of the twenty-first century. The creation of a Jean Talon Resource Library, focused on Canadian history, demography, geography, art, culture, technology, government, sport, leisure, etc, will provide a rich and lasting legacy which can be built on by future generations of Canadians.

It is also intended that the Project will help to unify the currently fragmented Canadian market for educational software and other educationally oriented electronic products. It is visualized that a more unified market will offer greater opportunities for the Canadian educational software industry and will provide educators, students and researchers with a wider selection of products at lower prices.

Given the broad interest expressed by provincial and territorial government education authorities, the project presents an important and unique opportunity for both levels of government to work cooperatively on nationwide educational applications. It will also bring into the public domain the rich body of information which exists within government information banks, museums, archives and other collections but which is not currently accessible.

It is planned that the IMM products will comprise four major streams:

The National Stream will include special modules on Canada's political system, scientific achievements, international role and architectural heritage.

The Cultural Stream will include the electronic recreation of major cultural institutions such as the National Gallery, the Museum of Civilization, the Royal Ontario Museum and La Musée Quebecoise de la Civilisation, which will allow users to make surrogate 'visits' to these institutions from their homes or classrooms and access entire collections and information banks on artists, artifacts and other elements of Canada's cultural heritage.

The Carto-geographic Stream will comprise products on ecology, demography, agriculture, urbanization, industrialization, the evolution of cities and so on.

The Provincial/Regional Stream will comprise contributions from each province on its own history in the twentieth century.

Each of the products described above will contain still and moving images, sound, text, data and graphic images. It is planned that the Jean Talon products will be modular and flexible to accommodate the varying needs of teachers, students and researchers. The modules will be designed to be used in two ways. Firstly, random search will allow for individualized instruction and the use of the modules for research purposes. By adding 'downloading' features, ministries, school boards or teachers will have access to specific combinations of information to create customized courseware or lessonware. Secondly, each province will be able to develop 'guidance systems' for each module; for example, data on the Canadian environment could be selected from a general information bank and used to accommodate the specific curriculum needs of a particular province and/or the requirements of a particular course of studies or grade level. The new interactive multimedia technology makes it possible for the first time to develop national products that can also fully preserve the curricular jurisdiction of the provinces. This represents an exciting breakthrough for Canada's decentralized system of education.

Another important aspect of the Jean Talon multimedia materials is that they will develop computer literacy and computer-based learning among young Canadians, enabling them to be active participants in the knowledge-based society of the future.

Pilot project description

Research conducted into the nature and direction that the Jean Talon Project should take has identified four topics or areas of study that would be particularly enhanced by the availability of multimedia learning materials:

• Canada's threatened environment;
• Learning about Canada's geography;
• Canada in the world; and

- Science and technology in Canada.

A demonstration project, entitled *Canada: Responding to Change*, is being piloted. An interdisciplinary approach will be employed which will include elements of history, literature, economics, anthropology and geography. The central theme of the database is social change as driven by environmental issues, demographic shifts within society, global economics and technology as well as other contemporary trends and realities. Insofar as the pilot project deals with the evolution of Canadian society, it will address aspects of Aboriginal Canadian history, culture, values, land use, etc. The inclusion and presentation of data on Canada's first peoples will be reviewed with their involvement. Future Jean Talon products could totally pertain to Aboriginal Canadians. Should this be so, project planning and implementation would be pursued with their direct involvement.

The products will be designed to demonstrate information technology as a driving force for socioeconomic change. They will provide users with insights and skills that will enable them to participate more fully as citizens in society and to influence developments and decisions that affect community, national and global wellbeing.

Specifications for the pilot project, which will target students in junior high school and adults experiencing literacy problems, include the following provisions:

- The database, while modelled on the grade nine social studies curriculum of the Province of Alberta, will be developed from a Canadian national perspective to ensure that it will serve as a curriculum resource in all provinces and territories.
- The database will be developed in both official languages and with attention to different levels and types of users in the multicultural classrooms of Canada.
- The information base will be a resource for the general public. However, the products will also contain software features for teacher-guided and self-guided inquiry. These features will serve to augment the use of multimedia materials in structured classroom settings and to facilitate independent open-ended study and distance education.

Digital Video Interactive (DVI) was selected as a development platform for this pilot project to show the rich potential of interactive multimedia technology for educational purposes. The platform is particularly suited to the creation of databases/learning products that contain a large volume of full-motion video. Recognizing that the required hardware will not be widely available in the schools for some time, products may also be developed on other platforms which are more limited in scope but can be operated on existing technology.

The budget for the pilot project is approximately CAN$800,000 and the proposed time frame is for development and production in April 1992–June 1993 followed by teacher preparation/field trials in August 1993–May 1994. Partners in this pilot project are the Department of the Secretary of State of Canada, Multiculturalism and Citizenship Canada, Alberta Education, the Faculty of Education of the University of Alberta and IBM Canada. Cooperation will be sought with local school authorities for the implementation and testing phase of the project.

University of Alberta Faculty of Education resource staff, curriculum consultants, teachers and adult literacy specialists will serve as consultants in the developmental, pilot testing and field trial phases of the project. Of special note is the proposal to establish consulting groups of learners who will work with the project developers on the learner interfaces, the nature of the information and the guided inquiry structures to be incorporated into the product. A number of school jurisdictions will be involved in the developmental process and field trials. For the adult literacy component, trials will be conducted in locations such as shopping malls, public libraries and community halls. The project will also include an in-service component for teachers and tutors. Qualitative and quantitative research will be conducted in regard to the design, production and storage methods of the multimedia products, the implementation and application of the technology in classrooms and other settings, the impact on learners, learning processes and teachers, and the implications for teacher training.

Industrial strategy

In addition to their intrinsic value, it is intended that Jean Talon products will pioneer practical arrangements for the multimedia publication of government information in the form of alphanumeric data, images and sound. It is visualized that such arrangements could lead to the creation and adaptation of standards and guidelines that would enhance Canadian electronic publishing ventures. It is widely recognized that there is a great need for standardization to assist the interfacing of electronic files containing information from multiple government sources. A common standards framework would be useful to government departments and agencies and Canadian industry engaged in multimedia-based activities and would assist in achieving compatibility in a range of information technology products. As Canada's largest publisher, and with its natural role as developer and promoter of national standards, it is appropriate for the federal government to set the pace in this area.

The Jean Talon Project will encourage increased government/ private sector cooperation in electronic publishing of material, which, in turn, could offer the government a variety of advantages including generation of revenue, reduction of publishing expenses and provision of a wider range of services. The vigorous pursuit of this technology will create an opportunity for a coherent national market for electronic teaching/learning materials. Licensing standards and functionalities would enable any software producer to develop materials for Canada's education system. This would not only be advantageous in terms of an industrial strategy but also in terms of providing Canadians with a shared knowledge base of their country.

It is envisaged that the Jean Talon Project will continue long after its formal elements have come to an end. The products can continue to be of value, particularly in education, well into the twenty-first century and a continuing stream of benefits can flow from the project's pioneering work towards greater standardization of electronic publishing and from increased government/private sector cooperation.

Research findings

Five separate studies were commissioned by the Department of the Secretary of State over a two-year period beginning in 1988. These studies examined the feasibility and explored the market potential of multimedia resources on Canada for education and public information purposes. A number of private consulting companies were contracted to carry out this research. (The studies have not been published but they are given in the references at the end of this chapter and are available on request from the Secretary of State of Canada, Ottawa.)

Feasibility study (1988)

This explored the feasibility of developing an interactive multimedia project for educational and commercial purposes. The findings were based on 41 interviews with specialists from private business, publishing houses, technology firms, all levels of government and educational institutions. Numerous reports on mutations in technology and their impact in education and other sectors were also analysed.

The respondents in this study reported that the Jean Talon Project should be directed at the (broadly defined) education system. It was recommended that priority should be given to content that would be of interest and use at all levels of education. A modular thematic approach to product development employing well-crafted and user-friendly software was recommended so that each educational jurisdiction could access and select information consistent with its specific curriculum requirements. To take advantage of future technology, it was suggested that decisions concerning hardware and software platforms should not drive the material/courseware development process.

Respondents strongly suggested that a user-needs survey should be conducted which would further define the demands of the educational market; experts should be used to undertake the project; a phased-in approach, including a series of pilot projects, should be considered; a flexible approach to technology should be adopted; political will and cooperation would need to be ensured; and, finally, particular emphasis should be put on the integrity and quality of the data contained in Jean Talon products.

User needs and current trends study (1989)

This study sought to develop an understanding of the needs of Canadian educators in regard to the introduction and uses of multimedia technology and the types of product that might satisfy these needs. An extensive literature review and 99 individual and group interviews were conducted across Canada with a threefold objective: to provide a point of departure for the study; to analyse the educational marketplace; and to explore multimedia developments in overseas educational contexts that might bear on the Jean Talon Project.

The respondents were asked to indicate their preferences among a series of suggested Jean Talon topics that were outlined in briefing documents. Educators expressed most interest in multimedia products in the following areas:

- geography (including environmental studies and urban development);
- science and technology in Canada (covering developments in pure and applied science);
- multicultural/genealogy studies;
- Canadian collections (including fine arts and cultural institutions);
- regional and/or provincial studies; and

- Canada in a world context.

The concept of a modular approach to product development, combined with the creation of rich data sets of a hierarchical nature that would allow exploration of each subject at varying levels of learning and interest, received particularly strong support. In general, respondents wished to see the creation of products that would be complementary to provincial curriculum requirements; would ensure a broad coverage of subject matter; were current and readily updatable; and would provide for a variety of viewpoints, thus enabling users to develop their own conclusions and interpretations.

The respondents agreed that Jean Talon products should be easy to use and that users should be able to train themselves to access and manipulate the data contained in the products. They also expressed the view that the software should be accompanied by print and other ancillary resources to enhance use by teachers. It was also stressed that since there is such a wide variety of computer systems in Canadian schools, the Jean Talon products should have software and hardware compatibility across a wide variety of platforms.

It was strongly recommended that Jean Talon products should be field tested widely. Educators reported that this would allow products to be refined in ways that would marshal the support of teachers and administrators as they experienced the potential of the products first-hand or learned about the field trials through seminars, workshops or conferences. This is an important consideration, as the rate of market penetration will be determined largely by teachers' assessments of the user-friendliness of Jean Talon products, their pedagogical soundness and their usefulness as classroom resources in specific curriculum contexts.

Educators expressed high expectations about the use of Jean Talon products as a reference resource for students. In particular, they emphasized the potential value of these products to help students develop the individual learning and research skills that will be needed in the knowledge-based society of the future.

Potential users of the products looked for long-term commitment and financial support from government at all levels. They were wary of committing themselves or resources to the project until they were convinced that a variety of products would be available and supported and updated as appropriate.

Product definition study (1990)

This study was initiated to test and further refine the 1989 study regarding the focus and design of potential Jean Talon products. In addition, the study undertook to develop an implementation plan for the creation, marketing and distribution of the recommended products for use in Canadian education. The findings were based primarily on interviews with teachers, administrators and consultants who were members of the Association for Media and Technology in Education in Canada (AMTEC).

The study concluded that the Jean Talon products must be designed for the most commonly owned and up-to-date computers in use in schools, libraries and homes. The respondents' primary concern for software development was that it should be easy to use for teachers and students. Software specifications had to stress interchangeability and downloading capacity. Since a number of Jean Talon products will utilize both magnetic and optical media, it will be necessary to design and implement the application software accordingly. In the respondents' view, the product would fail if there was no value-added interactive software, no matter how good the content.

The study recommended that the implementation plan should be based on four principles: governments to take the lead; government and business to cooperate on the project; all partners in the project to make a long-term commitment; and that market forces would eventually prevail. Furthermore, the collaboration and involvement of the educational community was seen as critical to the implementation process. The development of a consensus on the focus and content of Jean Talon products for the classroom, obtaining the necessary resources for product development and testing and applying these products in classrooms would take time. Hence a long-term implementation strategy was regarded as essential for the success of the project and the study recommended a decade-long, multi-phased implementation plan to bring the Jean Talon Project to fruition.

Of the 19 proposed products evaluated by the AMTEC representatives, the three most preferred for phase one development were Canada's threatened environment, learning about Canadian geography, and Canada in the world. Other products perceived to have a high level of interest were a multimedia encyclopedia/dictionary, science and technology in Canada, and exploring Canadian ecology.

The report recommended that products should be available in both official languages and while there should be one overall interface template, the products should respect the cultural differences of Canada's two language communities.

It was envisaged that in the early planning, research and development stages the government involvement would need to be high. This would gradually reduce and lead to the establishment of a separate agency, located at arm's length from government and mandated to create a market and sell the Jean Talon products. Once the programme was established and markets developed, it was anticipated that industry would assume the lead role in this enterprise.

Multimedia projects and products study (1990)

This study was commissioned to evaluate national projects and commercial products relevant to the Jean Talon Project and to identify successful elements that could be useful in the development of products aimed at the Canadian educational market. Some 40 national projects and 100 commercial products were reviewed.

The study established that, taken as a whole, the software development industry had generally failed to take the specific requirements of school curricula into account and had seriously underestimated the amount of in-service and preparation time that teachers required to become comfortable and competent with multimedia products. It was noted that many teachers continued to be sceptical about the effectiveness of the computer as a teaching/learning resource. Formative evaluation involving teachers and students was not apparent as an essential part of the software developmental process. Some excellent products, largely of non-Canadian origin, were identified but these were seen as more likely to be integrated into courses of study and classrooms as supplementary or reference material rather than as curriculum-specific instructional resources. The absence of specifically Canadian content in the majority of products was viewed by the educators as a serious impediment to their use in Canadian schools. It was again emphasized that any multimedia products for the Canadian education market should take into account the expectations and needs of the different linguistic and cultural groups within the education sector.

The introduction and acceptance of multimedia products in the typical school was seen to be further hampered by the costs, complexities and limited availability of, or access to, the sophisticated equipment required to achieve the technology's full potential in teaching, learning and self-directed study. While most of the national projects studied listed schools as a major market, it was found that, in general, these were aimed at single platforms that were neither common nor even likely to be introduced into classrooms.

It was noted that the majority of national projects tended to be characterized by multi-million dollar budgets, long time frames for development and undefined target audiences. By comparison, commercial products typically were driven or influenced by market factors and had a different set of priorities: to deliver quickly, to operate on as wide a base as possible and to reach their intended audience. The survey also found that the commercial developers were more likely to use a single development system to cross-develop products to conform to specific platforms and/or to meet a variety of user needs. Major upgrades to meet changed requirements are also much easier if the needs of the different target audiences are anticipated in the initial programme design and options allowed for.

Publishing government information in electronic form study (1990)

This study was undertaken to identify the most effective ways of facilitating the electronic publishing of government information and government/private sector cooperation. The study examined a number of Canadian government electronic publication ventures and entailed about 100 interviews with stakeholders concerned with access to, and dissemination and uses of, government information in electronic form.

A major finding was that government could improve the quality of its information systems and public access to these systems by levering the industry's energy, innovation and imagination to identify and fully exploit the market opportunities afforded by the new interactive multimedia technology. The various governments and governmental agencies collect and manage large and varied amounts of information intended for a variety of purposes. The study revealed a general perception that these instrumentalities on their own will not be able to respond effectively to the new demands and opportunities that will arise through new information technology. It was reported that it was difficult for parties outside government to discover what information is available in various government information banks and how best to access such information. The existing Access Register was not seen to be as helpful as it could be in such a process. Similarly, when information was located, it was often a complex and time-consuming task for the private sector to negotiate the rights to use such information in an electronic publishing venture. The lead time for a new electronics publishing idea or approach to a potential niche market is often remarkably short, but this requirement for rapid processing was not always understood by government managers. Their inexperience with marketplace realities, coupled with the complexity of contractual arrangements with government and the absence of clearly defined copyright/royalty provisions, militated against the industry's use of government data sources. Giving due regard to human rights considerations and privacy legislation, new arrangements were needed to simplify and speed up access to government information, particularly where more than one department was involved.

It was also noted that government departments were unable to use the revenues generated through providing such services to recover the costs incurred or to increase the efficiency of their publishing operations. As a consequence, departmental resources to ensure that all the information is correct and to deal with the contractual, policy and administrative aspects of the process were strictly limited.

The issue of copyright in multimedia product development was a significant concern for the industry. A large number of creators and copyright holders are likely to be implicated in these products. Given the overall context of these productions, issues such as the moral rights of the artists and the methods for determining the payment of fees have yet to be addressed. Automatic crown copyright was deemed by certain parties to be an impediment to database industry growth. The study recommended that the issue of crown copyright be the subject of a full and open discussion among all affected parties. Discussions between the government of Canada and the industry on this issue are ongoing.

The private sector also expressed concern about product ownership. It was pointed out that the 'added value' of the interactive multimedia products (the private sector contribution in converting government information into a marketable product) could be worth considerably more than the government information in its original form. As value-added products can contain property from several parties, multimedia product ownership is an issue that requires legal definition.

The study recommended that the government should consider the preparation of certain standards for its electronic information products, whether or not these were produced in-house or in cooperation with other parties. While not easily achievable because of significantly different product requirements, a common user interface would give products a similar 'look and feel'. Standard selection should be based on market considerations rather than dictated by supply capability. A standards review board could be established with joint representation from government and the private sector to ensure that standards were selected that were of maximum benefit to both parties.

The study made three priority recommendations:

- Departments and agencies should be given incentives to cooperate with the private sector in electronic publishing. They should be allowed to generate revenue and use it for the development of better products.
- A continuing dialogue between government and the private sector

should be maintained through annual and/or biannual colloquia to bring about an improved understanding of each other's needs and capabilities.

- A government unit should be established to assist departments in identifying government information that might usefully be published in electronic form, and to define product development opportunities for the private sector.

Conclusions

The first four studies, which were largely targeted on the education sector, underlined the strong support for the concept of the Jean Talon Project from the provinces and from educators. The project presents a real opportunity for federal and provincial government cooperation in the development of educational products with nationwide applications.

The research on Jean Talon has established that there is a lack of relevant and recent Canadian material in schools. The creation of a series of electronic multimedia products on various Canadian themes, topics and issues will contribute to the advancement of Canadian studies and to an increased sense of national identity. As a comprehensive information source on Canada and Canadian society, such materials will also help foster international awareness of Canada and its people.

The research indicated that a great diversity of computer platforms exists within the provinces as well as within provincial jurisdictions. Given this diversity, it is proposed that the project should issue its own products in both optical and magnetic formats to ensure that these can be operated on existing and emerging technology platforms in the schools.

The idea of a modular approach to product development received strong support from educators. Each module would be complete by itself or could be used in combination with other Jean Talon products to provide users with a comprehensive, interdisciplinary database. Modularity would also allow for future product enhancement and permit educators to choose those materials which best suit their curricula and previous software purchases.

At present, the Canadian education market is so fragmented that most multimedia productions do not generate a profit or, in many cases, even recover their production costs. It is projected that a unified market would create a major incentive for the Canadian electronic publishing industry to move to the cutting edge of new interactive software design and would offer new opportunities for the development and sale of a greater selection of electronic educational products at lower prices.

The Jean Talon Project proposes to use government information as a major data source in the development of its products. Government-industry cooperation in the use of government databanks for Jean Talon products is also seen as a way of encouraging the development of mechanisms to promote the more effective use of multimedia technology for publishing government information in areas other than education. Thus government cooperation with the private sector will strengthen multimedia enterprises in Canada and lead to more cost-effective solutions for meeting the government's electronic publishing needs.

Acknowledgments

Unpublished data reproduced in this chapter with the permission of the Minister of Supply and Services Canada, 1992.

This overview of the genesis and current state of development of the Jean Talon Project is a compilation of reports prepared for or by the Department of the Secretary of State of Canada. While many individuals have contributed to this paper, the responsibility for interpreting their work rests with the author. Acknowledgements are due to the following persons directly associated with the writing of this paper: James E. Page of the Department of the Secretary of State of Canada who, with Victor Glickman of Statistics Canada, has been a guiding force behind the Jean Talon Project since its inception and has provided many helpful suggestions; Neil Denison, a research assistant, who prepared an earlier synopsis of the research studies on Jean Talon; and David Mappin, Director of the Instructional Technology Centre, Faculty of Education, University of Alberta, who defined the direction and thrust of the Jean Talon pilot project, *Canada: Responding to Change.*

Project developers for *Canada: Responding to Change* are David Mappin, Sharon Jamieson and Robert Patterson of the Instructional Technology Centre, Faculty of Education, University of Alberta, Edmonton, Canada, T6G 2G5.

References

Abt Associates (1989). *User needs and current trends: Research report on the Jean Talon Project prepared for the Department of the Secretary of State of Canada.* Abt Associates, Toronto.

Barker, P. (1989). Designing multimedia workstations. In P. Barker (ed), *Multimedia computer assisted learning.* Kogan Page, London/Nichols Publishing, New York, 70–4.

Computers for People (1990). *Multimedia projects and products: Research report on the Jean Talon Project prepared for the Department of the Secretary of State of Canada.* Computers for People, Ottawa.

IDON Corporation (1990). *Product definition study: Research report on the Jean Talon*

Project prepared for the Department of the Secretary of State of Canada. IDON Corporation, Ottawa.

Info Gen (1990). *Publishing government information in electronic form: Research report on the Jean Talon Project prepared for the Department of the Secretary of State of Canada and the Canadian Workplace Information Centre.* Info Gen, Gloucester, Ontario.

Les Productions Louise Grenier Ltée and Le Groupe CIC (1988). *Feasibility study: Research report on the Jean Talon Project prepared for the Department of the Secretary of State of Canada.* Les Productions Louise Grenier Ltée and Le Groupe CIC, Montreal.

Glossary of terms

access (v) To retrieve information from a storage medium, such as videodisc, computer disk or tape.

access time (n) The total time required to find, retrieve and display data after initiation of a retrieval command. Typically a matter of minutes on videotape, two or fewer seconds on videodisc or CD, and milliseconds or microseconds on a computer.

algorithm (n) A plan of the exact sequence of steps needed to accomplish any task.

analogue video (n) A video signal that represents an infinite number of smooth gradations between given video levels. See also *video, digital video*.

application (n) The use of a technology to accomplish a defined purpose.

artificial intelligence (AI) (n) A computer software programming approach which allows a machine to use accumulated experiences and information to improve its own operations. The development or capability of a machine that can proceed or perform functions which are normally associated with human intelligence, such as learning, adapting, reasoning, self-correction, automatic improvement.

audiographics (n) A term used in educational circles to describe interactive teaching and learning between two or more sites using computing and audioconferencing technologies, typically with facsimile and printer as peripherals. See also *telematics*.

authoring language (n) A specialized, high-level, plain-English computer language which permits non-programmers to perform the programming function of courseware development. The program logic and program content are combined. Generally provides fewer capabilities or options than an authoring system.

authoring system (n) Specialized computer software which helps its users design interactive courseware in everyday language, without the painstaking detail of computer programming. In an authoring system, the instructional logic and instructional content are separate. Allows greater flexibility in courseware design than an authoring language.

bar code (n) A block of optically coded parallel lines, read by a scanner, wand or light pen which transmits a coded message to a microprocessor. Bar codes can provide commands for play functions on a videodisc player and can be integrated into workbooks, catalogues, location guides, etc.

baud (n) Commonly used unit of transmission speed to describe the rate at which binary data is communicated. One baud is approximately equal to one bit per second.

bit (n) Contraction of BInary digiT. A unit (either 0 or 1) of data equal to one binary decision. The smallest unit in computer information handling. Can be a single character in a binary number, a single pulse in a coded group of pulses, or a unit of information capacity. A computer's processing capability is usually determined by the number of bits which can be handled at one time.

button (n) A graphic component to an interface that represents some embedded function. For example, in Apple's HyperCard program, the user can create buttons that, when clicked on, branch the user to another location in the program.

byte (n) A generic term to indicate a measurable number of consecutive binary digits which are usually operated upon as a unit. Bytes of 8 bits ('by eight') usually represent either one character or two numerals. A computer's storage capacity or memory is figured in kilobytes (K or Kb); one K is actually 1,024 (2^{10}) bits.

CAV (n or adj) Constant angular velocity. A mode of videodisc playback in which a disc rotates at a constant speed, regardless of the position of the reading head or stylus. Thus, each frame is separately addressable. In laser videodisc technology, each track contains two video fields that comprise one complete video frame. CAV discs revolve continuously at 1,800rpm (NTSC) or 1,500rpm (PAL), one revolution per frame. Program time is 30 minutes or more per side on a 30cm disc, 14 minutes per side on a 20cm disc. Also a method used to address information stored on magnetic storage media such as disk. See also *CLV*.

CD (n) Compact disc. A 12cm optical disc that contains information encoded digitally in the CLV format. CD-A (compact disc-audio) is a popular format for high fidelity music. The standards for this format (developed by NV Philips and Sony Corporation) are known as the Red Book.

CD-I (n) Compact disc-interactive. A compact disc format which provides audio, digital data, still graphics, and limited motion video. The standards for this format (developed by NV Philips and Sony Corporation) are known as the Green Book.

CD-ROM (n) Compact disc read-only memory. A 12cm laser-encoded optical memory storage medium with the same constant linear velocity (CLV) spiral format as compact audio discs and some videodiscs. CD-ROMs can hold about 550Mb of data (the equivalent of about 250,000 pages of text). CD-ROMs require additional error-correction information to the standard prerecorded compact audio disc. The standards for this format (developed by NV Philips and Sony Corporation) are known as the Yellow Book. See also *CD-ROM XA*.

CD-ROM XA (n) Compact disc read-only memory extended architecture. An extension of the CD-ROM standard billed as a hybrid of CD-ROM and CD-I, and promoted by Sony and Microsoft.

CDTV (n) Commodore Dynamic Total Vision. Consumer multimedia system by Commodore. System includes CD-ROM/CD audio player, Motorola 68000 processor, 1Mb RAM, and 10-key infrared remote control.

CLV (n or adj) Constant linear velocity, an alternative format for laser videodiscs. CLV (or 'extended-play') discs allow twice as much playing time (up to one hour) per side, but many of the user-control capabilities of the CAV format are forfeited (eg, no still-framing is possible). The CLV disc can be read in linear play only, but can provide chapter search capability. Also the method used to address information stored on all CDs. See also *CAV*.

CMC (n) Computer-mediated communication using computers and communication networks to compose, process, store and deliver information that can benefit remote or networked learners.

combi-player or **combination player** (n) A player that can accommodate a variety of disc formats.

compressed audio or **compressed video** (n) An audio or video signal that has been digitally processed using a variety of computer algorithms and other techniques to reduce both the amount of data required to represent accurately the content and, therefore, the space required to store that content.

courseware (n) Instructional software, including all discs, tapes, books, charts, and computer programs necessary to deliver a complete instructional module or course.

cyberspace (n) A computer-generated artificial environment that is designed to to maximize the user's freedom of movement and exploration. See also *virtual reality*.

digital audio (n) Audio tones represented by machine-readable binary numbers rather than analogue recording techniques.

digital video (n) A video signal represented by computer-readable binary numbers that describe a finite set of colours and luminance levels. See also *analogue video, video*.

disc/disk (n) Flat, circular rotating medium that can store and replay various types of information, both analogue and digital. 'Disc' is typically used in reference to optical storage media, while 'disk' refers to magnetic storage media. See also *videodisc, CD*.

disk operating system (DOS) (n) A computer operating system designed for use with a disk. Languages, application, and utility programs can be transferred quickly between CPU memory and the disk storage. DOS is the preferred usage for both the Microsoft Disk Operating System (MS-DOS) and IBM's Personal Computer Disk Operating System (PC-DOS).

DVI (n) Digital Video Interactive. A technology that allows real-time compression and decompression and display of digital graphics and full-motion video with audio. While presently optimized for the data rate of CD-ROM, the technology is independent of storage medium. The highest video quality is achieved by using off-line, non-real-time compression on powerful parallel processing computers. However, the technology can provide lesser quality real-time compression. Developed by RCA's David Sarnoff Research Centre, then purchased and marketed by computer chip manufacturer Intel Corporation.

E-Mail (n) Electronic mail which allows messages and assignments to be sent to electronic mailboxes for named individuals and accessed when the named user logs on.

fibre optics (n) The technology by which information is transmitted through a glass fibre strand capable of transmitting light.

frame store (n) A device that stores one complete video frame. Also known as frame grabber.

generic courseware (n) Educational courses that are not specific to one organization and thus appeal to a broader market; as opposed to custom courseware, which primarily meets the needs of one specific client or audience.

graphical user interface (GUI) (n) A visual metaphor that uses icons representing actual desktop objects that the user can access and manipulate with a pointing device. Developed and popularized by Xerox, Apple Computer (in its Macintosh computer), and Microsoft (in its Windows environment). See also *user interface, video user interface (VUI)*.

HyperCard (n) A Macintosh-based software product developed by Apple Computer. Using the philosophy of hypertext, the program enables users to organize information in a random manner like that of their own thinking. HyperCard programs ('stacks') are made up of 'cards', often augmented with short program routines ('scripts') or other small programs known as XCMDs (external commands) and XFCNs (external functions). The cards contain 'buttons', which, when activated, branch the user to another location in the program. HyperCard programs are written in 'Hypertalk', a simple object-oriented programming language.

hypermedia (n) An extension of hypertext that incorporates a variety of other media, in addition to simple text.

Hypertalk (n) Apple Computer's simple object-oriented language for writing HyperCard programs.

hypertext (n) The concept of non-sequential writing which allows writers to link information together through a variety of paths or connections. Hypertext allows users to seek greater depths of information by moving among related documents along thematic lines or accessing definitions and bibliographic references without losing the context of the original inquiry. Hypertext is the driving concept behind Apple's HyperCard program.

icon (n) A symbolic, pictorial representation of any function or task.

instructional design (n) The methodology and approach used to deliver information in a manner that achieves maximum learning.

interactive media 1. (n) Media which involve the viewer as a source of input to determine the content and duration of a message, permitting individualized programme material. 2. (n) A philosophy of media production designed to take maximum advantage of random access, computer-controlled videotape and videodisc players.

interactive video (n) The fusion of video and computer technology. A video programme and a computer program running in tandem under the control of the user. In interactive video, the user's actions, choices and decisions genuinely affect the way in which the programme unfolds.

ISDN (n) Integrated services digital network. An international digital telecommunications standard developed to enable transmission of simultaneous high-bandwidth data, video and voice signals (all digital).

JPEG (n) Joint Photographic Experts Group. A working committee under the auspices of the International Standards Organization that is attempting to define a proposed universal standard for the digital compression and decompression of still images for use in computer systems.

kilobyte (K or Kb) (n) A term indicating 1,024 bytes of data storage capacity. A typical personal computer floppy disk has 1440 kb or 1.44 Mb of memory. See also *byte, bit*.

kiosk (n) The housing for an unmanned, self-contained, free-standing, interactive system, generally located in a public place.

laser 1. (n) Light Amplification by Stimulation of Emission of Radiation. An amplifier and generator of coherent energy in the optical, or light, region of the spectrum. In the laser videodisc system, a laser is used to read the micropits on the videodisc which contain the picture and sound information. 2. (n or adj) Generic name for reflective optical videodisc format promoted by NV Philips, Pioneer Video, Hitachi, Sony and others. See also *optical videodisc, reflective optical videodisc format*.

laser disc (LD) (n) Common name for reflective optical videodisc. 'LaserDisc' is a trademark of Pioneer Electronics USA for its reflective optical videodisc products. The firm has released the term 'laser disc' for use by any marketer of laser videodiscs, and the term has been used in the consumer market to describe all videodiscs. A standard disc offers up to 55,000 frames of information, each with its unique electronic address or frame number.

levels of interactive systems Three degrees of videodisc system interactivity proposed by Nebraska Videodisc Design/Production Group in 1980:

- *Level One system*: Usually a consumer-model videodisc player with still/freeze frame, picture stop, chapter stop, frame address and dual-channel audio, but with limited memory and limited processing power.
- *Level Two system*: An industrial-model videodisc player with the capabilities of Level One, plus on-board programmable memory and improved access time.
- *Level Three system*: Level One or Two players interfaced to an external computer and/or other peripheral processing devices.

Note: Some commentators have advocated additional levels (Four, Five, and up), suggesting that the addition of digital audio, touch screens, etc creates new levels of interactivity. However, the industry has never settled on any single standard for these higher levels, and any innovation mentioned with such 'higher levels' falls into Level Three.

light pen (n) Stylus with a light-detecting mechanism used as a graphics input or user interface device to identify cursor position on the computer screen. See also *bar code*.

master 1. (n) An original audio tape, videotape or film. Used for broadcast or to make copies. 2. (v) The process of producing master, mother, and stamper videodiscs, which are used for replicating videodiscs.

master videodisc (n) First stage disc in videodisc manufacture. On the master disc, conductivity to receive the converted video signal is produced by evaporation or plating. The disc is then nickel-plated.

Media Control Interface (MCI) (n) Platform-independent multimedia specification (published by Microsoft and others in 1990) that provides a consistent way to control devices such as CD-ROMs and video playback units.

mega– Prefix meaning 'one million', as in 'megabyte' or 'Mb' (one million bytes).

Microsoft Windows (n) GUI operating environment developed by Microsoft for use with personal computers under its MS-DOS operating system. See also *graphical user interface (GUI)*.

MIDI (n) Musical instrument digital interface. An industry-standard connection for computer control of musical instruments and devices.

mouse (n) A hand-held, rolling remote control device for a computer which guides the cursor on the computer screen.

MPEG (n) Motion Picture Experts Group. A working committee under the auspices of the International Standards Organization that is attempting to define standards for the digital compression and decompression of motion video/audio for use in computer systems.

MS-DOS/PC-DOS (n) The disk operating systems of IBM Personal Computers, developed by Microsoft Corporation. See also *disk operating system (DOS)*.

multimedia (n or adj) Refers to the delivery of information, usually via personal computer, that combines different content formats (text, graphics, audio, still images, animation, motion video, etc) and/or storage media (magnetic disk, optical disc, video/audio tape, RAM).

NTSC (n) National Television Systems Committee of the Electronics Industries Association (EIA) that prepared the standard specifications approved by the US Federal Communications Commission in December 1953, for commercial colour broadcasting.

object-oriented programming (OOP) (n) A programming methodology in which every element in a program is self-contained, having within itself all the data and instructions that operate on that data that are appropriate for that object. One element sends a message to another and the recipient carries out the task for itself.

optical videodisc (n) A videodisc that uses a laser light beam to read information from the surface of the disc. The information in optical videodiscs is encoded in the form of microscopic pits pressed into the disc surface. The pits or holes modulate the laser in a manner that can be decoded by the videodisc player. Information stored in these pits is 'read' by a laser beam and transmitted to a decoder in the player. See also *reflective optical videodisc format*.

OROM (n) Optical read-only memory. A 13cm laser-encoded optical memory storage medium, which features a concentric circular format and constant angular velocity (CAV). Used primarily to store digital data (not video or audio). OROMs have faster access time than CD-ROM discs, but less storage space (250Mb as opposed to 500Mb). See also *CD-ROM*.

OS/2 (n) Operating System/2. Multi-tasking higher-level operating system developed by IBM and Microsoft for the PS/2 series of microcomputers equipped with the 80386 microprocessor.

OS-9 (n) A 'real-time' operating system on which the CD-I operating system is based.

overlay (n) The facility to superimpose computer-generated text and/or graphics onto motion or still video.

PAL (n) Phase alternate line; the European standard colour system format, except for France. See also *NTSC, SECAM*.

palette (n) In digital video, the total number of colours available for pictorial presentations.

Photo CD (n) A system developed by Eastman Kodak Co for adding up to 100 35mm images onto a CD ROM which can be accessed by a computer's CD ROM drive, a CD-I player or a specially modified CD audio player.

pixel (n) An abbreviation of 'picture element'. The minimum raster display element, represented as a point with a specified colour or intensity level. One way to measure picture resolution is by the number of pixels used to create images.

processing 1. (n) In computing, the manipulation of data from one state to another, usually at the request of an operator or user. 2. (n) In film work, the photographic development of the film negative.

QuickTime (n) An extension of the Macintosh system software which integrates time-based data types into mainstream Macintosh applications. Time-based data types contain data that can be stored and retrieved as values over time. In QuickTime, the time-based data are referred to as 'movies'.

random access memory (RAM) (n) That part of a computer's memory which can both read (find and display) and write (record) information, and which can be updated or amended by the user; the largest part of a computer's memory, used in its day-to-day work. See also *read-only memory (ROM)*.

read-only memory (ROM) 1. (n) A computer storage medium which allows the user to recall and use information (read) but not record or amend it (write). 2. (n) The smaller part of a computer's memory, in which essential operating information is recorded in a form which can be recalled and used (read) but not amended or recorded (written). See also *random access memory*.

real time (n) The actual time in which a programme or event takes place. In computing, refers to an operating mode under which data is received and processed and the results returned so quickly that the process appears instantaneous to the user.

reflective optical videodisc format (n) Reflective optical (laser) videodiscs contain their information imbedded as pits or holes in reflective surfaces sandwiched between layers of polymethyl methacrylate (PMMA). The shiny surface reflects the laser light into a mirror, which in turn reflects it to a decoder. The clear PMMA protects the information from dirt and superficial scratches. Reflective discs must be turned over to read information on both sides. Because this format uses a laser instead of a stylus to retrieve information, there is no physical contact between the reading mechanism and the disc itself, hence no wear or degradation during playback. Promoted by NV Philips, Sony, Pioneer, Hitachi and others. See also *laser disc, optical videodisc*.

remote control (n) Command of a computer or interactive videodisc programme through an electronic device independent of the computer or disc player (ie, keypad, touch screen, joystick, mouse).

resolution (n) Number of pixels per unit of area. A display with a finer grid contains more pixels and thus has a higher resolution, capable of reproducing more detail in an image.

scan 1. (v) In basic television and video transmission, the rapid journey of the scanning spot back and forth across the scan lines on the inside of the screen. 2. (adj) In interactive videodisc technology, a mode of play in which the player skips over several disc tracks at a time, displaying only a fraction of the frames it passes. Scanning can be done in forward or reverse. 3. (v) In data capture, the process by which a document or hard copy image is converted to machine-storable image format.

SCSI (n) A small computer systems interface (pronounced 'scuzzy' or 'sexy'). A device-independent interface used for a wide variety of computer peripherals.

search (v) In interactive video systems, to request a specific frame, identified by its unique sequential reference number, and then to instruct the player to move directly to that frame (forwards or backwards) from any other point on the same side of the disc or tape.

SECAM (n) 'Sequential couleur à memoire' (sequential colour with memory) format, the French colour TV system, also adopted in the former USSR. The basis of operation is the sequential recording of primary colours in alternate lines. See also *NTSC, PAL*.

shell (n) An outer layer of a program that provides the user interface or the user's way of commanding the computer. See also *user interface*.

simulation (n) Representation of a system, sub-system, situation or device, with a degree of realism. The simulation mode enables users to learn the operation of equipment without damaging it or harming themselves or others. Extremely useful in training applications which involve potentially dangerous activities.

software (n) The programs, routines, sub-routines, languages, procedures, videodiscs, charts, workbooks – in fact, everything that isn't hardware used in a computer or videodisc system.

speech recognition (n) A computer input technology in which a human utterance is recognized within the computer terminal and then converted into machine-usable binary code.

speech synthesizer (n) A device that produces human speech sounds from input in another form.

stack (n) In reference to data and programs for use with Apple's HyperCard, a complete file of 'cards', along with any special programming routines ('scripts'). In short, a complete program set. See also *HyperCard*.

standards (n) A uniform set of machine protocols defining how devices communicate with each other.

step frame or **step** 1. (n) A function of optical videodisc players which permits the user to either move forward or reverse from one frame to the next. 2. (v) To advance one frame forward or reverse.

still frame 1. (n) A single film or video frame presented as a single, static image. 2. (adj) Refers to information recorded on a frame or track of a videodisc that is intended to be retrieved and displayed as a single motionless image. Playback is achieved by repeating the play of the same track, rather than going on to the next; as opposed to a freeze-frame, which stops the action within a motion sequence.

surrogate travel (n) A multimedia application in which physical travel is precisely simulated using videodisc and computer, allowing the user to control the path taken through the environment. See also *virtual reality*.

telecommunications (n) Communication from one computer terminal or system to another via telephone lines.

teleconference (n) A general term for a meeting not held in person. Usually refers to a multi-party telephone call, set up by the phone company or private source, which enables more than two callers to participate in a conversation. The growing use of video allows participants at remote locations to see, hear and participate in proceedings, or share visual data (video conference).

telematics (n) A term used in educational circles to describe the electronically based equipment, processes and strategies used to enable interactive teaching and learning between two or more remote locations. See also *audiographics*.

touch screen (n) A video and/or computer display which acts as a control or input device under the physical finger touch of the user. Basic functions are executed by touching certain parts of the screen and specific responses made by touching appropriate words, messages, or pictures as they appear. Different touch-screen technologies use infrared grids, small wires separated by air spaces, changes in electronic capacitance, acceleration detection, plastic membranes or other methods.

turnkey (adj) An off-the-shelf product or system that is ready to run when delivered – simply 'turn the key'.

user interface (n) The software which allows the computer user to communicate with the computer. The user interface may be a simple line which allows commands to be entered, or may be as sophisticated as the Apple Macintosh 'desktop' metaphor. See also *graphical user interface (GUI)*, *video user interface (VUI)*.

video (n) A system of recording and transmitting information which is primarily visual, by translating moving or still images into electrical signals. These signals can be broadcast (live or prerecorded) using high-frequency carrier waves, or sent through cable on a closed circuit. The term video properly refers only to the picture – but as a generic term, usually embraces audio and other signals which are part of the complete programme.

video user interface (VUI) (n) A proposed 'next-generation' computing interface metaphor, which will employ a full-motion video window as part of the user interface. Like GUI, VUI may use iconic representations to facilitate intuitive navigation. See also *user interface, graphical user interface (GUI)*.

videodisc (n) A generic term describing a medium of information storage which uses thin circular plates of varying formats, on which video, audio and data signals may be encoded (usually along a spiral track) for playback on a video monitor.

virtual reality (n) A computer-generated 'reality' which users may 'enter' by virtue of bodily peripherals such as data gloves and head-mounted computer graphic displays. Also in desktop interactive multimedia.

voice-activated (adj) Computer or videodisc programme executed or controlled by the sound of a human voice. See also *voice recognition*.

voice recognition (n) A computer input technology in which a human utterance is recognized within the computer terminal and then converted into machine-usable binary code.

window 1. (n) A segment into which the interactive videodisc user may enter at any point without missing the chapter stop. 2. (n) A defined portion of a display screen in which a video image or other information may be shown. 3. (n) In graphical user interfaces, a rectangular portion of the screen in which an application or document is viewed. Each program runs in its own window on the desktop.

Windows – See *Microsoft Windows*.

WORM (n) Write-once/read many times memory. A type of permanent optical storage that allows the user to record original information on a blank disc, but does not allow erasure or change of that information once it is recorded.

This glossary contains data kindly supplied by:

Multimedia and Videodisc Monitor
Post Office Box 26
Falls Church Virginia 22040 USA

Phone: 703/241-1799
Fax: 703/532-0529

Index

Author index

Subject index